BREAKING THE CYCLE
OF COMPULSIVE BEHAVIOR

Martha Nibley Beck
and John C. Beck

Deseret Book Company
Salt Lake City, Utah

Library of Congress Cataloging-in-Publication Data

Beck, Martha Nibley, 1962–
    Breaking the cycle of compulsive behavior / by Martha Nibley Beck and John C. Beck.
        p.   cm.
    ISBN 0-87579-290-1
    1. Compulsive behavior—Patients—Rehabilitation. 2. Repentance—Christianity.   I. Beck, John C., 1959–   . II. Title.
RC533.B39   1989
616.85'227—dc20   89-25862
                                                           CIP

Printed in the United States of America   18961-4545

10   9   8   7   6

To our parents

TABLE OF CONTENTS

....

Preface   ix

Acknowledgments   xiii

1   Introduction   1

2   The Body and Compulsive Behavior   25

3   The First Step: Feelings of Isolation   42

4   The Second Step: Actions of Self-Indulgence   64

5   The Third Step: Feelings of Self-Hatred   95

6   The Fourth Step: Actions of Self-Concealment   128

7   Breaking the Compulsive Cycle   172

8   The Joy Cycle   258

Index   299

PREFACE

. . . .

The idea for this book was born on a snowy night in Cambridge, Massachusetts, as we walked home from a visit with one of the most active of the small but tightly knit group of Latter-day Saint students in the Boston area. Earlier that day our friend's older brother had been excommunicated from the Church because of a problem we would later come to call a behavioral addiction, or a compulsive cycle. That night, though, as we talked the matter over with our shocked and saddened friend, we had no such label for the older brother's actions. We had only the vague impression that the story we were hearing shared similarities with accounts we had heard from other Latter-day Saints.

The problems these people described seemed very different on the surface, but the same themes appeared to underlie the stories of many faithful Church members whose lives had become painful or even unmanageable. Whatever temptations troubled them, these people described a similar pattern of behavior related to those temptations. They all felt a growing preoccupation with certain behaviors, a widening distance from loved ones, a profound loss of self-respect, and the feeling of being unable to control their own actions.

We began to recognize these similarities on that cold New England night, but it took four years and hundreds of hours of interviewing Latter-day Saints who were also

ix

behavioral addicts to convince us that compulsive cycles lay at the heart of many tragedies that might otherwise seem unrelated. This book considers the stories of three Church members whose compulsive behaviors fell into the most common categories: eating disorders, substance abuse, and sexual addiction; however, we saw compulsive behavior emerge involving many types of activity that do not fall into these categories. What all these behavioral addicts shared was a recognizable cycle of feelings and actions that came to absorb a huge proportion of their personalities and to destroy their happiness. We grew to believe that understanding the pattern is the key to escaping from it.

That is the first reason we decided to write this book.

The second reason is that we saw some of our interview subjects transform their compulsive cycles into a parallel pattern of behavior we call the joy cycle. These people became not only free from their addictions but more able to cope with virtually every aspect of their lives. We wish to share their experiences to reassure those struggling with compulsive behavior that their problems are not inescapable: there is hope.

Finally, this book is a testimony to our belief that "all things which are good cometh of God." (Moroni 7:12.) The process of breaking the cycle of compulsive behavior is contained in the gospel of Jesus Christ. We have never seen an individual, Latter-day Saint or not, who escaped from a behavioral addiction without following the steps outlined in the doctrines of the Church and without the help of a loving Father in Heaven.

This book is meant to assist behavioral addicts and their loved ones in understanding the problem of addictive cycles. We suggest a way in which that problem might be solved. We do not purport to offer a sure cure for any individual's addiction. We have attempted to use some of the training we received as social scientists in conducting our research, but we make no claim whatever to scientific objectivity in analyzing our results. We accept as inspired the teachings of The Church of Jesus Christ of Latter-day Saints, and we have approached the problem of addiction from that standpoint. On the other hand, statements we make about doctrine are our own interpretations and do not represent official Church policy. We make these caveats because we openly acknowledge that there are many imperfections in this book. Nonetheless, if we can convince one person trapped in the seemingly unconquerable grasp of a compulsive cycle that the problem can be overcome, or if we can help one would-be rescuer to understand the problem in a way that might enlighten or assist, we will have accomplished our objective.

ACKNOWLEDGMENTS

Many friends, knowingly or unknowingly, helped us formulate and clarify our ideas. Special thanks are due to Dr. Robert Bennion for his wisdom and insight and to Carol Christiansen for her willingness to offer deserved criticism and undeserved encouragement. Eleanor Knowles, executive editor of Deseret Book, had the kindness to listen to an idea proposed by two college students in 1984 and still remembered us four years later when our research was finally completed.

This book would never have been finished without Krista Boyd Stevens's unflagging willingness to help with the logistical problems of research, writing, and maintaining our family.

Finally, we would like to thank the many individuals who allowed us to interview them in the course of our research. Their patience, honesty, and courage were truly inspiring.

1

INTRODUCTION

It was six o'clock on Saturday morning. Ellen Schor forced her eyes open and slid wearily out of bed. She had been told that September in Utah would be hot and dry, but the morning air felt clammy and chilly on Ellen's skin. She quickly pulled on her sweatpants and running jacket, shook herself to get her blood moving, and sat down on the hard dormitory carpet to stretch before her run. Her legs were stiff and reluctant. As she pulled her left knee toward her chin, Ellen felt it sending murmurs of discomfort to her brain, requesting that maneuvers be cancelled at least for the day. She pushed the leg a little farther as a disciplinary measure.

At ten past six Ellen arranged her limbs in a delicately uncomfortable Yoga position and opened her scriptures. The night before, she had cut down her regular half-hour scripture study to twenty-five minutes in order to finish an English paper. She would make up that time this morning.

"Wherefore," she read from 2 Nephi 9:51, "do not spend money for that which is of no worth, nor your labor for that which cannot satisfy." Ellen nodded emphatically. That was her philosophy. She had worked hard to develop frugality and single-minded determination. In fact, the control she had gained over her time and her energy had become the central fact of Ellen's life.

"Hearken diligently unto me," the verse continued,

1

"and remember the words which I have spoken." Diligence. That was the key. Diligence and absolute adherence to principle. Ellen made a fresh resolution to live the day righteously. She had been taught, and she believed, that perfection itself was not too lofty a goal. She read on. "And come unto the Holy One of Israel, and feast upon that which perisheth not, neither can be corrupted, and let your soul delight in fatness."

Ellen unfolded her still-aching legs, thinking that the problem with Jacob was that you were never really sure what he would say next. "Let your soul delight in fatness." What a revolting concept. Purely metaphorical, of course; that was obvious. And besides, for every scripture in favor of obesity—spiritual or otherwise—Ellen could quote at least ten that recommended fasting, sparsity, discipline, self-denial, and control of appetite. For herself, Ellen knew that she felt much better, much purer, when she ate as little as possible. She knew so few people who had gained real mastery over that facet of their lives. While her fellow Americans had devoured literally tons of appealing poisons over the past four years, Ellen had spent that time mastering her lurid desire for cookies, ice cream, red meat, and the other temptations of the Natural Man. Now, as a sophomore in college, she had succeeded in eliminating all foods except whole grains, fruits, and vegetables from her diet. She scheduled every minute of her day to include only constructive and wholesome activities. She studied harder than anyone she knew. She ran ten miles a day, and she finally felt almost pure, almost clean, inside and out.

Almost. Ellen winced momentarily as she remembered one evening the week before. It had happened again, she had to admit. How had she gotten so out of control? She hardly remembered buying the ice cream and the corn chips, hardly remembered eating them, alone behind the snack shop like a dog skulking off with a stolen bone. All she remembered was the guilt she'd felt afterwards, the sickness of mind and body. How true it was that junk foods were poison. She'd felt like vomiting. In fact, she'd considered it seriously. It wasn't so much the stomachache as the guilt she'd wanted to be free of. Ellen shook her head hard, shooing away the memory. That had been a moral lapse, to be sure, but the incident was over. She would overcome the disgusting tendencies of her wicked body. In fact—think positively, she told herself—she already had.

Her greatest remaining sin was vanity: despite repeated attempts to repent, Ellen could not help feeling unseemly pride in the fact that size one pants dangled loosely from her hips and that her roommate outweighed her by eighty-five percent. Every morning, every night, and during her three other formal prayers every day, Ellen gave thanks for the strength of will which had made her so elegantly thin and prayed for the endurance to become even slimmer. She finished this particular morning's devotions at precisely six-thirty A.M. After a quick weigh-in on her forty-dollar medical scale, which reported ounces as well as pounds on its digital readout, she trotted down the dormitory stairs to the lobby on legs that trembled with weakness and resolve.

Few people were on the street yet, which pleased Ellen greatly. She had once been as gregarious as she had been gluttonous, but now she limited the people with whom she came in contact, just as she did the ingredients for her negative-calorie salads (which cost more energy to chew than they provided and were thus less fattening than eating nothing). True, she sometimes felt lonely, but certainly loneliness was better than indiscriminate association with people who might lead her away from the path she had chosen. Ellen clenched her teeth to shut out the ache that surged briefly from its hiding place beneath her consciousness. It was just hunger, she told herself, just a sign of righteous self-denial. Fasting and prayer could lead only to happiness: the pain was an illusion — there, it was gone. The exhilaration and the energy were back. If she could lose about five more pounds, Ellen thought as she jogged stiffly into the brilliant Rocky Mountain sunlight, she would be light enough to float straight up to heaven.

The buzzing of his alarm clock slammed into Bill Stewart's solar plexus almost before he was aware of hearing it. By the time the sound had fully registered in his ears, Bill's hand was already slapping at the "snooze" button like a hysterical housewife killing a cockroach. When he was sure the sound was dead, Bill closed his eyes and took a long, quavering breath to calm his nerves. Six thirty.

Bill did not want to get up. No. No, no, no. It was too early, and he felt terrible. Terrible! Another deep breath did little to ease the pounding pain in his head and the shivering thud of his heart. He opened one eye and peered at the merciless red numbers changing from 6:31 to 6:32 to 6:33. . . . Get up. He had to get up. The thought made the headache worse and brought on a wave of nausea that intensified with every thunderous quake of his heart. His hand, still clutching the clock, twitched in time with his pulse, and the veins on it bulged blue and sickly gray.

Bill had expected to gain muscle and a tan during the summer, working with Dad on the Idaho ranch. He always had before. The summer after his high school graduation he'd grown two inches and put on nearly twenty pounds. But last summer Dad had suggested that since the younger boys were old enough to help now, Bill might have a better time staying around school and keeping that terrific campus apartment and his job. . . . Of course, Bill had known what Dad meant. With nine children in the family, and everyone getting ready for college and missions and weddings, it was probably a good thing that the oldest child should be independent from now on. Mom and Dad had

4

given him the wings to fly, and while he was testing those wings, the other kids had grown so much they filled the nest without him. That was fine. That was reasonable. That was final. So Bill stayed at school and sold appliances part-time while the smell of summer filled his memory with images of cool mountains, and tall grass, and the bright blond heads of his little brothers and sisters.

That was when the world had begun to go gray, and Bill with it. Everything seemed to be like the screen of an old TV, growing slowly more fuzzy, slowly more ghostly, slowly more colorless and uninteresting. Except, of course, for Jenny. Jenny had worked at the store in the mall across from Bill, and she smiled a gorgeous smile at him every day until he had timidly asked her out. "Finally!" she laughed, confident in her expensive clothes and perfect haircut.

Bill smiled through his morning headache, remembering the first few dates he'd had with Jenny. He still wondered what could have made a smart, rich, beautiful girl like Jenny so generous toward a country bumpkin like him. As the summer wore on, he'd grown more and more glad he wasn't stuck in his tiny hometown, with a family as wholesome as oatmeal and just about as interesting. Jenny brought him into the real world. He had never realized how narrow-minded, how provincial he had been before he met her. She introduced him to new friends and more expansive ways of thinking. He discovered that the sense of humor he'd learned from his mother in their kitchen could be used to make people laugh in places with far more panache. "You're getting pretty interesting for an Idaho potato," Jenny would tease him, laughing. Bill would laugh, too, proud to have escaped his narrow-minded, puritanical, countrified upbringing with some degree of sophistication. Jenny brought out that sophistication. She shared everything with him—friends, jokes, ideas about how he should dress and walk and talk. And cocaine.

It was nearly a quarter to seven. He *had* to get *up*. Even if he hurried, he'd have to skip breakfast if he wanted to open the store on time. He'd probably end up running halfway. That was why he was getting so thin, he told himself. He spent half the day running from work to school to Jenny's. Bill had been saving to buy himself a car, but he'd ended up spending a little more on drugs than he'd expected. A lot more, in fact. At first he just took what Jenny gave him, but a guy has to keep some self-respect. And besides, he liked to have the stuff on hand when he had a reason to use it. Because of course Bill didn't just take drugs for no reason, like some sick junkie. That would be disgusting. None of Jenny's friends — his friends — were junkies. As Jenny explained to him, they just used drugs to get more out of life.

Bill hadn't really understood what she meant until school started. One day he went to class high, after a date with Jenny, and was astounded by how acutely he understood everything the professor said. He began to use a little "help" for special occasions, like finals and term papers. But if drugs were useful then, he began to reason, then taking them more often would keep up his batting average, help him learn more, do more — as Jenny had said, get more out of his college experience. He was a little surprised when his grades began to drop, but then again, this was his sophomore year and he'd never heard of a sophomore who didn't have trouble motivating himself to keep working. Bill started taking more drugs to counteract the sophomore slump and considered gratefully that at this rate, without them he'd probably be failing. Of course, as soon as he was out of this academic pressure, he'd stop using the stuff. He only took it when that was the logical thing to do. It cost a lot, but Bill resigned himself to the cost. As an investment in his education, it was worth it.

Six forty-seven. Bill's headache was worse than ever, and the world outside his half-opened lids was pale and out of focus. He had a terrible taste in his mouth. A little chemical assistance would help right now, he thought. But no. It was Saturday. He never took drugs on weekends. For one thing, he didn't need them just for work and church. For another, he had to admit that he was pretty much at the limit of his budget right now. But good grief, he felt rotten! He probably had a cold. It probably wouldn't be good for him to try to go to work without *something*. Everybody takes something when they're sick, Bill reasoned.

Bill's hand was shaking so hard that he could hardly open the drawer of his nightstand. Clearly, he really needed an extra boost this morning. For a moment he couldn't find the tiny canister of white powder, and his hands trembled even more violently as he rummaged, first methodically and then in something close to panic, through the drawer. Ah! He found it! There it was! He relaxed and his headache felt better already as he inhaled a tiny pinch — just a little, he didn't ever overdo it — and settled back into his pillows.

The gray song of a gray bird wafted through the window on a shaft of gray sunlight. Just for a moment, the sound filled Bill's mind with the gold, blue, and green of an Idaho morning and the cheerful chaos of his family sitting down to breakfast. The shaking and the headache grew worse, but only for a moment: the chemicals began to focus and clarify his world, and the simple lines of his terrific campus apartment took on a clarity that calmed and dimmed his memories. The tears that had incongruously gathered in his eyes dried there, unshed, as his vision grew brighter and his headache vanished. The relief was marvelous. The world was marvelous. Bill was marvelous. With a chuckle of satisfaction and a rueful grin at his susceptibility to silly farmboy sentiments, Bill Stewart threw back the sheets and got up.

At seven A.M. in Los Angeles the air was still relatively clear. Warren White turned off his alarm and looked out his eighth-floor window at the gentle golden hills of the horizon. It was a beautiful morning. Warren rubbed his stinging eyes and ran a hand through his hair. He hadn't slept well, hadn't even felt drowsy until sunrise was underway. Something was wrong, he thought, as he stumbled groggily toward the shower. It had been wrong last night, it was wrong long before that, and it was still wrong. No amount of California sunshine could drive it away.

Warren hung a towel next to the tub. He glanced at himself in the mirror and noted dispassionately that he was very handsome: tall and muscular, with black hair and startlingly blue eyes. His apartment, reflected beyond the open bathroom door, was expensive, immaculate, and furnished with perfect taste. Even his parents, when they'd seen the place, had been impressed enough to comment on Warren's success. They had barely even murmured about how nice it would be to have a woman's touch around the house, and there had been no mention at all of pattering little feet. Five years ago, when Warren had come home from his mission, the hints had rained down on him like hailstones on a tin roof—small, annoying, and promptly deflected. As much as he loved his family, Warren had been glad to move. He wondered if his parents knew what was wrong. They must. It must be obvious. They must be able to see it, hovering around him like his own personal smog bank.

He turned the shower on cold and let it shock the skin on his face and chest. He was so tired. Tired of worrying, tired of guilt, tired of wrestling his own feelings in the desperate hours that preceded sunrise, tired of a constant striving to attain an ideal for which he felt no desire. No, he told himself, that wasn't true. He did want a family. He wanted to build a home as full and warm as his own

8

had been, to give his time, his effort, and his love to his own children as his parents had to him. Warren thought about the passage in his patriarchal blessing that had filled him with new hope when he was seventeen years old. It said that he would find a wife who would understand him, whom he could love. It said that he would be a good father, one who could help his family attain the celestial kingdom.

When he'd received his blessing, Warren had been sure that everything would change. One day very soon he would wake up and find himself the typical, promising Mormon boy everyone thought he was. When he reached nineteen and nothing was different, Warren had decided that his mission would solve the problem. His first few months in Germany almost convinced him that it had. He had felt his testimony growing by the day, along with a deep affection for the people he taught. How ironic that it was one of them who had delivered the final blow to his new and vulnerable optimism.

Warren and his companion had been sure that the young man was Golden. He was sincere, introspective, and sensitive, with a real thirst for truth. He had accepted all the discussions avidly. He had only one argument.

"Eternal marriage is a wonderful concept," he had agreed. "But if I am a Mormon, does it mean that I have to marry a woman?"

Warren and his companion had stared at their investigator, thinking that he must have used a phrase they hadn't learned yet.

"I'm sorry?" said Warren's companion.

"Well," said the investigator, "I believe in eternal companionship, but I would like to marry a man."

There was an awful silence. The young man looked at Warren and his companion. "No?" he said quietly. "I thought not."

Warren cleared his throat nervously. "You're right. If you were to become a Mormon, you would have to marry

9

a woman. It says in the Bible that neither the woman nor the man is complete without the other. Marrying a—what you're talking about would be a serious sin."

The young man looked at them resignedly. "Well," he said, "then your church must not be true. Or if it is—I was beginning to think it was—then I'd be better off *not* joining it. I would get a worse punishment than I already deserve. I'm homosexual. I was born that way, and nothing will change me. They've done studies, you know. There's no way for me to change."

What Warren remembered most about that moment was that his teeth had begun to hurt. Maybe he'd clenched his jaws or something; at any rate, he had never heard anyone else describe the onset of despair as a toothache. He also recalled thinking that he had never really looked it in the face before, never really thought through the facts. The facts were that he was a homosexual. That he had been born that way. That he could never change. That he would never reach the celestial kingdom. That he was lost.

Warren turned off the shower and stepped into his well-furnished, empty apartment. Even though it was Saturday, he decided to check in at the office to make sure the half-day secretaries weren't having any problems. He dressed carefully in a pin-striped suit, a white shirt, and a subdued but distinctive tie—Warren had always had a conscientious devotion to his work and superb taste in clothes. As he stepped out of his apartment at precisely fifteen minutes to eight, Warren remarked to himself that he really had very little else.

If anyone had been able to see Ellen, Bill, and Warren all at once that Saturday morning, the observer would have thought that they shared very little. Their thoughts, their concerns, their situations, and their actions seem highly disparate. On Sunday, however, the observer would have said that the three had everything in common. That morning, they would all be seated on similar pews in similar churches, bowing their heads for the same sacrament and seeking the comfort of the same Spirit. The need for such comfort, as well as their membership in the Church, would be an invisible link between the three—but they would also have in common the outward appearance of contentment and invulnerability. What the casual observer could not have seen below this facade would be something to which none of the three young people would casually admit: an involvement in a pattern of behavior that had become something like an addiction and that was inhibiting their progress toward becoming like their Father in Heaven. Ellen, Bill, and Warren themselves might have been shocked to discover the similarities in their behavior and in the emotions and conflicts they each encountered within themselves but never expressed to others.

We suggest that there is a common pattern underlying much of Ellen's eating disorder, Bill's substance abuse, Warren's sexual temptations, and a host of other such phenomena that have become horribly familiar features of a troubled world. We call this pattern a compulsive cycle.

We thank the individuals who allowed us to set down in this book the experiences we have described, for Ellen, Bill, and Warren (though not the names we have given them) are real. They are some of the Latter-day Saints who graciously shared their stories with us over a five-year period of research and interviews, which began with a Sunday School class in 1984. As newlyweds, we were called to teach a class in our university ward. Since both of us were fledgling social scientists working on doctorates, we decided to offer our training in research as an extra feature of our calling. We promised the members of our Sunday School class that we would do our best to research their questions and provide information to them appropriately.

The response surprised us. The first class members who called us were usually concerned with questions they had encountered in their dealings with nonmember room-mates, friends, and classmates. As we mentioned a few of these in class, more and more telephone calls came in, and the callers spoke more and more candidly about struggles they had observed in Church friends, family members, and even themselves. These were some of the most stalwart, thoughtful, faithful Latter-day Saints we had ever met. Their testimonies were fervent and eloquently expressed. They were devoted to missionary work. They came from exemplary families. They endeavored to eschew all behavior that might impede their spiritual growth, to avoid temptations, and to repent completely if they succumbed. Outwardly, they were ideal young Latter-day Saints. And yet, some of them were engaged in struggles with self that absorbed huge amounts of energy and led them time and time again to the edge of despair.

We approached each new problem raised by our class members from three different angles. First, we listened very hard to the Church members who presented various problems to us. As often as possible, we attempted to interview the individual, Latter-day Saint or not, who was personally struggling with problem behavior. Second, we looked to the teachings of modern-day Church authorities and interviewed Church leaders about insights they had gained in their years of counseling and praying for members who experienced such problems. Finally, we considered the writings of secular social scientists whose work included investigations of the issues raised by ward members.

The research that had started as an adjunct to our Sunday School calling soon became a personal project, one we discussed on long walks, over dinner, and in favor of our schoolwork. We mentioned the project to our Latter-day Saint friends, who mentioned it to theirs, and we continued to receive phone calls and visits from people who were wrestling with what we came to see as various manifestations of a compulsive cycle. Our research soon gave us a clue to why so many of our age group seemed to be struggling with this type of behavior, for we read that the compulsive cycle, in all its many guises, tends to develop most easily during the stage of life when individuals have attained or nearly attained adult status but still have relatively few commitments or structured requirements in their lives. College and graduate school, we read, are typical situations where such behaviors tend to arise.

As we continued to conduct research on and off, through school commitments and the births of our children, the events we observed in the lives of compulsive-cycle victims led us to a conclusion that made us want to write this book. We found that although more individuals may become trapped in a cycle of compulsive behavior during a certain phase of life, the compulsion does not pass with the phase. Simple passage of time is not enough to free the addict from the cycle.

The people we interviewed grew older along with us, and as we encountered them again and talked with them about their struggles — sometimes after years without seeing them — we found that they had fallen into very different paths. We were thrilled to observe some whose lives had changed dramatically. These were the people who had broken out of their compulsive cycles, who felt free at last from their demons, who had turned even the nightmares of their experiences into a source of insight for themselves and others. In these people, the true message of repentance seemed to have reached its joyous realization. Those around them sensed their depth of understanding and their inner strength, without knowing that these qualities were the result of a long and terrible repentance. Tragically, other people we spoke with after long separations seemed to have given up the struggle and embraced their addictions. They looked at us with disdain, disgust, and disbelief if we suggested they might still change. They seemed to have lost the desire to do so. They had resigned themselves to the fallacy that breaking out of their cyclical patterns of destructive behavior was neither possible nor desirable. Finally, we spoke with those who were still locked into behaviors that they knew were inhibiting their progress toward perfection, who were struggling on with exhausted courage, who held despair at arm's length while they looked everywhere for hope.

These individuals and those who love them and counsel them and wish to help them are the people to whom we address this book. We do not know how many such Latter-day Saints exist, for no census can be taken of actions that are often hidden and denied. We do not mean to suggest that the Church is teeming with secret sins, for that is not the case. We believe that the vast majority of Latter-day Saints are, if not quite perfect, at least working effectively to become so. But we also believe that the troubled individuals we spoke with are not the only Church members caught in the terrible conflict between a true and inspired testimony of the restored gospel and patterns of behavior which they do not fully understand and therefore cannot yet fully control.

The implication that understanding addiction is fundamental to controlling it is based on our interpretation of the changes we saw taking place in the lives of recovering behavioral addicts. We hasten to point out that every victim of the compulsive cycle is unique and complex and that there can be no single, pat solution to every addict's problem. Nevertheless, among the subjects we interviewed, we discovered common patterns of behavior that we feel may be instructive to most people suffering from addictions. Generally speaking, the behavioral addicts we spoke with were caught in a repetitive, self-reinforcing cycle of destructive feelings and actions. We never saw anyone simply abandon that cycle. What we did see were individuals who managed to replace each step on the compulsive cycle with a constructive feeling or action. These people were still involved in a self-reinforcing cycle of feelings and actions, but it was a cycle that seemed to propel them upwards into happiness and freedom rather than downwards into misery and captivity. This positive pattern we call the "joy cycle." We came to believe that it is discernible in the lives of all righteous people. It, like every innate element of the human soul, is essentially divine. And, as he has done with every divine aspect of this mortal life, Satan has created a counterfeit—in this case, the compulsive cycle. This book is devoted to describing, in detail and with illustrative case studies, the nature of the compulsive cycle and some of the ways in which the joy cycle may be substituted for it. A quick description here might clarify the general direction of our discussion before it is overwhelmed by specifics—in other words, we will sketch a map of the forest before we plunge into the trees.

The compulsive cycle, as we see it, has four steps. Two of these steps are "feelings" the behavioral addict experiences emotionally; the other two steps are "actions" the behavioral addict performs in response to those feelings. The compulsive cycle begins with what we call "feelings of isolation." Various people we interviewed described these feelings as loneliness, a sense of having been abandoned, the belief that they were unworthy or incapable of being loved, or as a "homesickness for heaven." Perhaps this last definition was the most accurate, for though many of our subjects were surrounded by people who loved them, all of them were living in a world where the unity and oneness that are the natural condition of our spirits had been temporarily replaced by the fragmentations and separations of mortality. Whatever its cause, the behavioral addicts we interviewed expressed an almost universal feeling that a void existed within them. Although they described the void in different words, all agreed that it was an emptiness that cried out to be filled.

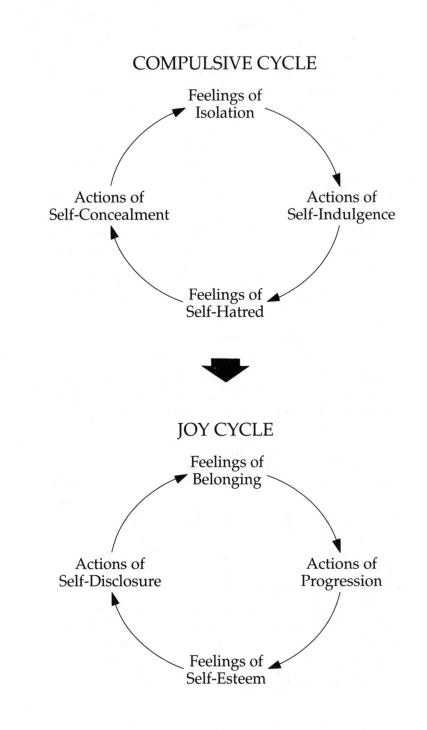

COMPULSIVE CYCLE

Feelings of
Isolation

Actions of
Self-Concealment

Actions of
Self-Indulgence

Feelings of
Self-Hatred

JOY CYCLE

Feelings of
Belonging

Actions of
Self-Disclosure

Actions of
Progression

Feelings of
Self-Esteem

In the case of the behavioral addicts, each individual had stumbled across some activity that did not fill this void, yet for a time produced physical or emotional sensations strong enough to block the person's awareness of the feelings of isolation. Because these actions involved the gratification of some immediate appetite at the expense of the person's (and other people's) long-term well-being, we have labeled them "actions of self-indulgence." The most common addictive actions we encountered involved the three areas we have chosen to consider in our case studies: eating disorders, the use of mood-altering substances, and sexual behavior. It seems, however, that almost any pleasurable activity, from shopping to reading, can become compulsive if the individual finds it effective in blocking feelings of isolation. Few of the actions were intrinsically evil. The harm we saw in them came from the addict's loss of ability to control the action. A true victim of the compulsive cycle typically will become more and more absorbed in the action of self-indulgence, will ignore responsibilities and relationships in favor of participating in the activity, and will eventually realize that he or she is unable to stop the behavior, even by the most determined effort.

The loss of self-control and the deterioration of lifestyle and relationships that accompany a behavioral addiction seem to lead directly into the next step on the compulsive cycle: "feelings of self-hatred." Immediately after the action of self-indulgence has been performed, when the appetite for it has been temporarily satiated, the addicts described experiencing an intense emotional and physical let-down, characterized by sadness, regret, discouragement, and guilt. That was true even when the action of self-indulgence was not considered a sin. But when the behavior was something explicitly forbidden by Church doctrine, the addict's feelings of self-hatred following the action of self-indulgence were overwhelming. Their guilt was not the healthy recognition that their behavior was unworthy of their status as beloved children of God. It was a judgment of self so severe, so punitive, and so absorbing that it all but drowned the addicts in their loathing for themselves. Compulsive-cycle victims at this stage almost always labeled themselves as disgusting, contemptible, and bad.

Feelings of self-hatred move the behavioral addict along to the second action step on the compulsive cycle: "actions of self-concealment." The addict's reaction to the addictive behavior is shame, and the reaction to shame is almost always a life-style of deception designed to hide the addiction. At the root of all actions of self-concealment lies deceit. The lies behavioral addicts tell to protect themselves from the recrimination of others—especially loved ones—may be lies of commission or of omission, of words or of silence, of actions or of failure to act. Because an addiction of any sort often grows to consume huge amounts of the addict's time and attention, more and more lies are required to disguise the compulsive cycle as it progresses. Ultimately, almost every aspect of a compulsive-cycle victim's interaction with those who do not share the addiction may be so riddled with self-concealing lies that even the addict cannot sort out truth from falsehood. At this point, the addict has developed a kind of double identity: a "good" self and a "bad" self. The bad self is seen by the addict as the real self and the good self as a false image carefully projected to others. The addict hides the part of the self that he or she feels is most fundamental from many other people, usually including the family members and friends who love the addict most.

The very real isolation caused by the behavioral addict's self-concealment adds to whatever the original conditions were that made the person feel alone and isolated. The addict's actions of self-concealment thus not only lead him or her back to feelings of isolation but also intensify those feelings, so the void within the person becomes larger than ever. To block consciousness of the feelings of isolation, the compulsive-cycle victim turns again to the action of self-indulgence that brought temporary relief in the past. After engaging in the activity, the addict feels worse than ever—the suspicion that the self is fundamentally bad has been confirmed. It thus seems even more important to keep that "true" nature secret from others . . . and so the cycle continues, growing more difficult to break out of with every turn.

Very often, people who are trapped in compulsive cycles know only that they repeatedly perform actions that they feel are wrong. Attempts to "break the habit" by simply abstaining from these actions seem to intensify the pressure resulting from the remainder of the cycle. The individuals we saw who succeeded in freeing themselves from compulsive cycles did more than simply vow to stop performing the action of self-indulgence. They recognized and addressed the whole cycle at once by a process of substitution rather than by simple abstinence. For every step on the compulsive cycle, recovering addicts must sub-stitute a feeling or an action that moves them toward hap-piness. That process is not one that can ever be accom-plished by the behavioral addict alone. Because so much of the compulsive cycle is related to the addict's relation-ship with others, the transformation of the compulsive cycle to the joy cycle always involves the participation of people around the addict. Many of the recovering addicts we interviewed gave grateful tribute to professional coun-selors, although finding the "right" counselor for the in-dividual addict seems to be crucial, and this choice should be made with great care. Others gave part of the credit for their recoveries to family members, Church leaders, or friends. We did not observe one case of a victim overcom-ing a compulsive cycle alone. The process of replacing the compulsive cycle with the joy cycle, then, is one in which not only the addict but also loved ones and counselors must be determined participants.

For addicts themselves, we believe that the focus of change must be on the two action steps on the compulsive cycle. On the other hand, those who desire to help the addict should turn most of their attention to the two feeling steps of the compulsive cycle, resisting the temptation to place heavy emphasis on restricting the addict's actions.

Because it is impossible to change one's feelings spontaneously without altering one's behavior, victims of the compulsive cycle must alter their actions first and then allow new feelings to arise in reaction to the new patterns of behavior. Actions of self-indulgence must be replaced by what we call actions of progression, and actions of self-concealment must be replaced by actions of self-disclosure. In the simpler terms of the scriptures, addicts must "confess and forsake" their sins.

The particular actions of progression that should replace the actions of self-indulgence will be different for each addict, depending on the personality and preferences of the individual. To qualify as an action of progression, however, an activity must fill two requirements: it must increase the addict's ability to learn or understand, and it must also increase the addict's ability to love. Exercising talents and serving others are the classic general examples of actions of progression. At first, a recovering addict might not find any activities as rewarding as the addictive behavior. Eventually, however, the intrinsic interest and enjoyment of actions of progression will come to seem more appealing than the actions of self-indulgence—provided that the addict is also careful to replace actions of self-concealment with actions of self-disclosure.

Actions of self-disclosure are performed almost constantly by most people. They are simply the small ways in which one shares one's self with other people. Conversations between friends or even acquaintances very often consist largely of individuals relating to each other how they feel and what they are thinking. Countless small self-disclosures tie most individuals to the community of people around them in a way that allows them to feel understood and included. Compulsive-cycle victims, because they hide such a large part of their activities, thoughts, and feelings from those who love them, understandably lack this security. To remedy this situation, we believe that addicts must at some point confess the real story of their compulsive behavior to some person or group of people whom they respect. Eventually, the story should be told at least to every person who has been somehow affected by the addict's actions. In the case of sins serious enough to require official Church action, Church leaders must be included among those to whom the addict discloses his or her "real" self. This disclosure is not to punish or humiliate the compulsive-cycle victim but to dispel the addict's belief that he or she will not be accepted or loved once the truth is revealed.

The positive effect of actions of self-disclosure can be all but destroyed if the person to whom the addict confesses reacts with an attitude of harshness or rejection. Therefore, those who desire to help the addict are most effective when they concentrate on helping the addict replace feelings of isolation with feelings of belonging and feelings of self-hatred with feelings of self-esteem. When a rescuer hears the whole story of an addict's struggle and then expresses interest in and love for the individual concerned, a huge step has been made toward making the first of these replacements. We have never seen a more dramatic transformation of personality than occurred in addicts we interviewed who finally told the horrible truth and found themselves loved nevertheless. On the other hand, the rescuer must avoid what researchers call "enabling" behavior: forgiving the addict so unconditionally that he or she sees no reason to forgo the addiction. To replace the

Reaction by those that the addict confesses to.

addict's feelings of self-hatred with feelings of self-esteem, he or she must learn to recognize and deal with the social consequences of addictive behavior. The example of Christ, who loved sinners without giving any quarter to sin, is the single greatest field guide for helping addicts overcome self-hatred without giving in to their weaknesses.

If all the steps on the joy cycle can be substituted simultaneously for all the steps on the compulsive cycle, the addict will have begun a repentance that may prove to be the greatest source of happiness he or she has ever known. Usually many attempts at substitution must be made before the compulsive-cycle victim is completely freed from old habits and destructive responses to stress. Nevertheless, if the attempt at repentance is persistent, and especially if loved ones are there to provide unflagging encouragement, the addict can eventually become so firmly entrenched in the joy cycle that the compulsive cycle is all but forgotten. As the person develops the habit of sharing self with others in actions of self-disclosure, the emotional and spiritual closeness to others that follows will manifest itself in feelings of belonging. These feelings, which bring irrepressible happiness, tend to overflow spontaneously in actions of progression, which in turn give the former addict increasing feelings of self-esteem. Self-esteem makes the individual more able and willing to perform actions of self-disclosure, which bring even more feelings of belonging, and so on and on the cycle goes.

The description we have given of the compulsive cycle and its cure may sound convincing—we hope so, because it represents more than four years of careful observation and analysis on our part. Nevertheless, the discussion as it stands is incomplete. Compulsive or addictive behaviors are extraordinarily, frighteningly powerful. They are more than simple human errors: they are some of the destroyer's most effective tools. We believe that to ignore the spiritual aspect of an addict's affliction is to doom any therapy to eventual failure. The single thing of which our research most firmly convinced us is this: only the power of God and the atonement of Jesus Christ are sufficiently powerful to free victims of compulsive cycles. Every recovered behavioral addict we have encountered, either in person or through printed accounts, mentioned a submission to God (however they conceptualized Him) and a spiritual rebirth as turning points in their recovery. Most could recount a moment at which the power of the Atonement (whatever they called it) became clearly manifest in their lives. For others the process had been more gradual but equally unmistakable. The testimony these individuals gained of the Lord's infinite love and of the magnitude of His sacrifice for them became the central reality in their lives. To our surprise, these addicts and their loved ones often expressed gratitude for the very addiction that had led them to this testimony by all but destroying their lives. The knowledge that our Heavenly Father lives and that He loves us was worth more to them than the price they had paid in suffering.

It is our fervent desire that this account of our investigation into the compulsive cycle and its effects on believing Latter-day Saints will provide instruction or at least encouragement to someone whose life is being marred by addiction. Our understanding and our explanation of the compulsive cycle are far from perfect, and for that reason we urge the reader not to accept what we have written without careful thought and earnest prayer. We have seen, many times, the Lord's fulfillment of His promise to those who seek His counsel in understanding: "Be of good cheer, for I will lead you along. The kingdom is yours and the blessings thereof are yours, and the riches of eternity are yours." (D&C 78:18.)

If you think that the long despair of compulsive behavior has irrevocably separated you or a loved one from this promise, you are wrong. The gift of the Atonement

23

is easily within reach and with it is a real, immediate, and immeasurable happiness. Behavioral addicts are no different from other mortals in their absolute need to take advantage of that gift. Nor are they different from others in being infinitely loved and valued by their Heavenly Parents, despite their sins. The destructive force of addiction is impressive, even awesome, but it pales in comparison to the power of the love of God. The reality of that love, rather than the horror of the compulsive cycle, is the central message of this book. We hope that we can somehow communicate the divinity and perfection of the plan of repentance through our own very human and imperfect efforts.

2

THE BODY AND
COMPULSIVE BEHAVIOR

. . . .

Before we ever saw our second child and first son, Adam, we knew a great deal about his personality. When he was only an embryo, four inches long from head to toe, we learned that he would be a calm, friendly, sociable baby, eager to please, with a strong sense of humor and a pronounced stubborn streak. Four months after we were given this information, Adam made his entrance into this world. He conformed very closely to the description of his character we had been given before his birth. No one was surprised. There was nothing mystical about the foreknowledge we had gained. The information had come from a photograph of enlarged cells, which were taken from the fluid that surrounded Adam during his prenatal development. The photograph showed that each of our baby's cells contained an extra chromosome—the tiny packets of genetic information that tell an individual body how it should be built. Most human beings have twenty-three matched pairs of chromosomes. Adam has that, plus an extra chromosome in the twenty-first position. This condition, known as Down's syndrome, is understood to influence many aspects of physical and mental development. We were somewhat surprised to find how much it also directed the formation of Adam's personality and the way he responds to objects and events.

During the period that followed Adam's diagnosis and preceded his birth, we learned a great deal about the devastating effects a "genetic accident" can have. We found out more than we wanted to know about the many mental and physical problems that might characterize people with chromosomal anomalies of various kinds. But we also learned to feel lucky that our son has Down's syndrome rather than any number of other birth defects, for his condition carries with it the many wonderful attributes we have already mentioned. We have often been assured, and we have noticed in our own dealings with the handicapped, that Adam's loving, cheerful, buoyant personality is common to a great many people with Down's syndrome. As we awaited his birth, and as we watch his development, we also learned more profoundly than ever before about the nature of mortality and the significance of the physical body for so-called "normal" human beings. We have come to realize poignantly that for us, as well as for Adam and people like him, *every* aspect of behavior, including personality traits we may think of as completely metaphysical, might very well be influenced by our physical natures. Not only are our muscles and bones, our language ability, and our spatial cognition influenced by our genes but so are our moods, our feelings, and our responses to the world around us.

In our research, we have found that the behaviors we call compulsive cycles focus on some specific action of the physical body, such as eating, using drugs or alcohol, or engaging in sexual activity. As we will point out, we believe that the very potential for behaviors to fall into cycles is in part an attribute of the body. The physical nature of a compulsive cycle is perhaps most obvious in substance abuse, where a recognizable chemical addiction exists, but we found close parallels to this type of addiction in behaviors as diverse as shoplifting and looking at pornography. We also found that many compulsive-cycle victims we spoke with shared concepts about their physical natures that were not congruent with gospel teachings. Instead, their understanding of their physical natures was based on ideas about the body and the spirit that were derived from secular and non–Latter-day Saint religious sources. We found that these misconceptions helped keep individuals locked into addictive behaviors by clouding their understanding of their physical natures and hence of their moral dilemmas. Before we discuss compulsive cycles, then, we would like to point out some of the fallacies about the body and the spirit that pervade our society.

When a Latter-day Saint hears the question, "Why are we here on earth?" the answer is likely to pop out automatically: "To gain a body and to be tested." At the present point in the eternal progression of our existence, these two factors are indeed the focus of our education, and they are inextricably connected with each other. We believe that our spirits were already well-defined, knowledgeable, and intelligent before we were allowed to come to mortality. One primary thing that separated us from God was the experience of living in a physical body to learn to master it. That is an experience we were unable to comprehend in the premortal existence. It is the experience that even Jesus Christ lacked before his mortal ministry. It is this experience that all of us must have to become like our Father in Heaven. And so it is that even the noble and great spirits, whom Abraham saw in the premortal existence, must trail their clouds of glory into the ignominiously awkward and disobedient bodies created by mortal parents. Some spirits, like our son Adam's, find themselves born into bodies that might never fully accommodate them in this world. But even the original Adam, when he first came to the earth, found his incomprehensibly powerful spirit subject to a physical body with an unfamiliar nature of its own. One of his most important tasks was to come to an understanding of the body and its nature that would allow him to work in harmony with its powers and master

27

its temptations. Latter-day Saints believe that all of his posterity share that important task.

The fundamental significance of that objective is matched by its difficulty. Satan has taken great pains not only to tempt the physical man but to mislead his intellectual and spiritual understanding of the body and its role. People who believe the sacred and secular philosophies that surround Latter-day Saints, especially in Western societies, view as strange or nonsensical the Latter-day Saint belief that the body is a central feature of mortality. "What importance could the body have?" might be the question put to Mormonism by the Judeo-Christian religious tradition that undergirds Western society. "The body is nothing but dross: vile, corrupt, and ephemeral. It is to *overcome* the body that we are here—to confine its appetites, flout its desires, and finally to escape from it into the bliss of a spiritual existence unencumbered by physicality. That is our purpose on earth." To most Western religions, the body is not only inessential but contradictory to the divine nature in man.

The influence of that idea is evident all around us. Our culture seems bent on forcing the "bad" body into a stereotype as far from nature as it can be. Our ideal of beauty is so rare that almost no one's body conforms to it naturally and certainly not for more than a few years. The physicality of the physical is futilely denied by the media myth that the natural attributes and capacities of the body—from six-week acne to childbearing to aging—are in fact unnatural things we should all hope to avoid. The bodies we see on television, in magazines, at the movies, do not seem to look or act or ache like ours do. The heroine never loses her tan, though she ostensibly lives in Siberia, and the hero springs back after seventeen brutal beatings, wincing only slightly, to whisk her away for a romantic interlude that seems to have no connection with procreation. They are not human figures. They are more like the gods of Valhalla or Olympus: eternally lovely, eternally young, eternally nothing like you or me. *Our* bodies, our cultural tradition tells us — our sinful, decrepit, mortal bodies — are disgusting shadows of these immortal figures.

And yet, with incalculable audacity, Joseph Smith dared to propound the notion that our bodies, the very ones we now possess, are themselves divine. Some Latter-day Saints seem to believe that in the resurrection we will become much like the movie stars whose appearance and abilities our society idolizes. Perhaps it is more likely that we will gain the wisdom to see beyond the "traditions of our fathers," which teach us that our bodies as we now know them are unacceptable and crude.

The religions that shaped many of our culture's attitudes have filled our environment with the idea that we can and should deny our physical nature. As members of the societies that formed around those religions, Latter-day Saints are constantly exposed to these erroneous ideas, often in the guise of truth itself. "Truth," says Eliza R. Snow in one of our most beloved hymns, "is reason." (*Hymns of The Church of Jesus Christ of Latter-day Saints*, 1985, no. 292.)

Truth as reason is the central tenet of the other major contributor to Western philosophy besides the Judeo-Christian religious tradition. Since the Age of Enlightenment, the gospel of rationality has occupied the premier position among the ideological doctrines of secular Western society. The response of this philosophy to the Latter-day Saint idea of mortality is opposite to the view of orthodox religion, but it is no less derogatory. "Here to *gain* a body?" the secular humanist might say. "How ridiculous. You cannot gain a body, for you *are* your body. We must celebrate the body, yes — we must use its capacities for enjoyment to the fullest — for *there is nothing else.*" Western rationalism teaches that the spirit is an illusion, fabricated by the conjunction of molecules in our brains, and that those brains are dictated by laws of physics, which are

29

utterly accidental and devoid of meaning. The truly honest and reasonable man, so the logic goes, must face the fact that his ideas of an immortal spirit are merely the desperate self-deceptions of a brain genetically programmed to deny the possibility of its own annihilation.

The cultural outgrowth of this philosophy might seem to be a negation of the Judeo-Christian denial of the physical. In fact, the two join hands in a sort of mad and paradoxical dance that dominates our popular culture. I am everything but my body, says the Judeo-Christian ethic. I am nothing but my body, says the tradition of rationality. And so as we are taught to loathe our bodies as nothing, we are also taught to indulge them as everything. If the body seems prone to gluttony, lust, or greed—fine! We deserve these little treats, don't we? After all, we're only here for a moment before we vanish into oblivion. "Eat, drink, and be merry, for tomorrow we die." On the other hand, as you eat, make sure you don't gain any weight. As you drink, make sure you do it suavely, like the aristocrats in the commercials and not like the sad, sick figures you might see on the street or in a detoxification center. And before you make merry, get your teeth capped so that the manic grin of a mortal facing death will appear to be the brilliant smile of one impervious to mortality. Even the most mundane products of our culture, far divorced though they may be from overt philosophical thinking, can often be traced to these paradoxical ideologies, which claim that the body is everything and that the body is nothing. Woven together, these two traditions form much of the fabric of the society in which we live.

The ideas of the Judeo-Christian ethic and of rationalism are seductive not only because of the glamor they have each been accorded in our culture but also because they claim to rely on the two great principles of human understanding: faith in the revelations of God and development of the divine capacity to reason. The worldly corruptions of these two sources of knowledge are two of the most neatly packaged and effectively marketed products sold by the adversary.

Under the attractive wrappings, however, these ideas contain the same fundamental error: the assertion that the physical cannot be immortal. This single error forces mortal beings to fix their identity on either the spirit or the body: to choose between the two. This choice is more than unnecessary. It is deadly. The Lord has revealed to us, both anciently and through latter-day prophets, that "the elements are eternal, and spirit and element, inseparably connected, receive a fulness of joy; and when separated, man cannot receive a fulness of joy." (D&C 93:33–34.) Satan would like nothing better than to see us cut off from "a fulness of joy." What better way to deceive the faithful and the honest in heart than to persuade them that faith or honesty must lead to the conclusion that *either* the spirit *or* the body is the soul of man?

This is not to say that Latter-day Saints have nothing to learn from those of other faiths. Like many of Satan's most effective lies, the lies of the world concerning the relationship of the mortal body and the eternal spirit are not outright inventions but twisted truths. These are the most effective forms of deception because they satisfy part of our need to continue discovering truth, which is born in each of us. After all, poison is most likely to kill when the fatal dose is mixed most imperceptibly with the tastiest and most nutritious food. We must all learn, as we must all eat, if we wish to continue our existence. The task is not to reject any "dish" of ideas served to us, for then our minds and souls would starve. The Lord has commanded us to "seek learning, even by study and also by faith." (D&C 88:118.) The object of that study and faith must be to discern the truth of an idea from the error it might contain, accepting what is good and nourishing and rejecting the errors, which can poison and destroy.

Our research convinced us that although they are flawed and incomplete, both the non–Latter-day Saint religious understanding of the body and the scientific findings that emerge out of rationalism do have a place in our understanding of our physical natures, of sin—especially addictive sin—and of the Atonement, which affords us the inestimable gift of repentance. We are told many times in the scriptures to "walk not after the flesh" (Romans 8:4), and yet latter-day doctrines teach that God Himself has a body of flesh and bone. Clearly, the Lord does not wish us to rid ourselves of the flesh. What, then, is meant by this injunction to "walk not after" it? Part of the answer might be found in the rationalist's claim that the body is "programmed" to seek its own comfort and maximize its own well-being. There is certainly some truth to this argument. In the scriptures we are told over and over that the natural man is an enemy to God. Successful and effective branches of human knowledge, especially the social sciences, are based on analysis of the ways in which human beings "naturally" behave; however, Latter-day Saints add to that understanding of man's nature the crucial belief that there is an immortal intelligence placed in the body, which, until this mortal stage of existence, has been separate from it. That intelligence is not subject to the same inclinations as the physical body. There are instances, as we have seen in our son with Down's syndrome, where the body can cloud the spirit's understanding. Like Adam, if not to the same extent, we are all affected by the nature we inherit in ways that may be complex and difficult to understand.

The idea that genetic inheritance has a profound effect on our behavior is vividly illustrated by the predictable ways in which behavior changes for individuals whose genes are abnormally constituted. But a physical or mental handicap is not the only reason such confusion of the spirit may occur. Consider the terrible ways in which the "sins of the fathers" might be "visited upon the children." One example might be an abused child who grows into a well-meaning adult. Having been abused by his parents, such an individual might abhor the thought that he himself would ever strike his children. And yet, studies show that when he finds himself under pressure and unable to cope with those children, the grown abused child is very likely to become a child abuser. Once we understand that this behavior is the only instruction in parenting that he ever received from his own parents, we might feel that it is terrible but nonetheless natural that he might resort to such behavior. Less frightening and more familiar is the example of a child whose parents offer food as consolation for every injury and reward for every success. "Naturally" such a child might grow up with a tendency to use food for emotional sustenance. A similar "natural" process seems to be at work in people with compulsive sexual behaviors: a great many of them appear to have experienced sexual molestation as children.

The behavioral sciences, which have uncovered these patterns in human action, have helped many people understand the roots of problem behaviors. The "natural man" — which is the only part of man such science acknowledges — does seem to base its actions on some kinds of conditioning. That is the learning of the carnal mind, which teaches the body to avoid pain and seek pleasure. Untempered, the carnal mind leads to the selfish and destructive fulfillment of appetites. As Alma told Corianton, "all men that are in a state of *nature,* or I would say, in a carnal state, are in the gall of bitterness and in the bonds of iniquity; they are without God in the world, and they have gone contrary to the *nature* of God." (Alma 41:11; italics added.) Here Alma uses the word *nature* to refer both to the sinful state of man and to the essence of divinity. What is the difference? The man who is in a state of nature is in a carnal state, but that does not mean merely that such a man possesses a body. After all, Alma has just informed his son that at the resurrection "the soul shall be restored to the body, and the body to the soul." (Alma 40:23.) The human body in and of itself does not constitute that carnal nature that is contrary to the nature of God. Rather, it seems that the submission of the intelligent spirit to the "natural" inclinations of the mortal body lies at the root of the problem.

In Doctrine and Covenants 93, the Lord elucidates the relationship between our physical nature, with its conditioned behaviors and selfish appetites, and the nature of the immortal spirit. This remarkable revelation explains much of the apparent contradiction between our carnal nature and our divine nature:

"For man is spirit. The elements are eternal, and spirit and element, inseparably connected, receive a fulness of joy;

"And when separated, man cannot receive a fulness of joy.

"The elements are the tabernacle of God; yea, man is the tabernacle of God, even temples; and whatsoever temple is defiled, God shall destroy that temple.

"The glory of God is intelligence, or in other words, light and truth.

"Light and truth forsake that evil one.

"Every spirit of man was innocent in the beginning; and God having redeemed man from the fall, men became again, in their infant state, innocent before God." (Vv. 33–38.)

According to this great scripture, we are not born into sin by inheriting mortal bodies. On the contrary, by taking on a physical nature we become "the tabernacle of God." Nevertheless, mortality does expose us for the first time to the temptations of the natural man. But the Lord points out that His evaluation of our actions rests on our understanding of our own behavior. As infants, at the stage of mortality when we are most selfish, most dominated by the nature of our bodies, we are paradoxically "innocent

34

before God." Why is a baby incapable of sin? Not because he is unselfish or because he denies the appetites of his body but because he is incapable of *understanding* the nature of selfishness or appetite. He has not yet had the opportunity to evaluate his actions through "light and truth," which constitute intelligence. Once he is able to understand his actions through godlike intelligence, once he has eaten from the tree of knowledge, he will be capable of defiling—or glorifying—the temple of his body.

One great problem of mortality is that we do not grow from our infant state of innocence into a state of knowledge without receiving pressures from the physical condition of the world, from the errant ways of those around us, or from Satan, who claims to be the god of this world. Often, like children who are mistaught in their infancy, we fall victim to sin before we are fully capable of understanding why. Our mentally retarded son Adam, because of the nature of his body, may perform behaviors that are against the laws of God simply because he does not fully comprehend the nature of his actions. His case is extreme, but it is not unique. Each of us inherits a body, which acts before we have divine understanding of its motivations. Doctrine and Covenants 93 continues:

"And that wicked one cometh and taketh away light and truth, through disobedience, from the children of men, and because of the tradition of their fathers." (V. 39.)

Satan and his servants are working on us, unfairly and treacherously, from the moment we assume mortality. Sometimes, as this scripture tells us, in committing acts of disobedience we simply follow their counsel instead of the Lord's. Sometimes, like the child abuser, the overeater, or the sexual offender mentioned above, we owe part of our transgression to the "tradition of our fathers." That these actions may be unconsciously motivated or result from the misused free agency of others does not mean that the actions are not wrong. The fact that the child abuser was

35

himself abused might make his actions understandable, but it does not make them good. Nor does our ignorance transform even the smallest of our sins to virtues — and we all have sins. In all of history, there has only been one Person on the earth who did not succumb to any of the various pressures of mortality. "If justice be thy plea," says Shakespeare's Portia to Shylock, "consider this: that in the course of *justice*, none of us should see salvation." That is why, Portia continues, "we do pray for *mercy*." (*The Merchant of Venice*; italics added.)

Commenting, as Shakespeare does, on the universal sorrow that would result from the nature of men in the course of simple justice, Alma explains the way in which mercy is offered to all of us: "And thus we see that all mankind were fallen, and they were in the grasp of *justice*; yea, the justice of God, which consigned them forever to be cut off from his presence.

"And now, the plan of *mercy* could not be brought about except an atonement should be made; therefore God himself atoneth for the sins of the world, to bring about the plan of mercy, to appease the demands of justice, that God might be a perfect, just God, and a merciful God also." (Alma 42:14–15; italics added.)

God did not create us with the potential for unintended sins or uncontrollable appetites and then abandon us to the consequences. He did not make us vulnerable to the pain and pressure inflicted by the free agency of the wicked and then condemn us for being hurt or twisted. In order that we might have the subjective experience of weighing and feeling both good and evil and emerge from that experience whole, Jesus Christ assumed the consequences of our sins Himself. "Surely he hath borne our griefs, and carried our sorrows. . . . he was wounded for our transgressions, he was bruised for our iniquities: the chastisement of our peace was upon him; and with his stripes we are healed." (Isaiah 53:4–5.)

Each human being is given the light of Christ by which he may know whether his actions are good or evil. That is all we need in order to overcome the sins of the natural man, for we are not expected to pay the consequences for every action that falls short of godliness. The Lord merely entreats us to repent of our incorrect behavior when we recognize that it is wrong. As we stumble through mortality like bulls in a china shop, smashing objects we are far too poor to replace, He requires only that we recognize the damage and do our best to correct it. He has paid for our destruction already, so that we might have the chance to go into the shop without bankrupting ourselves. The Lord's prophets "say nothing but repentance unto this generation" (D&C 6:9), not to condemn us for our imperfections, but to encourage us to accept the Atonement, which ransoms us from paying the price of nature by ourselves. Repentance is not a burden. It is a gift.

Part of the process of repentance is that we learn, through our errors, to understand our physical nature so that we may become one with it. Because of the Lord's unimaginable sacrifice, there is only one group of mortals for whom "there is no forgiveness in this world nor in the world to come." (D&C 76:34.) These are they who, "having denied the Holy Spirit after having received it, and having denied the Only Begotten Son of the Father, having crucified him unto themselves," will "go away into everlasting punishment." (Vv. 36, 44.) The difference between this type of sin and all others is that the denial of the Holy Spirit, which by definition "enlighteneth our understanding" (Alma 38:28), is committed in full personal understanding of the sin and its implications. "For behold," says Alma, "if ye deny the Holy Ghost when it once has had place in you, *and ye know that ye deny it,* this is a sin which is unpardonable." (Alma 39:6.) Just as we have no need for the Atonement until we obtain some understanding of our behavior, we do not become ineligible for forgiveness

37

until that understanding is complete. A son of perdition, having partaken of the light of Christ, understands the plan of salvation. He has been filled with the light and truth that Alma defines as godlike intelligence. He knows himself and the consequences of his actions, and he chooses *with full understanding* to deny Christ and refuse the gift of the Atonement. The Lord will never violate our free agency, just as He could not deny Lucifer's when that son of the morning knowingly chose damnation. Even the supernal gift of the Atonement cannot force redemption on one who understands sin with the understanding of a God and chooses it nevertheless.

Most of us never have the opportunity to make such a choice. Our sins are sins of partial comprehension, of ill-gotten conditioning, of mistaking the desires of the carnal mind for those of the spiritual intelligence. The sins of the natural man are not the choices of Lucifer but the blunderings of spirits who search for a half-remembered heaven by pursuing the weak rewards of earth. Psychologists who claim that our brains and bodies are programmed to follow such reinforcements seem to be right in many cases. What their mechanistic theories do not account for, however, is that *understanding* our errors can often allow us to correct them. If the child abuser, overeater, or sexual offender can learn to identify the true causes for the undesirable actions, the person will have a better chance at controlling them — an idea that constitutes one of the cornerstones of modern psychology. The sciences that claim that we are only carnal beings, and nothing more, can show that comprehension often brings control. But they do not logically explain what it is within us that can change conditioned actions through the process of understanding. They cannot. For they do not acknowledge the existence of the spirit, and it is the spirit that understands, the spirit that changes, the spirit that makes it possible for us to allow Jesus Christ to atone for the sins of the natural man. The study of the physical body and its nature is part of the spirit's gaining that understanding. The role of the spirit, as the scriptures show, is not to eschew the nature we gain when we assume a physical body but to direct that nature toward the good.

"Bridle all your passions," said Alma to his son Corianton, "that ye may be filled with love." (Alma 38:12.) This simple and profound phrase is evidence of the wisdom of a prophet who understood that the spirit and the body are both integral parts of the soul. A bridle is not an instrument with which a vicious beast is forced into submission. It is a tool of guidance, of communication, between a valuable animal and its human rider. Left without governance, an unbridled horse, like the natural man, will turn to the satiation of its appetites because it sees no reason not to. If the horse is abused or tormented or forced to abandon altogether the good and wholesome aspects of natural appetites, it will use every device at its disposal to escape, circumvent, or flout the impossible demands of an unreasonable master. But if it is loved, valued, and guided by a hand that understands its needs and nourishes it without overindulgence, the horse, like the body, can take its rider to objectives that can profit both of them—objectives that the animal would not reach without the rider's knowledge and the rider could not reach without the horse's strength.

We believe that compulsive cycles arise "naturally" in some individuals when they are exposed to certain conditions. Research suggests that at least some forms of addictive behavior have a physical component. Alcoholism is a good example. Many scientists believe that the potential to become severely addicted to alcohol is carried in some individuals' genetic makeup. If a person who is genetically predisposed to alcoholism is exposed to liquor, so the theory goes, he or she is more likely to become severely addicted to alcohol than is a person with different genes. Some researchers have claimed that other addictions, such as sexual promiscuity and homosexuality, are also "in the genes." They use this claim to argue that such behaviors should be accepted by society. Although we disagree with this claim, this book is not designed to argue against it. We are not "value-neutral"; we write to believing Latter-day Saints who wish to rid themselves of addictive behaviors, and not to others who wish to defend those behaviors as morally acceptable. Our research has convinced us that whether or not a genetic predisposition is involved, some individuals seem more likely than others to respond to a particular experience by becoming addicted to that type of behavior. Certain surrounding conditions — for example, the intense pressure and minimal structured time of a college student's schedule — seem to make the individual even more likely to develop such an addiction. Compulsive behaviors come in infinite variety, but the common pattern described by all the people we interviewed makes us believe that the course of almost all these addictions is remarkably similar. The natural man seems prone to this pattern of behavior. It develops without conscious effort and often in spite of the resistance of the addict.

That is the pattern we have called the compulsive cycle. It is one of the most devastating errors of the natural man, for those who become trapped by it often do not understand the nature of their dilemma — and understanding is an integral part of change and repentance. One of the most pronounced differences between the people we spoke with who managed to free themselves from their addiction, and those who remained addicted, seemed to be that the first group understood that the sin was part of a cycle. This understanding was a key element in these individuals' repentance. For, as we have pointed out, the intelligence, or spirit, is able to control the behavior of the natural man insofar as it understands that behavior. The testimonies of the compulsive-cycle victims we spoke to — including the accounts of the three individuals, Ellen Schor, Bill Stewart, and Warren White, whose cases we follow in describing the cycle — were often unsettling and sad. Nevertheless, in general the self-descriptions of these compulsive-cycle victims were marked by courageous honesty. Especially in the cases of those who repented of their sins, we believe that they told us the truth about their lives. In their accounts of their addictions we have seen enacted the simple and eloquent words of the Savior: "If ye continue in my word, then are ye my disciples indeed; and ye shall know the truth, and the truth shall make you free." (John 8:31–32.)

3

THE FIRST STEP:
FEELINGS OF ISOLATION

. . . .

There is no true "first step" in a cycle: by definition, a cycle works as an unbroken continuum. The behavioral addicts we spoke with in our research did not remember a distinct beginning to their compulsive cycles, although they sometimes remembered the first time they became involved with their particular actions of self-indulgence. Looking back over their lives, people who were in the midst of an addiction often remembered themselves before the problem began as "accidents waiting to happen." These people seem to have decided retroactively that the behavior to which they were addicted had always been a part of their natures and that their entrapment in the compulsive cycle was therefore inevitable. They remembered themselves as leaves floating along on a stream that had eventually dragged them under. By contrast, people who had successfully repented of habitual sins saw this "selective memory," which they had exercised during their addictions, as part of the addiction itself. Recovering compulsive-cycle victims felt that their recollections of childhood were more balanced and accurate after they had broken the cycle than those memories had been when they were actively involved in the addiction. They thought they could remember a time when they were not involved in addictive behavior. Unlike the actively addicted subjects, they did not think they had been floating on a current of potential

42

addiction all their lives. They did not think they had "always been this way." They could pinpoint times when they believed they had fallen or been pushed into the stream of compulsive behavior.

Despite these differences in their personalities and experiences, all the people we interviewed recounted remarkably similar *feelings*, which they claimed had led them to behavioral addiction. Feelings of emptiness and loneliness were the water of the stream that had surrounded them before the compulsive cycle caught them. Those feelings did not change qualitatively when they entered the cycle; the water simply became deeper and the current stronger. We have labeled these painful sensations "feelings of isolation." Because they seem to be so universal and can begin so early in life for so many reasons, feelings of isolation constitute the stage of the cycle which most nearly approaches the first step.

One of the most frightening aspects of mortal life is the capacity each of us possesses to feel utterly and irredeemably alone. Perhaps feelings of isolation were present in previous stages of our existence, but surely the loneliness of this "lone and dreary world" can be as devastating as anything we might have experienced elsewhere. Jesus Christ, who sought solitude often during His mortal ministry, nevertheless entreated His disciples to "watch with me" (Matthew 26:38) as He approached the terrible suffering of Gethsemane. Instead, they fell asleep, and as the resurrected Christ later told Joseph Smith, "I have overcome and have trodden the wine-press *alone*." (D&C 76:107.) It was in the garden and later on the cross, as He took our sins upon him and "descended below all things" (D&C 88:6), that Jesus experienced the ultimate spiritual isolation possible in the human estate. There is no more powerful image of this loneliness in all literature than that evoked by Jesus' exclamation on the cross: "My God, my God, why hast thou forsaken me?" (Matthew 27:46.)

Each of us, as we sojourn on the earth, experiences

43

some shadow of the agony of Christ's isolation during His atonement. The great promise of the gospel, made possible by that ultimate sacrifice, is that we need not be alone forever. Many of the most sacred ordinances of the Church concern the sealing of human beings to each other and to God, with a power that will maintain those relationships throughout eternity. Each of us knows from personal experience that "it is not good for man to be alone." (Moses 3:18.) The search for companionship, for the unconditional love that binds souls to each other, is one of the most powerful forces that drives us from our infancy onward. The ultimate source for that love is of course the Lord Himself, who *is* love. Most of us, however, first come to a mortal understanding of that love through the medium of our fellow human beings. And yet the physical conditions of this world, including factors like death and time, which are unfamiliar to our spirits, create inexorable barriers that separate us. One great challenge we face on earth is the same one that Christ himself underwent — to confront temptation and suffering within the confines of our own free wills, to "work out our salvation in fear and trembling" in a condition of isolation.

The people we talked to who had been trapped in compulsive cycles did not describe their feelings of isolation in quite such ultimate terms. What they mentioned without exception, however, was the core of loneliness that lay at the heart of their behaviors. No matter *what* the behavior, the *why* seemed invariably to come down to loneliness: to a sense of being different or alien, to the feeling that the person involved in this behavior was ultimately not lovable. Interview after interview followed a common pattern. The first response to the question, "Why do you perform this habitual action that you know is destructive?" would be something unique to the respondent's personality or situation: "I learned it from a friend and just got hooked," or "I guess I kind of wanted my parents' attention," or "It just seemed fun." If that first response was followed up by a second question—"Why did you get hooked?" "Why did you want your parents' attention?" "Why did it seem fun?"—the answers that came back would begin to speak of loneliness, isolation, and the person's own conviction that he or she was unlovable. "I felt like one of the group when I was doing it." "I just wanted to know my parents cared." "While I was doing it, I would forget for a while that I was basically a bad person."

Let us repeat that these people did not appear at all unusual. In fact, most of them seemed to have better than average evidence in their lives that they were worthwhile and loved. But what we came to realize, as we conducted our interviews, is that every person who ever comes to earth has some difference, some real or imagined inadequacy, some factor that might indeed set him or her apart from others. There are as many ways to feel different and alone as there are human beings, for each of us is unique and our understanding of one another is far from perfect.

At the times when we spoke to them, many of our subjects were in the midst of a long-term addictive behavior. This fact no doubt dominated their responses during the interviews. Nevertheless, it was interesting to see that all of them were unconvinced, emotionally and spiritually, that they could be loved unconditionally by other people or, especially, by their Father in Heaven. Although they agreed to the concept intellectually, they did not believe it in their hearts. If asked directly, they would willingly admit to the feeling that some part of them, the part they often identified as "the real me," was unlovable and therefore utterly, achingly, endlessly alone. Involvement in destructive cycles fed into this isolation and eventually created the terrible degree of loneliness we saw in people with long-term problems. But we believe that at some point it was the feeling of differentness, the ubiquitous "certain something [that] whispers 'you're a stranger here' "

45

(*Hymns of The Church of Jesus Christ of Latter-day Saints,* no. 292), that enticed our subjects into an addictive action and pushed the compulsive cycle into its first deadly revolution.

Often, the experiences a person had had within the family of birth had contributed to the form the compulsive cycle took in that particular person. Occasionally it was clear how "sins of the fathers" had translated directly into similar actions by children. For example, a child who had seen his parents take drugs thought nothing of doing so himself as soon as he found an opportunity. A girl whose mother was abandoned by her father tried to replace him by engaging in promiscuous relationships with men. But the vast majority of the people we spoke with emphasized that they came from good families, that their parents loved and provided for them, and that they had been taught correct ways throughout their lives. Their involvement in compulsive cycles seemed to be less tied to anything their families had done incorrectly or had failed to do correctly, than to a combination of many influences in their lives and the ways they interpreted or misinterpreted others' actions—and always, to the sense that for some reason, they were different and alone.

The examples of Ellen Schor, Bill Stewart, and Warren White might serve to illustrate how very different situations can create similar feelings of isolation and contribute to the beginning of a compulsive cycle. The comparison of these three case histories is notable for the differences between the individuals mentioned but also for the common themes. It is important to point out that, while these three subjects are in many ways exemplary of the people we interviewed, we have no empirical basis for claiming that they are typical of all those with similar problems. We are not experts on the addictive behaviors exhibited by these individuals. Nor do we claim that the incidents we record here were necessarily the factors that "made" Ellen, Bill, and Warren turn to their addictions. The case histories that follow are simply the stories told to us, in retrospect, by three people who had worked through addictive behaviors. The following incidents are their subjective accounts of important events that might have helped direct them into problem behavior.

Ellen Schor was a surprise baby, one who had been born several years after her parents believed their family was complete. Although the entire family was thrilled by her birth, Ellen always knew that they had not planned on it. She was an accident, however happy that accident might be. She wondered if that had had some detrimental effect on her development, for as she grew up, Ellen realized she was different from other little girls. For one thing, she liked books on science and history better than dolls. For another, she was not turning out to be the beautiful princess she was supposed to be. She had a rather large nose and extremely short legs, and no one on television looked anything like her. Ellen pinned her hopes for loveliness on the Grimm brothers' tale of the ugly duckling and retreated into her schoolwork when the other girls talked about clothes or hairstyles.

Her academic diligence soon earned Ellen a reputation for being aloof and bookish, which made her teachers favor her and her peers avoid her. Out of devotion to the teachers, who clearly liked her even when the other children didn't, Ellen worked harder than ever to rise to the top of her class. By the time she was twelve she was so far ahead of her classmates that she was encouraged to skip from the seventh grade directly into her freshman year of high school. Accepting the consensus of her parents and teachers that this advancement would be a remarkable experience, Ellen started high school at thirteen.

She soon discovered that her teachers and parents had been right. It *was* a remarkable experience, being singled out and given so much attention—much, Ellen thought,

47

like being chosen to sit on the trapdoor at a carnival so people can throw baseballs at you in hopes of knocking you into a vat of water and watching you drown. Ellen was even less socially adept, by comparison with her new schoolmates, than she had been in her own age group. To make matters worse, the onset of adolescence had added acne and a slight but distinct chubbiness to her private catalogue of unacceptable physical attributes. She decided that those must be the reasons everyone else in her new school seemed to have so many friends and so much fun while she ate lunch alone and filled her after-school hours with more study than ever. High school seemed to be populated exclusively by girls who looked like Miss America, and boys who looked at the girls, and, of course, smart fat ugly pockmarked accidental little Ellen, who looked for comfort in too many chocolate chip cookies.

Ellen had almost given up on the Brothers Grimm and their famous duckling when a wonderful thing happened. She caught hepatitis. She missed the last month of classes and nearly died while the disease ran its course, something she vastly preferred to attending school. Ellen spent most of that time in an exhausted daze, with neither the strength nor the desire to get out of bed. On the June morning when she finally managed to totter dizzily down the stairs to her sister's bedroom, she was met by an astonishing spectacle—her own reflection in her sister's full-length mirror. There she was, a month older, years wiser, and—glory be—nearly twenty pounds thinner than the last time she had seen herself. Ellen leaned against the doorjamb and gazed in rapture. She, Ellen Schor, was thin! She admired herself with unabashed delight. Certainly her face would never amount to much, but from the neck down, she thought, she could be on a magazine cover. Thin! Ellen made a happy little leap into the air and passed out cold.

That summer, as she regained strength, Ellen made a secret pact that she would not regain weight. She began to read up on the latest diets, trying them all with varying degrees of success. She memorized calorie charts and carefully measured her food. When her weight began to creep up, she started a jogging program and brought it back down. Staying thin took a lot of effort. Nevertheless, Ellen found that she could control her body. With this realization came a self-confidence she had never felt before. She bought herself new clothes as rewards for self-discipline, accumulating a modest but attractive wardrobe. When school started, she found herself no longer intimidated (well, not so very much) by the gorgeous specimens of femininity who flocked through the classrooms. Nor was she so afraid that the boys who lined the halls at class break would jeer at her as she walked past. She began to smile and talk to acquaintances, and soon she found some of them becoming friends. They laughed at her jokes and even seemed to admire her academic prowess. They apparently didn't realize that she was younger than they. They convinced her to try out for the pep squad. She made it.

For the first time she could ever remember, Ellen felt that she belonged. She now did everything done by everyone else her age, with one notable exception: she never ate with anyone. For deep in her heart Ellen knew the source of her newfound popularity, and she therefore knew that food was her deadliest enemy. When she returned home from school in the afternoons, she could see in every family portrait the hideous image of the old friendless Ellen. She wished she could burn the pictures. She hated their evidence that somewhere, frozen in the past and lurking behind every corner of the future, was Ellen the Fat. Obviously, she thought, it was her weight loss that had transformed her from the unappealing lump she had been into the vivacious person she now pretended to be. She shuddered to think what would happen if her new friends found out that she had once been so fat—or, worse,

49

that she could become that heavy again. With every ounce of her impressive determination, Ellen clung to and nourished the behaviors that she knew could keep her monstrously rebellious body from achieving its former unbelievable bulk. For she believed without question that if the pounds returned — or even one pound, for that matter — the fragile sense of belonging she had built would vanish like the fairy tale it seemed to be. Ellen at fourteen was enlisted in a self-proclaimed war between her body and her happiness. The compulsive cycle had begun to turn.

Bill Stewart was the oldest of nine children, and for ten years the only boy in his family. As a child he was constantly aware of the need for him to be the "little man of the house," to imitate his kind but silent father and offer constant support to his mother and sisters. Bill's personality, however, was closer to that of his exuberant mother than his father. When he was still very small, Bill's mother would spend hours singing to him, and he would join in lustily with his baby voice until she burst into laughter and the song stopped. These were the happiest times of Bill's life. When his twin sisters were born, Bill decided quite without prompting that the singing sessions were over. It was time for him to be a man, and men sang only in church. At age three, Bill had bid a sad farewell to his childhood — a fact that would have horrified his parents if they had known.

Bill imitated not only his father's quiet demeanor but also his independence and self-sufficiency. Samuel Stewart had been a child during the depression, when his part-time job at a lumberyard had provided a sizable proportion of the income for his entire family. He had learned to place hard work and frugality among the premier virtues possible — especially for a man. When Samuel married, he thrilled with quiet pride at his ability to provide a comfortable and well-appointed home for his bride. Watching her flourish in the house he bought and maintained with the labor of his own hands, Samuel felt rewarded for every weary hour of work. Bill never knew that on the day he had come home from the hospital, while his mother had been sleeping an exhausted sleep, Samuel had picked up the fragile bundle in his callused hands, kissed the baby reverently on the forehead, and promised without words that someday Bill would know the same joy he felt at that moment. He would teach his son to build a family as he had done, without complaint and without assistance. He could think of no greater gift.

What Bill did know, although it was never spoken openly, was that his father expected him to provide for himself. Even in grade school, he sensed that asking for money for the toys and snacks his friends bought would be unacceptable—he never even tried it. When he lost a two-dollar reader from the school library, Bill went straight to the librarian to ask for work in order to pay back the money. He was sure if his father found out about his loss of this valuable object, there would be no forgiveness. He had no idea that the librarian had called his father to praise his honesty and resourcefulness and would never have believed that Samuel had nearly burst with pride and love for his son when he had received the call. Nothing was said. In Bill's eyes, his profligacy remained a dreadful secret.

The unmanly Bill, he decided, the Bill who lost money and threw away opportunities, was the same infant Bill who had joined in his mother's musical effervescence and sense of humor. Ashamed of his weaknesses, Bill would have sent that part of himself into a lifelong solitary confinement, if it had not been for one thing. To be more accurate, eight things. As the eldest, Bill was often assigned to help his mother with the care of his younger siblings. The quiet, studious teenager who did his schoolwork and assisted his father in stoic silence was transformed when

51

Bill found himself alone with his younger brothers and sisters. They were surrounded by a magic world where the need for self-sufficiency was irrelevant, and the secret Bill, greedy for a sense of connection, could romp in heady freedom. Bill was the idol of his siblings. When he was not with them, the memory of their admiration made him struggle even harder to be a strong and independent man.

When Bill's father suggested that he not return from college for the summer after his freshman year, the public Bill had hardly even noticed. Certainly, that was the logical thing to do. It made perfect financial sense, and the public Bill accepted it without a second thought. It was the secret, weak Bill, nearly invisible now, whose unmanly heart had ached at the thought that he would not see his youngest sister's "terrible two's" or teach his four-year-old brother to throw a football. He refused to listen to the voice of the secret Bill. He refused to acknowledge that it even had a voice. He could not understand his vague but inescapable malaise and never consciously called it loneliness.

Jenny burst into that loneliness when it had grown so large that Bill felt little else. She was the opposite of everything Bill had tried to become. She was energetic and outgoing, like his mother. She wanted him to laugh with her. With Jenny he was three years old again, never caring about the need to stay wrapped inside himself. Jenny had one trait his mother did not: she spent money as though it rained on her from the sky. Jenny had never saved a dollar, and she worked to supplement an already generous allowance from her parents. Bill's extreme carefulness with money and the seemingly impossible task of saving for a mission while he supported himself at college had become a kind of necessary obsession. But he was tired of thinking about money—how to earn it, how to save it, how to spend it, and, more to the point, how not to spend it. Jenny never, ever, thought about such things. Money and fun flowed from her equally freely, without being measured, divided, or reserved. To Bill, her life seemed to consist of every forbidden and wonderful thing.

Still, he was plagued by his own stiffly trained exterior. The secret, soft, spendthrift part of Bill had been isolated for so long that it seemed reluctant to come out into the light. Bill longed to be a part of Jenny's group of friends, but he lacked the familiarity with their way of life to fit in effortlessly. He felt awkward, and sometimes lonelier than ever. The first time Jenny offered him recreational drugs, the public Bill was appalled. But the child he remembered when he was with Jenny had been ignorant of danger and easily manipulated, and in a way it was that child who trustingly agreed to join in the "fun." Bill quieted the part of him that screamed a warning against the drugs by assuring himself that it would only be this once. "This once" turned out to be the first time since leaving his family that not even the smallest part of Bill felt cold and lost and alone. It would be years before he broke free from his compulsive cycle.

When Warren White was three years old, his uncle Joseph turned to Warren's mother and said, "Whew! This one's a lady-killer, just like his dad!" Susan Paxton White blushed and laughed, agreeing. Warren's translucent skin, his opal blue eyes, and his dark thick hair reflected every nuance of his father's handsome face.

To Susan and her husband, Don, Warren was the perfect child, the unexpected reward after a long and discouraging wait. It had been nearly ten years after their marriage that Warren was conceived, long after the tests and procedures and treatments for the Whites' infertility had been given up as useless. They had thought of him as their miracle baby before he was born, and after his birth he lived up to the promise. Bright, sweet, beautiful, and affectionate, he was everything Don and Susan had ever imagined in a son. Watching him, Susan often thought — though she never would have said so — that the luster from the other side of the veil had never quite left Warren. From the time he was very little, she noticed him playing privately in a world formed and peopled in the endless reaches of his imagination. Toys and television were there to be enjoyed, but Warren seemed happiest with the playthings Susan could not see.

If she had been able to enter Warren's invisible world, Susan probably never would have left. It was a marvelous place, full of colors and sounds seldom seen on earth, with people of heroic stature and character doing thrilling, wonderful things on every hand. Warren was the king, except on the days he was the deputy sheriff. (Usually these were the days when the sheriff — his father — was out of town.) As chief ruler and protector of the populace, Warren's sworn duty was to rid the world of evil and injustice.

That was one reason it upset him so to have both his uncle and his own mother label him a lady-killer. Apparently, there was some hereditary component to this alarming identity, for Uncle Joseph had specifically mentioned Don White as sharing his son's subconsciously murderous inclinations. Warren looked at his mother and Uncle Joseph gravely. Joseph repeated his outrageous accusation. "Isn't that right, Warren? You're going to be some lady-killer when you grow up!" Susan saw Warren's face go pale, and each of his cheeks showed a bright red spot where the blood always rushed when her son's emotions ran too high for him to contain them.

"No!" Warren shouted.

Uncle Joseph looked startled.

"Mommy, I'm not a lady-killer! I don't kill ladies! I save ladies!"

The laughter that ensued echoed for years as Joseph and Susan related Warren's childish misunderstanding during different family gatherings and nostalgic visits. The imagination Warren had shown and the passion with which he responded were some of the qualities his family loved most in him — and in each other, for both the Whites and the Paxtons were known for their willingness to dream wonderful things and to bring them about through steadfast energy of purpose. Everyone on both sides of the family was proud of little Warren. And no one ever explained to him exactly what they meant by "lady-killer."

He soon forgot about the incident. Still, it raised questions that never quite stopped bothering him. What was this thing, referred to so often by adults and especially on television, magazines, and movies, that he did not quite understand? What knowledge were grown-ups privy to that he was not — knowledge that seemed so central and important to the workings of the world? For a while Warren incorporated this unknown Thing, this bad and dirty Thing, this alluring and wonderful Thing, into his imaginary world. He was not quite sure what it would turn out to be, but he knew it was important.

Secretly he hoped it would be a friend. Warren was lonely in his imaginary world, just as he was at the parties his parents held for their friends, where he would listen as the adults talked and laughed about things Warren neither cared about nor understood. For his adored parents' sake, he sat quietly in his uncomfortable bow tie through endless evenings with no one but grown-ups. But he retreated often to the wonderful world in his mind where vicious pigs and alligators fell before his sword as he, King Warren, quested through the land in search of someone with whom he could plan and plot and play.

When he was five, the quest ended. Warren knew vaguely that babies grew in their mommies' tummies, and he had also noticed that his mother was gaining some girth around the middle, but he never put the two together until one day Don and Susan asked him if he would like a little brother or sister. Susan laughed merrily at the blank look on her son's face, at the sudden look of understanding that brought the familiar pallor to his face and the two hot pink spots to his cheeks. "Yes!" Warren shouted, and ran to his room for a furious session of saving his mother from the pigs and alligators who would undoubtedly pursue her during her daring mission as his new brother's protector. He knew it was a brother. How else could the baby become the next Deputy Sheriff, once he, Warren, had inherited his father's badge?

One night, Warren awoke with the hair standing up on his arms and the back of his neck. He lay there, trembling, wondering what the sound was that had awakened him, when it came again. It was his mother's voice, but not his mother's voice: a strange, animal cry, half anguish and half despair, like nothing he had ever heard before in his life. He knew before his father came into his room that he was not to ask what was happening. He knew that when his Uncle Joseph and Aunt Della arrived in slippers and overcoats and told him everything would be all right, that he must not complain about his parents' sudden departure. He knew, during the long night they spent at the hospital, that everything was not going to be all right. And he knew, when his father arrived alone at dawn and told him Mommy would be home later, that his brother would not be coming home with her.

What Warren did not expect, what he was not prepared for in any way, was what he saw when he crept back into the living room for comfort after his father tucked him into bed that sleepless night. Uncle Joseph and Aunt Della were standing awkwardly in the living room, trying not to watch as Don sat on the couch with his hands over his face and sobbed. Della patted his father's shoulder helplessly.

"It's all right, Don. It's all right. I know how I felt when I had my miscarriage. It's terrible, but it passes."

Warren's father looked up through swollen eyelids and tried to laugh.

"I know, Della, I know. It's not the baby . . . well, yes,

it is the baby — did I tell you he lived for nearly ten minutes? I had a chance to bless him . . . so tiny. . . . "

Joseph and Della nodded.

"But, no, it's not the baby, it's Susan. She wanted this baby so much. She was so happy. What will this do to her, after all these years? It'll kill her. It'll kill her. And, I . . . I . . . "

Warren watched transfixed as his father's face contorted with pain and grief.

"I feel like it's all my fault! I did this to her! It's my fault—if it weren't for me she'd have all the kids she wanted. She'd be happy! It's all my fault!"

Warren turned and fled down the hall to his room. In some corner of his brain he could hear his Aunt Della's voice, sharp with reprimand: "Now, Don, you just stop that! It's not your fault, and you do make her happy, and the two of you'll be having children for eternity, so just you stop this!" But the memory of the agony on his father's face and the desperation in his voice dominated Warren's acute imagination. So this was it. This was how he and his father were destined to kill ladies. It fit, it resonated in Warren's mind. The fear and sorrow that flooded his small consciousness were almost too much for him to bear. He went to the imaginary world where he had always found comfort and happiness, but it had been laid waste by the horrible monster that was killing his mother and had killed, irrevocably killed, his brother. It was barren and hideous and frightening. Just before he fell into an exhausted sleep, five-year-old Warren closed the door to his ravaged imaginary world, locked it, and threw away the key.

Warren did not cry that night. He did not cry during the year that his mother smiled seldom and spent much time alone. In fact, no one in the first grade ever saw him cry—or the second, third, fourth, or any other grade. Warren's lack of emotional display made him an object of admiration among his classmates, especially when they were also his teammates. He was an excellent athlete, tall, strong, and coordinated, and he earned the nickname "Ice" for the deadly calm that seemed to settle over him like a frost when a game demanded his concentration. This concentration served him as well in school as it did in sports. He studied methodically even as a young boy, always turning in his work on time, well completed and immaculate.

Warren himself was rather impressed by his unusual control of his passions. He was always calm and reasonable, with a dry sense of humor that made him popular as he grew into adolescence. He rarely argued. He considered anger beneath his dignity and saw no need to succumb to it. With self-control came confidence. Warren knew he could be trusted, and others sensed that as well. He was called to leadership positions in his Primary classes, his Scout troops, and eventually in his priesthood quorums. He knew that he would never succumb to the temptations that seemed to be the obsession of some other boys his age. When he was thirteen, one of the boys in his group of friends found a pornographic magazine in an abandoned construction site. All the other boys seemed fascinated by it, but Warren, when he caught a glimpse of one of the pictures, had felt such revulsion that he thought he would choke. He walked away from the group without a word, not caring that the other boys would jeer, and was surprised when some of them followed him and the others looked ashamed. He was a natural leader, and among all the boys he knew, Warren was the most confident and self-assured.

When he was not among boys, however, he was a basket case. Warren liked and admired many of the girls in his ward and at school, but when it came to interacting with them he was hopelessly out of his element. The other boys all seemed driven by some invisible force to think about girls, to talk about and to girls, to make girls notice them. Warren felt no such compulsion. Nothing. Fortunately he had little opportunity to expose this weakness, for there were plenty of all-male activities in which to participate. In fact, for years Warren was able to maintain a very active social life without ever once having to interact with girls for more than a few seconds.

As his sixteenth birthday approached, Warren knew he was losing his camouflage. Soon, he would have no more excuse for his lack of interest in girls, and he had no idea how to imitate the way the other boys acted—something seemed to have been amputated from his mind. He turned sixteen quietly, hoping that no one would notice, but less than a week later he picked up the telephone and heard the terrifying voice of the prettiest cheerleader in the junior class. The dance next week was girl's choice, did he know? Oh, sure, yes, Warren mumbled. Would he like to go? Um, yes, sure, um, sure, yes. Warren began to sweat as he replaced the receiver. Now he was caught. Maybe he'd get sick before the dance—but it was right after the football game, and he had to play. Maybe he would be fatally injured during the game? No, he decided, not likely.

Warren paced the floor. What did this girl Julie expect of him? Did she like him, the way everyone talked about girls "liking" boys? How would she expect him to act? Would she be able to tell that he wasn't like other guys, that toward girls he felt as blank as an empty swimming pool? Would she try to—Warren stopped pacing and stared at the floor—*kiss* him? Worse yet, would she expect him to kiss her?

In the midst of his panic, Warren suddenly had a brilliant idea. One of the other cheerleaders was going to the dance with his best friend, Cameron West. That was it! A double date! Cameron was everything Warren aspired to become: warm and friendly and exuberant and socially facile. If Cameron were along, the guys could talk together most of the time, and then if Julie tried anything, Warren could watch how Cameron behaved and take his cues from that. It was perfect.

It was awful. Julie seemed impressed by the way Warren looked in his tuxedo, but after chatting with him all the way to the restaurant without eliciting a word in response, she turned around and directed her comments to Cameron and his date in the back seat. It set the tone for the entire evening. Cameron and the two girls talked and laughed comfortably during dinner, while Warren sat in a miserable silence that grew deeper every time Julie threw him a puzzled glance. At the dance Julie and Warren ended up watching the other couple pirouette gracefully around while Warren pressed his back against the wall of the gym and fought a desperate urge to turn and run. Cameron showed his date to her door with chivalric courtesy, a procedure that Warren tried to duplicate with Julie once they had dropped Cameron off at his house. He came across with all the grace of a rhinoceros on stilts. He was sure he heard Julie give a sigh of relief as the door closed behind her. He was just glad there had been no attempt at kissing.

That night Warren had trouble sleeping. He was paralyzed with embarrassment, terrified by the prospect of having to repeat this ghastly effort ever again in his life, and he was angry. At least he thought it was anger—he had never felt quite this restless, burning irritation, this unsettling discontent. He stared at the ceiling. There was Cameron, talking with his girlfriend Debbie. Warren rolled over and buried his face in his pillow. Cameron was chatting nonchalantly with Julie. Warren threw back his sheets and rolled over. Cameron and Debbie and Julie danced happily around his room.

It *was* anger he was feeling. He was angry. More than that, he was furious. No, that wasn't quite it. . . .

Abruptly, Warren sat up in bed. His face went pale, and two red spots burned on his cheeks as he realized what was wrong. He was jealous. He had never felt anything like this before. Waves of terrible emotion swept over him in suffocating floods. The feelings seemed to be endless in their scope and variety—love, anger, fear, desire, longing, excitement. Castles and forests flashed past his mind: slavering alligators and bold heroes and the chestnut horse he rode on with his stillborn little brother. A terrible thing began to happen. For the first time since he had watched in horror while his father cried, a deep wrenching sob began to rise from Warren's own chest. The sob seemed to bring his insides up with it: all the pain, all the joy, and all the love he had kept buried there since that night. And in this torrent of feeling, Warren felt more numb than ever before. For he knew now that he was and always would be alone. Utterly, unspeakably, irredeemably alone. The secret was out. The infinite yearning that filled his soul to the limits of his imagination would never be fulfilled. Yes, he was jealous. And he was in love. But it was not Cameron's attractiveness to girls that Warren wanted, nor Cameron's social adeptness, nor even Cameron's charm. It was Cameron. As the smothered sob broke from Warren's throat, filling the air with the sound of his terrible isolation, the compulsive cycle folded him quietly in its icy embrace.

The stories of Ellen, Bill, and Warren obviously have many differences. They also have many similarities. It is the similarities that provide clues to how compulsive cycles emerge from feelings of isolation. These three young people all came from loving Latter-day Saint families. All were bright, well-meaning, and happy youngsters. But each of the three felt lonely and different as children, for a number of reasons. All of them began to experience such feelings before they were old enough either to define them explicitly or to recognize that they were anything other than the natural state of the universe. Perhaps because of that, and because they misinterpreted cues they took from the behavior of people around them, Ellen, Bill, and Warren all kept their feelings of isolation private and unexpressed. At the same time, however, each of the three was searching for some means of alleviating the sense of isolation that characterized their everyday experience. A combination of traits and circumstances, which might occur in anyone's life without producing particularly devastating effects, led each of these three individuals to a very compelling experience with some kind of behavior. For Ellen the experience was losing weight, for Bill it was using drugs, and for Warren it was a relationship with a male friend. These experiences would probably have left many people relatively unaffected. For Ellen, Bill, and Warren, however, they broke through internal barriers that created feelings of isolation. They were therefore extremely powerful and alluring.

There was no sin involved in the conditions that created feelings of isolation in these three people or in many of the others we talked with in the course of our research. The feelings themselves are not destructive. On the contrary, they are essential to motivate us to regain the presence of our Heavenly Father. But the natural man, in his intelligent ignorance, often feels the presence of needs before he understands their nature. The compulsive-cycle victims we spoke with were bright, intuitive, and eager to form conclusions by which to conceptualize their experience. Sometimes this process outstripped the acquisition of wisdom. In such cases, individuals can misinterpret the objects of their own desires and the expectations of those around them. There is usually no way to place accurate blame on anyone or anything when a good person becomes addicted to a destructive behavior, except perhaps the very nature of mortality. But even when there is no obvious perpetrator involved in the creation of a compulsive cycle, there are inevitably many victims. The next chapter will discuss the way in which feelings of isolation can lead to the second step in a compulsive cycle with more and more inevitable consistency. The accounts of our interview subjects, as they discuss these actions of self-indulgence, will testify that the void that seems to haunt so many people in this mortality is never filled by behaviors that they expect will bring pleasure. If feelings of isolation bring the individual to the compulsive cycle, the compulsive cycle even more surely will bring isolation to the individual.

4

THE SECOND STEP:
ACTIONS OF SELF-INDULGENCE

One of the best-known aphorisms in latter-day scripture is Lehi's declaration, "Adam fell that men might be; and men are, that they might have joy." (2 Nephi 2:25.) In that one stunningly simple phrase, Lehi sums up the plan of salvation and the reason for our existence, the Good News reduced to its barest essentials and proclaimed with the resonance of a Hallelujah shout. It is the answer to the ubiquitous question, asked directly or indirectly by human beings in so much of their art, philosophy, and unexpressed thought: "What is the meaning of life?" In our popular media, pompous cartoon characters and the heroes of comedies may purport to answer this question. Or they may open an examination booklet to find it the only question on a test—the ultimate nightmare, because the question is generally considered to be unanswerable. The social consensus is that no one can tell us the meaning of life but that occasionally a brilliant scholar, philosopher, or scientist, working at full mental capacity for a very long time, can turn out something approaching part of the answer. Such an explanation must necessarily be extremely complex and erudite, far beyond the ken of the person on the street. Like the Israelites in the wilderness, many in our world perish "because of the simpleness of the way, or the easiness of it" (1 Nephi 17:41), working desperately to discover the meaning of life while the simple truth sits under their noses and waits vainly to be seen.

After all, we do not need Lehi to tell us that we seem designed to experience joy, that when we feel joy we are glad of our existence and happy to continue living. The "pursuit of happiness" is one of the "self-evident" truths that the Declaration of Independence acknowledges as the right of every human being. Every action taken by most of us is in some way an effort to become happier, to feel more of this sensation we call joy. In short, we all know perfectly well that, as Joseph Smith said, "happiness is the object and design of our existence." (*Teachings of the Prophet Joseph Smith,* sel. Joseph Fielding Smith [Salt Lake City: Deseret Book, 1938], p. 255.) This fact is so baldly obvious that Satan rarely even tries to convince us it is not true. Instead, he throws out a smokescreen of deceit to convince us that we can't really credit such a simple definition of life's meaning, that there must be more to it than we can understand. A vast pool of learned treatises, theological, philosophical, and artistic, parade as Satan's substitute for the fourteen words, "Adam fell that men might be, and men are, that they might have joy."

Substitutions such as these represent the adversary's chief line of offense against man's innate, spiritual response to things that make him happy. In baffling our recognition of how to achieve the joy we all know we want, Satan uses the ignorance of the natural man, with its natural appetites, to great effect. For every good and marvelous and joyful thing the Lord has given us, the devil is busily erecting a whole parade of shoddy counterfeits, covered with chrome and glitter to disguise the fundamental flaws in their design. Some of these appeal to the spirit: the Lord gives us revelation to enlighten and free our wills, whereas Satan (as Doctor Faustus and Macbeth discovered) gives us sorceries and priestcrafts to mislead and entrap. Some counterfeits seduce the mind, like those worldly philosophies that build towers of exquisite reasoning based upon incorrect premises, too proud of their rational coherence to question or even recognize the errors in their fundamental assumptions. But because the central task of this life is to gain and master a body and because the most powerful agents of joy we gain on earth involve the powers of the body and their proper use, Satan has put some of his most diligent efforts into designing counterfeits for joy that entrap us through our physical beings. Among them are the behaviors that occupy the second step of a compulsive cycle, behaviors that we have labeled "actions of self-indulgence."

In the context of a compulsive cycle, an action is simply a behavior, the movement of the physical body to achieve some specific end. The philosophies of our society, which discount the physical as either meaningless or temporary, belittle the significance of such physical actions. The argument is that since the intentions of the heart and thoughts of the mind are of primary significance in determining the moral context of our behavior, the physical manifestations of these feelings and beliefs are superfluous and irrelevant. As college students in a university that nourishes and glorifies the mind, we often heard arguments against the necessity of mere physical enactments to confirm metaphysical intentions. "Why should I have to be baptized if I can just believe in God and lead a good life?" was a common question, or "Why should we have to get married—we don't need a piece of paper to show that we love each other." If one believes that the physical body is just a casing to be abandoned by the spirit at death or that the mind dies with the body anyway, this attitude toward the physical acting-out of a spiritual reality is logical and justified.

But Latter-day Saints do not adhere to these views of the body and its actions. We believe so strongly in the influence of physical actions on the immortal spirit that we build temples and serve in them as physical proxies for those spirits who did not perform the ordinances of salvation while in mortality. The ordinances of salvation are not merely a show of good faith, wherein we confirm our spiritual devotion by submitting ourselves to meaningless or simply symbolic action. Action itself, the physical action of the physical body, possesses a power that we do not fully understand. It is not trivial. It is part of the power by which the worlds were created, and it is not to be trifled with. Every deliberate action we perform carries the whole soul, body and spirit, with it. For this reason the Lord has, at certain times in history, created explicit and carefully delineated rules of action by which His people were instructed to direct their lives. To the people of Moses' day, the Law was made the whole substance of the gospel for a people whose understanding of the Spirit proved insufficient to direct action. In the latter days, we have been given one such law, "for a principle with promise, adapted to the capacity of the weak and the weakest of all saints, who are or can be called saints." (D&C 89:3.) This is of course the Word of Wisdom, a simple code by which our actions are to be directed—not only because such action is the stuff of truth but also because it has the power to carry the spirit toward or away from the fulfillment of its divine potential. As the Lord told His chosen people before the coming of Christ, physical action is necessary to bring us closer to Him.

The power of adherence to laws of physical behavior is evident in many of the world's great religions. As students traveling in Asia, we once had a long discussion with some Malaysian Moslem friends. They were anxious to convert us, and we were eager to learn more about their religion. We asked them what they believed. "Oh," they said, "we pray five times a day, we study the Koran, we wash ourselves before meals, we fast during the day for a month each year, we hope to travel to Mecca . . . " They recounted a long list of ritual behaviors and observances. "Yes," we said in puzzled ignorance, "that's what you *do*.

67

But what do you *believe?*" Our friends looked at us in confusion. "We just told you what we believe," they said. "We pray five times a day — oh, yes, we face Mecca, that's important — we wash ourselves at certain times, we wear coverings on our heads, we abstain from foods that are unclean . . . " After another few minutes of recounting behavioral codes, they beamed at us in assurance that now we would understand.

We didn't. Our Christian upbringing, in a society dominated and undergirded by the ideological impact of the New Testament and the philosophers' emphasis on reason, had done nothing to prepare us to understand a way of thinking in which the enactment of the Law constitutes the essential fabric of religious faith. It was not that our Moslem friends did not understand the concepts of motivation and intention. They simply considered them secondary to the physical acting out of ordinances commanded by God. Our Western ideological training, on the other hand, made us much more amenable to the idea that what a person does is not the point, as long as his heart is in the right place. On the one hand is the idea that the acting out of physical behaviors is central to salvation; on the other, the firm belief that "it's the thought that counts." Both are partially correct, and both are in error. Physical action and spiritual or intellectual commitment are both necessary but insufficient to the salvation or damnation of the soul, which is spirit and body combined.

A good illustration of the relationship of intention and action can be seen in temple work for the dead. The physical ordinances must be performed in the body — there is no way around it even for the greatest of souls. The body must undergo physical baptism in water and all the other actions by which the soul is made ready for the presence of God. If that body has already passed away, then another body may be substituted as proxy, but a physical body it must be. In order for every soul to have the opportunity to accept these ordinances, Latter-day Saints aspire to what may seem the preposterous goal of performing temple ordinances for every soul who has ever lived on earth—a goal that we would never have imagined for ourselves if the Lord had not set it for us. And yet, even when this tremendous task has been accomplished, only a relatively small group of spirits will be willing and ready to accept the ordinances we have performed for them. In other words, these actions are absolutely essential to salvation, and the spirit cannot perform them without the body. But even when the body has carried out the actions, the spirit of the individual has the ability either to accept them or to reject them. It is the spirit's intelligence that guides the body's power.

That is why the Lord instructed Samuel that "man looketh on the outward appearance, but the Lord looketh on the heart." (1 Samuel 16:7.) All deliberate actions have great power to move the soul some given "distance" in our eternal progress. Some actions, by their natures, move us further than others. But the direction in which an action takes us—whether it moves the soul toward or away from our Father in Heaven and the joy which emanates from Him—is directed by the intentions and understanding of the spirit. Thus, a very powerful action, for example, the physical union of a man and woman, can move us much closer to godhood if it is sanctioned by the Lord. But it moves us equally far in the opposite direction when it is undertaken with impure intentions. To think that such an action can be performed without *any* consequences, however, is a terribly dangerous mistake. While the spirit determines the direction in which action takes the soul, the action itself cannot be divorced from the power it has to move us.

Of course, not every action performed by our bodies is significant to our eternal progress. It is doubtful that the Lord includes every sneeze, wince, and hiccup in the list of mortal actions that will save or destroy our souls. These actions are insignificant because they are unintentional. The physical behaviors that matter to our progression are deliberate actions motivated by the intelligence. They are expressions of the spirit. The actions of self-indulgence that occupy the second step on the compulsive cycle are not meaningless but pleasant behaviors like scratching an itch. Nor are they actions that yield pleasure as one component of a righteous search for joy, the way that the pleasure of physical intimacy accompanies the much broader and more encompassing joy of a celestial marriage. The term "actions of self-indulgence" refers to actions that are temporally enjoyable but that the actor mistakes for eternal joy, the joy that is the "object and design of our existence." The condition of the spirit that motivates this behavior—of which the behavior is an expression—is the sense of profound isolation discussed in the last chapter. It seemed to us, as we conducted our interviews, that for a person who becomes entangled in a compulsive cycle, some particular action has the capacity to provide a strong enough sense of pleasure to block for a moment the perpetrator's awareness of his or her loneliness.

For a person involved in an addictive behavior, then, the gratification involved in actions of self-indulgence is a counterfeit of the joy for which we exist. The people we spoke with who had been taken in by the counterfeit were not seedy or ill-intentioned; in fact, they seemed to be individuals who were particularly driven to seek for joy and were thus perhaps too eager to accept a substitute. The feelings of isolation that these people found to be intolerable are the precise opposites of the joy we are designed to experience. The happiness we are promised by the gospel is one of inclusion, of connectedness, of being in the presence of those we love most—including our Father in Heaven and His Son—and of being one with them. The ultimate hell our doctrine envisions, on the other hand, is the condition of "outer darkness." The sectarian image of hundreds of sinners roasting over communal coals is certainly frightening, but it does not strike such a terrifyingly familiar chord as the idea of a spirit separated from all love and all light. The feelings of isolation that accompany this mortal estate bring us close enough to that terrible experience to know that the pain of fire and brimstone is nothing in comparison to separation from God, who is both light and love.

This mortal world is the province of the adversary, and in it we seem to feel more of his agony than of God's joy. Death, physical injury, illness, abandonment, and all the other "thousand natural shocks that flesh is heir to" have to do with disintegration, with entropy, with things falling apart. Satan preaches the gospel of disintegration, of people and things withdrawing away from each other in a chaos of isolated fragments. The Lord's way, on the other hand, is one of integration, of bringing together, of sealing things both on earth and in heaven, of at-one-ment. That unity is the joy for which Lehi says we are designed. The Savior is the source to which we must look to fill the void that exists within each of us. The way to that eternal joy has been clearly outlined in the gospel of Jesus Christ. It is straight and well-defined.

Unfortunately, it is also difficult to follow for those wrapped in the ignorance of mortality and the unfamiliarity of a physical nature. As part of that nature, we are privileged on this earth to enact—*physically* enact—behaviors that are component parts of the joy of eternal life. Many of these behaviors bring with them great pleasure, which we could not have experienced without obtaining a body. The sensation of physical pleasure is one we have never known before this life. Its allure is a testament to the great intrinsic power of physical action. According to our interview subjects, the pleasure of some physical actions is so strong and partakes enough of the joy of eternal life, that for some people it can block awareness of the void within us caused by the fundamental disintegration of this lonely world. For those involved in compulsive cycles, in whom the awareness of their isolation is particularly intense, this relief from unhappiness is mistaken for joy itself.

It seems that almost any action can become an "action of self-indulgence." It is not even necessary for the behavior to be genuinely enjoyable. The only thing necessary to allow any action to qualify as an addictive behavior is that, for some people, this action is capable of blocking awareness of the feelings of isolation that characterize their everyday experience. A few actions are particularly addictive because they have great intrinsic power to capture our attention and create enjoyable sensations. The three types of action we have chosen for our case studies — eating, the use of mood-altering chemicals, and compulsive sexual activity — are the most common examples we encountered. But for some people the behavior might be gambling, shopping, stealing, falling in love from afar, jogging, working, watching television, or virtually any other activity. What differentiates a compulsive-cycle addict from anyone else who engages in these activities is that addicts find relief from feelings of isolation in performing the action and that they mistake this oblivion for joy. Since, as Lehi says, joy is the reason for our existence, compulsive-cycle victims erroneously locate the meaning of life in the pleasure obtained from the addictive action and hence in the action itself. The action consequently becomes the primary focus of the addict's life.

The surprising thing about our interview subjects' descriptions of their actions of self-indulgence was that different subjects' lives were affected in almost identical ways by a wide variety of very different behaviors. We spoke with many people who had engaged in some improper activity once or twice and then immediately stopped. We do not consider these people to have been in a compulsive cycle. People who are caught in a cycle describe a pattern

72

of behavior and feeling typified by several characteristics that are the same, no matter what the particular action of self-indulgence may be.

To begin with, many behavioral addicts report that before they ever began to indulge in a particular behavior, and even if they thought the action was wrong, they found it fascinating, exciting, or romantic. That may seem difficult to imagine for people who are not similarly attracted to such actions. Even victims themselves, after escaping the compulsive cycle, often mention that their own addiction seems disgusting or boring from the perspective of their new understanding. Nevertheless, entrancement with a particular action seems to characterize people who later fall into compulsive cycles. It was unclear to us whether the fascination is itself part of the cycle or whether it is merely a predisposing factor. What was clear from many of our interviews, however, is that fascination with a particular activity is not necessarily "built in" to the addict's personality. The people we spoke with who had escaped such addictive behaviors all reported that the longer the time since they had been involved in the cycle, the less interest they felt in the action to which they had once been addicted.

The addict's initial fascination with the action of self-indulgence often leads to the first commission of the act. Sometimes this is a distinct departure from the addict's ordinary life-style, an incident that stands out in the addict's mind as the moment when he or she capitulated to the compulsive cycle. In other cases the action is so mundane, so much a part of daily life, that it does not strike the individual as anything more than a slight exaggeration of ordinary behavior. But even if the addictive action is something the victim has done before, there is a distinctive quality to the action that initiates a compulsive cycle. The addict generally describes it as "the time when I got hooked." The "hooking" occurs when, suddenly, an action as exotic as taking drugs or as ordinary as eating moves into a particular position within the person's mind. It becomes the focus of the person's thoughts and feelings for several hours, days, or even weeks after the actual activity has ended. The action, whatever it might be, becomes the object of the addict's inordinate attention.

Once this initial exposure to the action of self-indulgence has taken place, the person involved in a compulsive cycle begins to act somewhat like a teenager experiencing puppy love for the first time — except for the fact that puppy love is a normal step in the process of coming closer to other people and one's own potential, while the fixation of a person in a compulsive cycle is a step toward isolation and pain. Young lovers are transported by the objects of their affection. They feel that their adored one is the answer to all of life's sorrows and inconveniences, the purveyor of such bliss that to be with this person is to rise above the petty woes of existence. Compulsive-cycle victims feel the same way about their actions of self-indulgence when they first feel the pleasure of the action replacing their feelings of isolation. Like a lover, a behavioral addict feels that whatever the addictive action — shoplifting, drinking, jogging, or any other of an unlimited array of behaviors — that action is the answer to everyone's problems. One of us was invited, while still in high school, to take drugs with a group of young acquaintances. Even after the invitation was firmly declined, the group drove to a meetingplace where they customarily assembled to smoke marijuana and experiment with other chemicals. What was astonishing about these people was not their behavior so much as their attitude. They claimed, and seemed to believe sincerely, that anyone's life would be enriched by recreational drugs and that once a newcomer was broken of initial "shyness," he or she would naturally relax into the use of such substances. To them, drugs seemed to stand as the essential center of all life, one they could not

74

live without and one that all people wanted in their hearts, no matter how much they denied it on the surface. They saw the world as divided into those who took drugs and those who were violently and maliciously opposed to drugs out of a frustrated desire to use them. Their complete refusal to believe that anyone could be simply uninterested in using recreational chemicals was nothing less than amazing. Nevertheless, it is typical of those in a compulsive cycle. The anorexic believes that thinness is everyone's top priority. The sexual addict thinks that physical intimacy is at the forefront of everyone's mind, all the time.

What makes this aspect of a compulsive cycle particularly baffling and infuriating to the friends and acquaintances of the addict is that all *their* actions are interpreted by the addict as though they were motivated by a similar addiction. Having found a pleasure that substitutes so nearly for joy, having determined that this action is the answer to all troubles and discontents, the compulsive-cycle victim simply does not believe that other people do not place it at the center of their lives. There is a chilling parallel to missionary zeal evident in many accounts of "actions of self-indulgence." Almost all of the behavioral addicts we interviewed had been literally taught and trained to indulge in their addiction by someone more experienced with that particular action. We spoke with a bulimic woman who admitted that during her high-school years she had taught "about fifty" of her friends and relatives to binge on food and then vomit it—an action she had decided was a wonderful way to eat her cake and not have it, too. With anguish she told us, "I honestly thought I was doing them a favor"—a belief that seemed grotesque and horrible from the perspective of a mature woman who had almost destroyed herself with that addictive action.

As terrible as the sin of transmitting an addiction might be, it is often motivated by a desire that is in itself inoffensive, the wish to have others share one's world view

75

and activities. That desire is strengthened by the fact that, soon after the person involved in a compulsive cycle becomes addicted to the "action of self-indulgence," he or she begins to realize that the obsessive preoccupation with this action does not fit in socially with the activities of others. That realization leads quickly to another typical feature of a truly addictive action: such behaviors are usually enacted either alone or in the company of a few people who are similarly addicted. Addicts begin to shut all other people out of their lives and thoughts. The exclusionary character of the activity is one of the things that mark it as an addictive action. For example, it is normal to enjoy playing handball with a few good friends. It is not normal to limit one's acquaintances to those friends and nobody else, to talk about handball to them and them only, to drastically decrease one's contact with all those who are not handball players, and to react with aggression or defensiveness when a nonplayer asks questions about one's handball games. Compulsive-cycle addicts, no matter what "game" they may be playing, become proprietary and solitary in the commission of the action.

Another characteristic of addictive behaviors is that they are planned ahead of time in the addict's mind. Remember that compulsive-cycle victims have decided that some action of self-indulgence is the source of all happiness because while they are involved in such an action, the feelings of isolation and pain they deal with during the rest of the time are blocked out of their consciousness. The problem is that addictive actions do not really heal the wounds of isolation. In fact, the action generally leaves the addict feeling worse than ever. Eventually, most compulsive-cycle addicts begin to notice that the action of self-indulgence—no matter what it is—simply does not occupy enough time to keep them from experiencing profound discontent and unhappiness. Compulsive-cycle victims therefore begin to "stretch" their addictive actions over time in a variety of ways. These ways almost always include spending more time to complete the activity as well as engaging in it more frequently, but these measures alone do not prove sufficient to totally block addicts' awareness of their own unhappiness. Therefore, they typically begin to spend more and more time simply thinking about the activity to which they are addicted. It is a very specific kind of thinking. It occupies a great deal, if not all, of the addict's attention. It most commonly takes the form of reliving past experiences with the action of self-indulgence and of imagining and planning in great detail some future experience. One question we asked the people we interviewed was "How much time do you spend thinking about this problem?" The typical answer for someone at the height of a compulsive cycle was that the addict thought about the action of self-indulgence and related topics practically all the time. As one addict put it: "If I'm talking to someone about something else, I of course think about what I'm saying. But as soon as the conversation's over, my mind snaps back to it [the addiction]. If I'm in a movie or something, every now and then I kind of break away from the movie, and I'm thinking about it again. I'd say about 99 percent of my thoughts are about this problem, either thinking about how I can do it or thinking about how I can stop."

Besides that kind of concentration, another way that compulsive-cycle victims enlarge the scope of the action of self-indulgence is to develop a kind of ritualized routine surrounding the activity. The routine is generally something that grows longer and more elaborate over time. A man we spoke with who habitually stole items from stores described the development of this kind of routine:

"I remember the first time I actually took anything . . . all of a sudden I was just sneaking out of this store with some stupid little thing—something I would never use in my life. I just was out of the store with it all of a sudden.

"That was the first time. Well, I didn't really blame myself for taking the thing because it was so cheap, and I just felt like it wasn't really even me that did it, you know—it just sort of happened and I wasn't really even aware of it. But then I started, like, wandering in stores hoping that it would happen again! I mean, in my right mind I wouldn't do anything like that, you know, but I kept hoping it would just happen, like a fit or something, so that I could do it and not feel guilty.

"After a while, even going to the store would trigger me to steal something. I would do things like go shopping for four items and then I'd only buy one, so I'd have to go back more times. After a while just getting in the car, I'd get in it for something else and I'd end up at a store. And then I'd spend a long time browsing around, and then I'd steal something. I always told myself that I was just window shopping, and then at the last moment I'd take something. Pretty soon I was spending a lot of time doing this. I would even end up late for work, or leave early so I could go to the mall. This happened over several years. I would try to stop, and then it would get worse. I was out of control. Finally I got caught."

This man's action of self-indulgence grew from a moment of time into an activity that occupied an enormous proportion of his life. Strange as his experience may seem, this pattern is not unusual among the behavioral addicts we interviewed. What is important about the shoplifter's story is that it points out how an action of self-indulgence is enlarged into a whole routine of related activities. As soon as addicts start into their routines—for this man, simply getting into his car or entering a store—they push away their consciousness of all painful feelings. They also push away the part of themselves that is appalled by their own actions, which despises such behavior and vows re-

peatedly to stop. When those involved in compulsive behaviors say they can't help themselves or that they are out
of control, their statements may sound very strange to
someone who has never been trapped in such a cycle. After
all, what could be so difficult about *not* going to the effort
of driving to a shopping center and purloining some unnecessary item? But when addicts describe themselves as
uncontrollable, the part of themselves that expresses the
feeling of being out of control is speaking with complete
honesty. That is the part of the self that addicts squelch
and silence while they are committing the action of self-
indulgence, and so it is the part that truly has no control
once the routine of an action has been begun. Once
compulsive-cycle victims are involved in such routines,
they have entered a different world, where knowledge of
right and wrong, of dangers and consequences, is muted
to a mere whisper and easily ignored.

Because it is this "other world" that protects behavioral
addicts from "feelings of isolation" and the pain arising
from them, compulsive-cycle victims allow it to grow — in
fact, no matter how strongly they may object to an addiction in principle, they nurture its growth at moments of
crisis when they cannot deal easily with life. Sometimes
the compulsive cycle grows slowly, filling a lifetime with
a few hours here and there of addictive behaviors. But
often it burgeons more rapidly, starting with a few relatively "innocent" escapades that hardly seem completed
before the compulsive-cycle victim becomes enmeshed in
a terrifyingly far-flung net of destructive activities. The case
histories of Ellen Schor, Bill Stewart, and Warren White
may help illustrate this process. Once again, these three
cases are typical of stories we heard from practically all
people caught in compulsive cycles, no matter how different their addictions seemed on the surface. It should be
noted that many behavioral addicts seem to enjoy talking
about their actions of self-indulgence to a sympathetic au-

dience. As long as they feel confident that their listeners share their belief in the desirability of their actions, they will spend a great deal of time recounting all the lurid details of their behavior. They also enjoy reading the accounts of others who describe an addiction similar to theirs with the same kind of fascination. "Locker room talk," both spoken and written in the form of verbal pornography, is an example of this kind of discussion. In contrast to this self-indulgent and provocative style of reporting actions, the stories we heard from compulsive-cycle victims who had broken free from their addictions were terse, dry, and to the point. To avoid crossing the fine line between description and titillation when discussing these "actions of self-indulgence," we here recount the stories of Ellen, Bill, and Warren's addictions in their own brief but honest words.

I was kind of an awkward kid, and I had always thought I was a bit too plump. When I was about fifteen, I lost a lot of weight during a bout of hepatitis. I think it was then that I first decided dieting was the key to happiness. Well, not dieting exactly. At first, what I wanted was to be thin — or so I thought. Looking back on it, it seems more as though I was looking for some way that I could control my life, and I decided that way was through controlling my weight. Even when I got very thin, my whole life still revolved around eating, dieting, exercising — every aspect of energy input and output. I can't believe I spent so much of my life on something so boring, but I guess I did it so that I could avoid facing the real issues of life. You know, if I could just focus on my weight or a diet, I wouldn't have to admit that there were elements of my life I couldn't control that simply.

Anyway, if you want to know what I actually *did* during that time, it's a long, boring story. The center of the whole complex of behaviors I got into was eating. Even when I didn't eat for several days at a time, I was always thinking about it. I thought about what to eat, what not to eat, and how I should eat or not eat it. A lot of behaviors went along with this obsession—memorizing diet books, exercising for hours, reading fitness magazines, looking through catalogues for pictures of especially thin models to "motivate" me. The real compulsion came to center on the habit I got into of bingeing on huge amounts of food. Afterwards, I would force myself to vomit to get rid of the calories and the guilt.

It all started after my illness, when I first lost weight. I became fixated on maintaining that body size. It seemed to me that everything good in my life hinged on staying thin. That's when I started thinking about dieting constantly. During that first year, my activities centered mostly on working hard at eating as little as possible. I weighed and measured all my food and switched to eating mostly low-calorie foods like vegetables and diet soda. I occasionally "slipped" and went off whatever diet I was on, but basically I kept my calorie intake very low. I know this because I kept a daily diary (which I still have) where I recorded lists of everything I ate each day, along with the calorie count, which I looked up in diet books. I think I must have bought every calorie-counting book ever published. I used to page through them for hours, memorizing the calories in any food I was likely to encounter. After a while I hardly needed to consult the books—I had an automatic calorie counter in my head. I added up the calories in everything I ate before I'd even swallowed it. All the time I spent thinking about food and dieting kept me from having to deal with the rest of my life.

I got pretty skinny after a year or so of this, as you can imagine. I think I dipped below the best weight for my body, because my metabolism dropped, which is what the body does to protect itself in times of starvation. This meant that it took less and less food for me to maintain my body weight. It also meant that I was cold all the time, that I felt weak and tired, and that I gained weight very easily while eating the same small amounts I'd been eating all along. But I still wanted to lose weight, so I took up a severe exercise program. I read that jumping rope burned more calories per hour than just about anything else I could do, so I jumped rope for hours in my bedroom. I also saved up to buy an exercise bicycle, and I jogged every morning before school. Of course I was always exhausted, and I hardly had time for anything but dieting and exercising. My parents and friends began to show some concern about me, so I "moved underground" and began to keep my dieting a secret. I imagined that I was some kind of spy on this secret mission to lose weight. I started thinking everyone was against me, that they were the "enemy" trying to make me fat. I was pretty crazy. The magazines and books I read—usually quack fitness publications— helped me convince myself that everyone who didn't live like I did was unhealthy and weak-willed. I was still shy and awkward, but now I decided it was because I was better than other people instead of worse.

By my junior year of high school, I was a physical wreck. People would tell me I looked like a concentration camp prisoner, which thrilled me. My parents took me to the doctor, but he couldn't find anything wrong with me and told them I must just be naturally skinny. I decided that I was happy at that weight. To stay there, however, was a constant battle, because my body was not made to be that thin. I managed to stay thin with the same methods I'd been using all along: constant preoccupation with food, exercise, and my body, calorie counting and calculations about weight loss (I kept a small notebook with hundreds of tidy lists concerning food and exercise), and doing every-thing I could to burn calories. I wrote in my journal that I couldn't imagine anything besides weight loss that might be interesting to think about. Can you believe that?

Anyway, after about another year of this compulsive behavior—and of being underweight—I began to get hungry. Not just hungry the way you feel when you've fasted twenty-four hours or forty-eight hours. That kind of hunger seems almost unnoticeable compared to how hungry I got. Until you've been undernourished constantly, for a long period of time, you have no idea what real hunger is. I still can't believe that there are people who feel that hungry, who would give anything for a little food, and here I was doing it deliberately in the midst of plenty. Most Americans don't realize what a terrible, compelling force hunger is. I once heard a psychologist say that anyone's will could be broken by hunger, if semistarvation went on long enough. Well, my will finally broke. That's when I started to binge.

Sometimes I hear people joke about going on some kind of binge—like they ate too much birthday cake or something. People laugh about that. Well, believe me, the binges involved in eating disorders aren't funny. As a freshman in college, I still maintained my dieting and exercising—more so than ever, in fact—but in all this effort to control myself, I would occasionally break down and eat enormous amounts. I don't want to go into detail about that particular behavior. Just talking about it, even after years, makes me feel awfully sad and degraded. What I didn't realize then was that I had cut myself off from everyone to the point where I was terribly, terribly lonely, and I was trying to fill that emotional emptiness with food. Even after my physical hunger was stuffed to the gills, that hunger for love was as strong as ever. When I binged, I felt as if I would never be able to get enough food. I would go on eating, as fast as I could, until I became horribly nauseated. Then I would feel so overcome with guilt and self-hatred and the fear of being fat that I would fast for weeks, or run for hours, or force myself to vomit. Of course, I had to keep this whole thing secret from the people around me. I didn't make any friends during the first two years of college, because I kept away from people to leave time for my obsession. I also became a terrific actress to hide the problem from people in my dorm. No one had any idea what my life was like.

During the year before I finally went to the college health clinic and asked for help, my life was totally out of control. My original ideal of staying thin and attractive was still there—I had never once felt I could count on being thin enough to please myself—but it had become a minor part of this nightmare of bingeing and purging. The more I kept bingeing, the more alone I felt, and the more alone I felt, the more I depended on bingeing to try to feel better. That may sound melodramatic, but I got to the point where I literally felt like I was in the power of some demonic force. I would get up in the morning promising that I would eat practically nothing that day. Then something would happen that would trigger a binge. At first it had to be something fairly drastic, like failing an exam or having an argument with my parents. But after a while it got to be so that almost anything—passing a candy store, talking to a friend, not getting any mail—could set off a binge. I would leave my dorm and go into store after store, buying the most fattening things I could afford and stuffing them down. That would go on for hours, until I ran out of money or the "demon" was satisfied and I could stop eating. Then, of course, I would go into the "purging" phase, where I'd find some quick way to get rid of all those extra calories. You can't imagine what a horrendous way this is to live—and I know I'm not the only one who's had a problem with it.

I knew I needed help when one day I went into "binge mode" before I could go to the bank and get cash. I went into a panic. I started running to the bank, but on the way I passed an all-night convenience store. I tried to walk past it, but I couldn't. I went into the store, picked up some goodies, and left — without paying, of course, since I didn't have any money. I was going to have cash in about two minutes, but the demon couldn't wait that long. Outside the store, I started to cry. I had never stolen anything before. When I was little, I was the kid in the neighborhood who talked the other kids out of stealing treats. I didn't know what had gotten control of my life, but I knew it wasn't me. It was as though I had been walking down a hallway where the walls kept getting narrower and narrower, and the ceiling kept coming down, and the floor coming up. I had finally reached the point where I couldn't go on, and I turned around to leave — and I found out there was no way back. I was trapped in this smothering little box, and I couldn't move. I couldn't call to anyone for help. I was completely immobilized. There's no way I can describe how I felt at that moment. And yet, I wasn't aware of feeling anything. I was completely numb. It was like I'd been killing myself for years, and now I was watching myself die — not just my body, but my *self* — without feeling a thing.

I never really thought about drugs at all until I was almost halfway through college. When I first started taking them, it was pretty much a social thing. My girlfriend and her friends seemed like really great people to me — well, they *were* great people, in a lot of ways — and they took drugs like it was no big deal. I just didn't consider the consequences. It's like when you're fly fishing. You hide the hook in something that looks really good to the fish, so good he doesn't even think about the hook. Then when he goes after the fly, the hook gets lodged in his mouth, and you end up taking the fly away anyhow. The fish ends up with nothing but the hook. And it's not just like he ate something bad for him, either. The hook drags him away from the water and kills him. That's drugs.

So, anyway, for me the bait was these parties I used

to go to with friends. I didn't get addicted to anything right then. I would take drugs with everybody else. I guess it helped me have a good time—yes, it did, because before that I was so shy. I just felt like a lump on a log. Never said anything, never smiled. I was self-conscious about my looks and my manners and everything. Mostly I just felt so dumb compared to the people who interested me—especially my girlfriend Jenny. When I took drugs, though, I felt completely different. I had a lot of confidence when I was using "uppers." I know now from talking to people who are on drugs that there's really no difference in how smart or how interesting people are when they're high and when they're not. In fact, when they're high, people are actually—in my opinion—less interesting, even though they can get very "hyper." Anyway, when I took drugs at parties I stopped feeling self-conscious, and that let me develop a lot of friendships, which was really a good feeling since I missed my family a lot.

Sometimes I would have a hard time unwinding after these parties. It got so I had a really hard time sleeping. I knew that I was awake because of the drugs, so I couldn't trust my body to fall asleep naturally. So I started taking "downers" to help me sleep at night, so I'd be able to function in class and at work the next day. I'd use just about anything to help me sleep—over-the-counter medications or sometimes a drug I'd gotten from a friend. Later on I found out the most effective thing was alcohol, and I really got hooked on that. That's probably the most dangerous drug I ever used, because no one thinks anything about it. Anyway, at the beginning I would take something to make me sleep when I got back late from a party. Then I would have only a couple of hours to sleep, so when I woke up I'd be so exhausted I could hardly move. Well, the answer to that was more "uppers." It got so I was completely regulating my life by chemicals—I never knew how my body actually felt, because it was sort of buried under this constant flow of drugs.

I think I just decided I couldn't trust myself to do anything without taking something to help me. I had no faith in myself. It was like insurance—like I couldn't even try to do something without drugs in case I failed. Any time I had to do *anything* I would pop something—whether it was sleeping, or waking up, or going to class, or going to a party, or going to play basketball. As soon as I knew I had to do something, I'd get terribly nervous that I couldn't do it on my own, or that people wouldn't like me, or something. Then I'd remember that I could take something, and I'd just relax and feel better once I'd decided to use drugs. Then after I took them, I felt really confident, which I never did otherwise. When I went to class high, I felt so smart—I felt like I was the smartest person on campus, and I could do better than anybody else because they didn't have drugs to help them. I actually started to kind of look down my nose at people who didn't take drugs, because I thought they were so stupid to be missing out on this great secret. It was like, drugs could solve all your problems, so if you don't take them you're really missing out. I know how my girlfriend felt when she gave me the drugs in the first place. After I'd been on them for a while, if I got to know someone I liked I would think, "boy, I bet they'd love to find out about drugs," because I wanted them to do well in school and everything. Now that seems so crazy, but then, that's just the way I thought.

Finally my roommate found out about my drug habit. He'd been suspicious for a long time, but one day he actually walked in on me while I was about to take some drugs. He took the stuff and flushed it down the toilet (he was a lot bigger than me or I might have tried to stop him), and he told me he was going to tell the bishop and my parents and that I'd better start to fly right or that he'd have me arrested. He talked to me for a long time. I really was furious at him then, but looking back I think he was amazing to get that involved. He was a really great guy.

I spent the rest of that night sitting in a chair staring at the wall. I thought my whole life was over. For a while all I could think about was "I've got to get some drugs or some booze or I'll never get through this." But for the first time in more than a year, I couldn't turn to anything like that to solve the problem. I really did some hard thinking that night, I can tell you. That was the beginning of my getting over the drug problem.

I don't know when my problems with homosexuality really began. I do remember the one time in high school [the prom date related in chapter 3] when I first decided that I was a homosexual. That day my life seemed to become divided into two separate "rooms." There was the good room, where I kept everything clean so that people could come in and walk around and see what a great guy I was. That good room was perfect, too. I was everybody's all-star everything. Never a problem. But then there was this bad room, connected to the good room by this little door. The bad room was filthy, had no windows, and was full of junk. I never cleaned it. It was where I went to relax, you know, in my mind. That's where I kept the "real" me. Well, the whole bad room was built just to hide the part of me that felt romantic feelings. I say "romantic," because that's what I mean. What I wanted—at least at first—was a loving relationship with one individual. If I had felt that for a girl, I never would have had to build a "bad room," to divide my life into two opposite halves. But I immediately decided that I was a homosexual, and that thought was so terrible that I locked all my feelings into this secret room. I could never tell anyone about them. I knew my parents, friends, and Church leaders would have been appalled if I had gone to them to talk about it. Besides, I wanted to keep the feelings of love that I felt, even if they weren't right. I wanted to protect them. So I put together this "bad room" and kept a secret, homosexual self there to grow without any input from anyone but myself.

At first I managed to ignore my feelings most of the time. But when I was lonely or sad, I would go into the "bad room" and imagine that I could just talk and relate to someone I felt very close to. That person was always a guy my own age. I think in a way that the person in the bad room was *me*—I wanted to feel loved by my own self. Does that make sense? Anyway, as a teenager I would imagine that I had this very close relationship with another male. I think our society relays the message—especially to men—that all love is sexual, because I couldn't imagine being close to someone emotionally without including a sexual element. It took me years to learn that love and sexuality are not necessarily the same thing. At any rate, my fantasies were relatively innocent for a while but eventually became more and more centered around sexual activity. It didn't seem to matter, because I had already decided I was "gay," so I felt there was nothing more to lose. I was lost already, right? I thought, as long as you've stepped over that line, you can't make things any worse. So as a teenager, I grew more and more obsessed with those fantasies.

I confessed those feelings to the bishop in preparation for my mission. He seemed very uneasy about the whole thing—didn't want to talk about it. I remember thinking, "He's just glad he wasn't born this way." The bishop was a good man, but he made me feel as though these homosexual thoughts were a sign that I was from some different species. I know that he was a wonderful counselor for some of my friends who had "normal" sexual temptations or who had even succumbed to those temptations, but he treated my problems as though they were really incurable. He just told me to try never to think about anything like that again, because if I did there would be no hope for me.

It was like being told you have a vein in your brain that's about to rupture and kill you if you move—it was paralyzing, but it didn't help the problem. I just sort of vowed I would never let anyone into that "bad room" again. Anyway, I kept myself pretty free from those thoughts for a while and went on my mission. I kept myself so busy I'd never think about anything like that. I made sure I was exhausted all the time. I was the hardest-working missionary in Germany! Plus that, the special gift and companionship of the Spirit that missionaries have made it easy to avoid any kind of temptation.

When I got back from my mission I tried dating some women, but I just couldn't seem to get interested. All my friends were dating and getting married, and I felt very lonely. I missed the missionary work, the sense of purpose it gave me, and the tremendous love I felt for the people I served. I really love kids, and when my friends started having their own kids, it would just remind me what I "was," and that made me lonelier than ever. To get away from these feelings, I started to fantasize a lot again. I started noticing men who were obviously homosexual and found that there were certain places in town where they seemed to congregate. I started going to those places "just out of curiosity." The people I saw there provided a lot of fuel for my imagination. I found some homosexual pornography in the parking lot of a bar and made the mistake of looking at it. That old "bad room" was getting quite a collection of experiences in it. I didn't like the effort of keeping that part of myself so secret, so I took a job in Los Angeles to get away from my family and Latter-day Saint friends. I heard a lot about homosexuality on the news and other places—how it was natural and should be given equal status with heterosexuality, and so on. A lot of the information sounded very persuasive, and I was swayed by it. I started to accept the "fact" that this was my nature, that God had made me this way and I deserved to act out my feelings just like anyone else.

In Los Angeles I sort of moved into the "bad room." My testimony just stayed in the "good room," and I never looked at it while I was thinking about my sexual behavior. I often swore to myself that I would somehow overcome my feelings and live in the "good room" forever, without loving anyone romantically or sexually for my whole life. But then I would go into a kind of trance that would take me, without any conscious thought, to the gay bars and other areas of town where I knew homosexual activities were taking place. It hardly even seemed like a big step to begin engaging in such behaviors. I had already given up on myself. As long as you have this "bad room," which no one ever sees, you're lost anyway, right? What does it matter how awful the things are that you do in that room? So, I started actually having relationships with some of these men I met during my nightly wandering. I cut off contact with my family altogether. When they called I would get furious at them because I hated myself so much and felt so alone and miserable, and I couldn't tell them why.

What amazes me most, looking back on those days, is how something that began as a search for love could have become so empty of real human relationships. The encounters I had were all pretty anonymous. They had nothing to do with love. Love enhances the rest of your life. This behavior seemed to be dragging the rest of my life into it like a whirlpool. I spent larger and larger amounts of my time engaged in these activities — sometimes in actual encounters with other people, but more often in wandering through "that section of town" or into bookstores that sold homosexual materials. It just took so much time! I was glad it did, because the rest of my life — except for my work, which was pretty isolating — was so empty. So night after night I spent hours wandering, dwelling on this "fascinating" topic. The way I see the world now, any kind of loveless sexual encounter seems so empty and hollow. But then, this type of activity seemed exciting and forbidden. It began to absorb my whole mind and soul.

I really hit rock bottom one day when I was sitting in a gay bar and I ordered a soft drink, because of course I never broke the Word of Wisdom. Can you imagine that? There I was, all geared up to commit the sin next to murder, and I was being all careful not to break the Word of Wisdom! I was standing between the "good room" and the "bad room," and I just couldn't believe the contrast. It just seemed so absurd, so ridiculous, and so disgusting. I knew the Church was true, I loved the Lord with all my heart, and here I was sitting in this horrible place where He could never, ever, reach me. And the terrible thing was that I knew—I *knew*—that even if I left right then I'd be back sometime in the very near future. I was totally out of control. If I had not had a testimony, that is the first time I think I might have just ended it all. As it was, nothing made sense to me. Not anything. It was the most terrible feeling in the world, and I wanted to just vanish altogether—good room, bad room, and all.

In considering actions of self-indulgence, as well as the other steps of the addictive cycle, the common elements in the stories of Ellen, Bill, and Warren are striking and important. Despite the apparent differences in these people's lives and personalities, and despite the dissimilarity of their actual addictive behaviors, all three stories fit a common pattern. Each of these actions of self-indulgence could be interpreted as a kind of demonic counterfeit for some aspect of life that is good, wholesome, and ultimately a contributor to the joy for which we are designed: Ellen mentions her preoccupation with the process of nourishment, Bill sees drugs as a substitute for the normal physical alternation of relaxation and alertness, and

Warren describes his homosexual behaviors as a misguided search for friendship and romantic love. All three of these people fell into the trap of mistaking an activity that blocks pain with an activity that brings joy and, therefore, of placing that activity at the center of their lives.

Bill, Ellen, and Warren all described a complex of behaviors surrounding their actions of self-indulgence that were quite similar. Each of them mentioned an early predisposition to be intrigued with the activity to which they later became addicted. Each described how the fascination grew once they had begun to engage in the behavior, gradually becoming an obsession that absorbed enormous amounts of time and energy and progressively cut them off from interaction with loved ones. All three case histories show the development of an "addictive routine," a series of activities leading up to the actual commission of the action, during which the victim blocked out everyday thoughts and feelings. They describe the way in which their routines became more and more time-consuming and the activities less and less congruent with what they themselves considered decent and good. Finally, Ellen, Bill, and Warren all described the terrible sensation of being "out of control" that assailed them at times when their feelings and consciences were not pushed aside by the excitement of a routinized, addictive action.

The pattern exhibited by these three compulsive-cycle victims in regard to the action of self-indulgence is typical of the addicts we interviewed. Not all of them showed every aspect of the pattern in exactly the same proportions. In some cases, one feature or another of a typical addictive action might be predominant, insignificant, or altogether missing; however, every victim we spoke with recounted experiences with most of the aspects of actions of self-indulgence we have mentioned. Perhaps the single most telling fact that identified an addict was the choice to participate in a behavior even at the expense of hurting or excluding loved ones. That was the source of much anguish for both the compulsive-cycle victims we spoke with and the people who cared about them. During the commission of the "action of self-indulgence," the addict invariably blocked the memory of this pain by becoming absorbed in the addictive routine, which seemed to have an almost hypnotic power of distraction. After the action was over, however — when the second step on the compulsive cycle had been taken and completed yet another time — the addict typically entered the guilt, shame, and self-hatred of the third step. This terrible consequence of the action of self-indulgence is the subject of the next chapter.

5

THE THIRD STEP:
FEELINGS OF SELF-HATRED

For many centuries, one of the most frightening and horrible illnesses of the many that afflict mankind was the
disease of leprosy. Leprosy was not feared for bringing
sudden death, as many infections can. A quick demise
would be merciful compared to the slow decay of leprosy,
which rots the body a little at a time, often for years, before
the victim finally succumbs to it. Nor is leprosy the most
painful condition to be suffered by the sick. On the contrary, this disease owes many of its deadly effects to the
fact that it anesthetizes the victim to the sensation of pain,
so that wounds and infections go unnoticed until they have
destroyed the body piece by piece. This is not a pleasant
subject, but it is an apt metaphor to use in describing
addictive behavior. For what leprosy does to the body, the
compulsive cycle does to the soul. The pain of being left
alone on earth to work out one's salvation in fear and
trembling is not easy to bear, but like any pain that comes
from happenstance rather than from evil, it can be a very
useful sensation. It tells us that we must search for the
companionship of other people and the Lord's love and
ultimately the eternal presence of all righteous beings. It
will not allow us to rest completely unless we are moving
closer to that happy goal. As we have pointed out in the
last two chapters, however, for some people this search
ends—or at least is suspended—when they stumble into
some action that anesthetizes them to the spiritual pain

95

that accompanies feelings of isolation. Mistaking the comfort of oblivion for that of the Comforter himself, such people often become involved in behavior which tears, wounds, and destroys the soul while the victim is desensitized to its effects.

Satan, however, is crueler than leprosy. He is interested in the anesthetizing effect of addictive actions only so long as they serve to entrap us and allow us to hurt ourselves. Once the injury has been inflicted, there is no need for him to allow us to ignore the pain of drawing further away from our divine potential. The action of self-indulgence may continue for some time, but eventually it ends. No appetite is unlimited. At some point even the most advanced addict reaches the point of surfeit, and the addictive action ceases. Then, inevitably, follows the third step on the compulsive cycle. We have labeled this stage "feelings of self-hatred," but that is a rather pale way to describe the emotions that flood through compulsive-cycle victims when they realize that they have once again broken all promises and resolutions not to engage in the addictive behavior.

This realization is what marks the end of the action of self-indulgence and the beginning of the next step on the cycle. To someone who has never experienced powerful temptation, the claim that behavioral addicts do not realize what they are doing until after the action of self-indulgence is ended might seem rather odd. After all, when someone plans several hours or even days in advance to perform some action and then carries it through with every indication of premeditated gusto, it seems ridiculous to say that the person does not realize what is being done. And indeed, addicts readily admit that in a certain sense they are aware of their actions while the actions are being performed. In another sense, however, they do not fully realize what the action means at the time when they commit it. The function of the routinized patterns of behavior that surround or precede the action of self-indulgence seems to be the removal of the addict from the real world. The further a compulsive-cycle victim goes into these behaviors, the more effectively the addictive routine blocks out awareness of even the most powerful reasons for avoiding the action of self-indulgence. The loved ones whom the addict truly wishes to protect and please, the fervent covenants to obey God's commandments, the expectation of horrific consequences, and every other obstacle to the addiction are simply pushed aside.

The addict does not do this out of spite but because the real world where promises and consequences exist is also the world that contains so much loneliness and unhappiness. As long as the action of self-indulgence is in the immediate future or the present, the addict is aware neither of this earthly isolation nor of the reasons for avoiding the compulsive cycle. Only when the action is over and the excitement inevitably fades does the victim *realize* — incorporate into the real world — what he or she has just done. When that realization occurs, it is as though an anesthetized person has unwittingly torn his flesh apart and then suddenly regained an acute sensitivity to pain. It may seem to an observer, watching an addict seek out an addictive action again and again, that the compulsive-cycle victim feels no remorse for sins or broken promises. On the contrary, however, the people we spoke with described the third step on the cycle as an overwhelming, all-consuming combination, of guilt, shame, bitterness, remorse, sorrow, and despair. Alma described this feeling to his son Helaman by telling him that it could not be described, referring to it as "inexpressible horror." (Alma 36:14.) The effect of all these emotions seems to boil down to a greatly reduced sense of self-esteem, or as we refer to it on our model of the compulsive cycle, self-hatred.

The feelings of self-hatred that follow the action of self-indulgence may seem natural and even constructive to both

97

a compulsive-cycle victim and the victim's loved ones. Everyone involved may see a healthy dose of guilt as a good indicator that the addict is on the way to reform. That is a natural error to make, for often, especially in instances that do not involve addictive behavior, shame and remorse do result in a sinner's abandoning his sin. The youngster who taunts a classmate may be so affected by the tears in her friend's eyes that she becomes more considerate for the rest of her life. The careless and overly confident teenager might become a much more careful driver after an accident that results in damage to his parents' car. An employee who steals a few items from a huge shipment of goods, thinking it will never be noticed, might be so smitten by conscience that he finds himself unable to enjoy the stolen objects, eventually replaces them, and resolves to be more honest in his daily activities. This kind of guilt—what the scriptures call sorrowing unto repentance—is healthy, normal, and constructive. (See Mormon 2:13–14.) It is one of the chief mechanisms by which we learn to live uprightly. It is given to us by the light of Christ to recognize when an action is unrighteous, and guilt is a part of that recognition.

The self-hatred of the addict following the action of self-indulgence, however, is different from the prickings of conscience just described. It is a horror that numbs and petrifies, rather than remorse that goads to repentance. Self-hatred serves to cement the compulsive cycle in place, rather than to free the victim from it. Victims and their loved ones who view this stage on the compulsive cycle as the guilt that will ensure that the addict "never does it again" are mistaken. Their well-meaning intentions to improve the preventative efficacy of guilt by dwelling on and exacerbating the feelings of self-hatred actually contribute to the problem. These feelings are a part of the compulsive cycle. They perpetuate the addiction. It is therefore very important that both behavioral addicts and those who wish to help them learn to identify these feelings and to distinguish them from the righteous guilt that should follow a misguided or destructive action.

All the behavioral addicts we interviewed described the same type of emotion as following the commission of their various actions of self-indulgence. Usually the addict mentioned that the feelings changed in intensity and nature depending on how long the addiction had been going on. The first commission of an addictive action, especially one that is not explicitly forbidden by the scriptures or social convention, usually inspired a kind of surprise in the perpetrator. "I couldn't believe I had done it" or "It seemed as though it must have been done by someone else" were common descriptions of an addict's reaction to his or her first experience with an action of self-indulgence. When the action was a serious sin, this surprise was more extreme and accompanied by a sense of horror and loss. No matter what the action, however, the feelings of self-hatred that followed this initial realization were less intense during the first revolutions of the compulsive cycle than they became later on. The first experience was usually followed by an immediate resolution never to participate in the activity again, and because the addict had not yet experienced the failure of breaking this commitment, it was usually made with great confidence. At the same time, however, the memory of the pleasure and the oblivion to pain that accompanied the action often occupied a large place in the addict's mind even after the action. This memory, of course, contributed to the recommission of the action and the perpetuation of the compulsive cycle.

By the time compulsive-cycle victims have been involved in their addiction for several months or years, their reaction to the action of self-indulgence is different from what they experienced at the beginning of the addiction. Many of the people who came to us for advice and volunteered their stories were at this terrible stage. Some had been there for years. Typical comments about the long-time addict's feelings after each occasion of indulging in the action of self-indulgence were, "I want to die," "I feel like killing myself," "there seems to be no hope," "I don't see how I can go on," "it's just too hard to keep trying," or "I'm just naturally this way; I might as well give up."

Not only is the addictive action followed by despair and agony but the pleasure has gone out of the action itself. After years of trying and failing to repent and forsake their addictions, compulsive-cycle victims find their lives transformed into a meaningless repetition of the same tired and hated activities, followed inevitably by self-loathing and despair. Their spirits have been wasted by this leprosy of the soul, until their only keenly felt desire is for the extinction of consciousness. Believing Latter-day Saints know death will not accomplish this end, and that makes the predicament seem completely inescapable to a compulsive-cycle victim in the advanced stages of an addiction.

Between the surprised remorse of the first reaction to sin and the despair of a long-time addict lies a history of deeply felt shame that follows each occurrence of the action of self-indulgence. From the very outset, however, there seem to be notable differences between the guilt of the compulsive-cycle addict and that of a nonaddict who commits a similar sin. Perhaps the most important of these differences is the tendency of behavioral addicts to label themselves evil, disgusting, or worthless. As we mentioned in the chapter on feelings of isolation, many people who are vulnerable to the compulsive cycle already have rather low self-esteem. Many of the very successful people we interviewed who were caught in such a cycle expressed an anxiety about their worth as human beings, which seemed astonishing in view of their impressive accomplishments. Some of these people seemed to be working extraordinarily hard to achieve success of all types, in order to disguise what they felt was their fundamental lack of worth. Other talented people we spoke with were so convinced of their inadequacy as human beings that they refused to work up to their potential in school, employment, or personal relationships. They felt doomed to failure before they began and were not willing to risk the hurt of attempting something that they felt sure would end in a confirmation of their low self-image. Where these people had picked up their original low self-esteem was something that varied with each person and is therefore impossible to sum up in generalized terms. What was obvious from the interviews, however, was that in the first place this skewed image of self increased the victims' sense of isolation, which made them more vulnerable to temptations, and second, that once they had succumbed to temptation, these people immediately decided that the sin was proof of their original estimation of themselves as low and blameworthy. As one woman put it, "When I realized what I'd done, it was like all the worst suspicions that I'd always had about myself came true."

That type of reaction is particularly devastating when the temptations encountered by compulsive-cycle victims are designated by labels that they can apply to themselves to make their self-disgust concrete. One of the most striking examples of labeling we saw in the interviews was evidenced in the difference between men who had some kind of sexual addiction and women who had similar problems. For instance, in the case of men who indulged in improper relationships with women, even repetitively and obsessively, no extremely pejorative title was readily available to affix to the sinner. Our society looks upon such men as impressive and admirable and often gives them such labels as "playboy" or "lady's man," which carry connotations of being dashing, successful, and desirable. A woman who engages in similar relationships with men, on the other

101

hand, is subject to a variety of titles so vituperative that we will not repeat them here. One of the most bewildering things we saw, in interviewing male-female couples who had fallen into precisely the same sin at precisely the same time, was that both partners often labeled the woman and felt concerned about her ability to remain faithful and chaste, whereas the man's sin was seen as a simple and understandable mistake. Surely part of this reaction can be attributed to labeling as well as to the social backgrounds and attitudes that create different types of labels for different types of actions.

Even more devastating than the examples of the labels given to promiscuous women, however, were the absolute designations of type our society assigns to individuals who commit sexual sins in something other than male-female relationships. Of the compulsive-cycle victims we spoke with who were involved in homosexual behaviors, for example, a large number remembered being approached by a much older person and molested when they were still quite young. Because this event had a powerful effect on them, they had decided that they must "be" homosexuals, a label given and heavily reinforced in our society to anyone suspected of such inclinations. One puzzling and saddening problem we faced in our research was that so many reputable theorists state, or simply assume, that one who has committed a homosexual action "is" a homosexual, and can never gain fulfillment in any other type of relationship.

This type of labeling, by the way, is certainly not limited to sexual behavior. According to many of the psychological theorists whose works we studied, once a person is an alcoholic, he or she is always an alcoholic; once an anorexic or bulimic, always an anorexic or bulimic; once a pathological liar, gambler, or kleptomaniac, always and forever a flawed and categorized person. Nevertheless, when psychologists deal with these afflictions, their assumption is that the addict can at least be helped to escape from the behavior, even if there is always some susceptibility to the problem, and great success in overcoming their addictions has been achieved by people in all these categories. This escape is assumed not to be available to people who engage in homosexual activities but who do not wish to be homosexual. It is politically inadvisable to suggest that homosexuals either can or should establish heterosexual relationships. The few stories that are available about homosexuals who attempt a heterosexual life-style often cite their eventual return to their "true nature." This belief keeps everyone within the bounds set by those who claim that homosexuals are a genetically distinctive group, entitled by an accident of birth to live a separate life-style. By far the strongest statements we found to the contrary were published by members of the Church, especially modern prophets. We have no wish to argue with homosexuals who are intent on claiming the right to be homosexual. We are addressing those who believe in the gospel, who do not wish to lead a homosexual life-style, and who wonder if the hope offered by the prophets is as convincing as the unanimous cry of the secular world. In our research we encountered a number of people who, at this writing, appear to have escaped from both the enveloping label of homosexual and the behaviors it entails. But the power of this title, and the encouragement given to those who are tempted to admit that they "are" homosexual, to establish an identity within themselves as homosexuals first and foremost, is by far the most devastating example of the power of labeling that we saw in our interviews.

The act of labeling oneself, of identifying with the sin one has committed before one identifies with any other aspect of one's being, is not part of healthy guilt. The Lord tells us over and over again through the scriptures and His spokesmen on the earth that judgment is not ours. It belongs to Him. We are instructed to recognize sin and to

103

abhor it, but to abhor the sinner is itself a sin. A person who sees himself or herself chiefly as a child of God, and who knows of the unlimited potential for goodness pertaining to this relationship, will see addiction as a dangerous behavior uncharacteristic and unworthy of a Divine heritage.

That is how the Lord sees us. It is how He wants us to see ourselves. The power that encourages us to judge, to label, and to hate the sinner as well as the sin comes from below and not from above. We interviewed many compulsive-cycle victims who actually seemed proud of their self-hatred, as though this loathing was a demonstration of their good intentions and their knowledge that what they had done was wrong. The more they could hate themselves, the more righteous they felt. What a paradox! It is Satan who despises us, and when we hate ourselves — even because of the basest transgression — he and all his angels rejoice that we have joined their ranks. Judgment belongs to the Lord. And yet, consider His actions when He confronted the woman taken in adultery — not "the adulteress," but "the *woman,* the daughter of God, taken in adultery." Knowing full well that He would suffer for her sins in Gethsemane, that He had every right under heaven to accuse her, Jesus told the woman, "Neither do I condemn thee: go, and sin no more." (John 8:11.)

That is all He asks any of us to do in assessing our own actions. In our hearts, most of us know that. But the fact is that "going and sinning no more" is the one action many of us are not willing to perform. The compulsive-cycle victim, in particular an individual who has been involved with an addiction for some time, is unwilling to forgo the addiction, no matter how guilty he or she may feel about it. Like many of the people described by Nephi, addicts seem to feel at some level that if they "sin a little," "God will beat us with a few stripes, and at last we shall be saved in the kingdom of God." (2 Nephi 28:8.) Inflicting those

"stripes" themselves, by a sort of emotional self-flagella-
tion following the action of self-indulgence, seems in many
cases to be part of the addictive ritual, the way in which
the victim pays for the sin so that there will be no need
to give it up. Unlike the feeling of sorrowing unto repentance, which makes the guilty person hurry to leave the
sin in the past and get on with a righteous life, the feelings
of self-hatred experienced by the compulsive-cycle victims
rivet addicts' attention on their mistakes and on their own
sinful natures, absorbing so much attention and energy
that the feelings actually interfere with other aspects of
living. Obsessed with the idea that they are dreadful persons whom everyone would despise "if they knew what
I really am," compulsive-cycle victims withdraw further
and further from loved ones and from the Lord. A behavioral addict may seem driven to work at a frenzied pace
or else refuse to work at all in jobs or school. The person
may sleep too much or too little and seem unable to enjoy
leisure activities. The Lord, who is our model for all behavior, clearly tells us that once we have truly repented
of our sins and forsaken them, He simply forgets them.
Compulsive-cycle victims in the throes of feelings of self-
hatred do not forget their mistakes, not any of them, not
for an instant. That is not a Christlike reaction.

One of the most instructive stories we heard about the
difference between feelings of self-hatred and sorrowing
unto repentance was told to us by one of several bishops
we interviewed about their experiences counseling people
with addictive problems. This Church leader recounted an
experience he had had while serving as bishop of another
ward some years earlier. A great deal of the bishop's attention in his calling was taken up in trying to help a
member of his ward—we'll call him Eric—who was addicted to alcohol. This ward member went on a drinking
binge every few months, whenever pressures at work and
in his troubled marriage became too intense for him to

handle. After each drinking bout, Eric reacted by plunging into a severe depression, during which he berated himself as a failure, a disgusting, drunken bum, and any other degrading label he could think of. His wife, who loved her husband despite their arguments and was deeply concerned about his drinking, tried to stop Eric by shielding him from consequences on one hand (making excuses for him at work, delivering messages for him while he was drunk, and so on) and on the other hand by reemphasizing his feelings of self-hatred. After a drinking binge, Eric would go through a period of being verbally abused by both himself and his wife. Then he would go to the bishop, confess his sins, and to quote the bishop, "hang his head like a whipped dog expecting to be kicked." After a few occasions the confession appeared to become part of the routine that surrounded Eric's binges. In fact, he seemed disappointed that the bishop did not "come down harder" on him, since the sting of shame seemed to allow him to feel that he had paid for, and thus repented of, his sins.

The bishop advised Eric many times to attend the local branch of an alcoholic treatment program. Finally, he told us, "I delivered him personally to a meeting and made sure he stayed there." At the meeting, Eric encountered some new perspectives about both his relationship with alcohol and his relationship with God. That night, at his home, Eric prayed for help in overcoming his addiction. He had said similar prayers many times before that, but this time Eric felt his prayer answered by a flood of warmth and love that was completely different from the vengeance he expected the Lord to pour out on him. The next day Eric made yet another appointment with the bishop. As the bishop later told us, "Eric was a different person that day. He was completely honest about his problem, but he didn't dwell on it. He didn't seem to be begging me to restore his self-confidence, and he didn't seem hopeless. In fact, he seemed to be really happy, even though he wasn't proud of his actions. That's really what it was. *He was still ashamed of his actions, but he was proud of himself.* Now, I grew up thinking that if you were really repentant, you'd go through all kinds of weeping and wailing when you confessed to the bishop. Well, Eric used to do that—in fact, he did it all the time. But this time he didn't shed a tear. He actually seemed excited. But this time the Spirit told me Eric had really repented for the first time."

Eric had occasional problems with alcohol even after this incident, but the different character of his reaction to his mistakes helped him use them as constructive, rather than destructive, lessons. At this writing it has been ten years since Eric took a drink. Both the professional and the personal sides of his life seem to be going well, and he is active and happy in his Church callings. What changed first for Eric was the quality of his reaction to the action of self-indulgence that tied him to the compulsive cycle. The crushing force of the feelings of self-hatred he had felt for years finally gave way to the sorrow that came from the knowledge that he was worth too much to waste, not that he was worthless until he repented.

The stories of Ellen, Bill, and Warren at the third stage on the compulsive cycle all fit the typical pattern of a behavioral addict who has not yet reached the realization of personal worth that rescued Eric. Their stories have in common a monotonous theme of self-destructive shame and guilt. The media of our society often portray addicts as tortured souls whose suffering is extraordinarily noble and romantic; however, anyone who consistently deals with people who are full of guilt—but not to repentance—soon comes to the conclusion that there are few things more common and less interesting than self-hatred. Still, the images of Ellen, Bill, and Warren suffering through these feelings may serve to illustrate the third step on the compulsive cycle, as well as to show that just as faith in our divine potential can bring us closer to the Lord, belief in our own worthlessness inevitably brings us closer to the adversary.

It was five-thirty in the afternoon, and already as dark as midnight. Ellen had a ballet class at six, and until lunchtime she'd honestly been planning to go. The dance class had been traumatic since she had gained nearly three and a half pounds (according to the digital readout on her new computerized scales), and Ellen was sure everyone in the class was scandalized by her obesity. She was constantly afraid that the teacher would comment. After all, she'd enrolled in ballet in the first place to make sure that she would stick to her diet and exercise program. Ballet people really cared about thinness, Ellen had told herself, and if she knew she had to show up in a leotard and parade around in front of several of them, that thought would certainly be enough to stop her from indulging in the eating binges that had recently been getting more and more frequent.

Somehow, the plan didn't seem to be working the way Ellen had expected it would. In fact, she had to admit that it seemed to be having the opposite effect. Whenever she thought about her ballet class and the necessity of staying thin to avoid the disapproval of her instructors and classmates, she was gripped by the terror that she would never be able to do it — that her true, fat nature would soon bulge out and reveal itself in the most public and humiliating way. The really infuriating thing was that every time this fear came over her, she had the same reaction. Well, approximately the same. Sometimes it was Chocolate Ripple, and sometimes it was Burnt Almond Fudge. But it was always an unbelievable amount, and she always ended up vomiting to get rid of it.

Ellen lifted her head wearily and stared at the rim of the bathroom sink. She couldn't afford to miss ballet again, but she certainly couldn't go now. This was where she'd spent the last class period, too—slouched against the cold tile wall between the fixtures of the only private bathroom in her dorm. Finding a place to rid herself of calories after a binge had been one of the most time-consuming struggles of her years of college. Now, though, she wasn't sure the private bathroom was a good thing. Knowing it was available seemed to have made her binges begin more easily and go on longer. Ellen winced. She didn't want to think about that, about the way she behaved when that terrible demon overtook her, about the contrast between her life and the lives of normal people. She would tell her ballet instructor that she'd had—uh—food poisoning. All week. That wasn't very far from the truth, really. A whole gallon of ice cream at one sitting was probably an overdose in the truest medical sense of the word.

Ellen closed her eyes and pressed her cheek against the cold tile wall. She knew what was coming. It had to come. After each and every binge it came, like the bills after a credit-card spending spree. Buy now, pay later. She hadn't enjoyed this latest binge at all—hadn't enjoyed eating for years—but at least while she'd been in the middle of it she hadn't had to think about anything. Especially she hadn't thought about herself: what a really low, abhorrent, filthy creature she was. Ellen put her face against her knees, pressed the heels of her hands against her forehead, and began to rock slightly back and forth as the realization of what she was and what she had done began to break over her in scalding waves. Familiar, time-worn nouns began to parade themselves through her mind: pig, slob, glutton, barbarian. . . . They were followed by the adjectives: fat, obscene, disgusting, hideous, gross, filthy. . . . There were more adjectives than nouns. They took longer to go through. They always did.

Ellen hugged her bent legs and pressed her eyes against her kneecaps until stars and comets twirled behind the lids. The verbs went by: swilling, hogging, stuffing. . . .

After four years of this, Ellen was a veritable thesaurus of degrading gustatory terminology.

She wanted to run, wanted to escape this thing that was ruining her life and filling her with inexpressible disgust. She rose jerkily to her feet and began to pace back and forth, back and forth, between the sink and the wall four feet away. There was no escaping the thing. The thing was Ellen. How could she get away? What was there in Ellen that *could* get away from the essence of what she had become? There was no place far enough, deep enough, dark enough, to hide Ellen from herself. Every day she walked and ran and danced and bicycled away from her Self, trying to make it dissolve around her, and everywhere she went the Self came with her. Every day—yes, she had to admit it had become every day—some part of her Self that was not Ellen filled her with food, food used like a weapon to hurt her and destroy her while it enlarged its Self. Every day she purged her Self, sometimes again and again, trying to spit her Self out and flush her Self away forever. The catharsis would ease the agony for a moment. But then it would return again, this Self that was destroying Ellen. And every time it came back, it was stronger.

Ellen began to pace faster, swinging in little circles between the bathroom wall and the door, panicking at being trapped in this tiny room with her most powerful and most hated enemy. She couldn't leave, couldn't go out where people could see her, her loathsome and bloated Self dragging her with it like a criminal locked in the stocks for people to jeer at. Ellen hated her Self, hated it with a passion she no longer felt for anything else. She could see it all so clearly now, everything her Self was doing to her. There must be a way, must be a way to win victory over it. Ellen was beginning to perspire from her frantic pacing in the tiny warm room. She stopped and jerked open the medicine cabinet. The panic receded slightly and her eyes brightened as she quickly made a mental catalog of the contents. One bottle of aspirin, two used cotton balls, a box of laxatives (those were Ellen's — she used them sometimes after a binge), and a disposable razor.

A razor! Ellen backed away from the medicine cabinet and did two or three more laps around the bathroom. She could win. Yes, she could win. She could destroy her Self, and then she would be free. Ellen clenched her teeth in a defiant snarl. Revenge, that was what she wanted. Revenge over this hideous Self that lured her into unspeakable actions, that had used her to gorge its Self until Ellen was driven half mad with hatred for it. Her Self had ruined her life, Ellen thought, and it was only by taking her life — taking it back — that she could ruin the Self. With trembling fingers Ellen lifted the razor from its shelf and tried the edge against her wrist. It was dull, coated with shaving cream and hard-water minerals, but it was sharp enough. She drove the corner of the blade into her skin.

A brilliant flash of pain shot up Ellen's arm and into her brain, and the razor dropped, clattering to the floor. Blood oozed from a small wound in her wrist, not even big enough to require a Band-Aid and pitifully inadequate to accomplish what Ellen had planned. She kicked the razor into the corner, shaking her arm furiously until the blood flicked over the mirror and the white tile of the bathroom wall. Her mouth opened in a silent scream — not because of the pain in her wrist but because of the pain in her soul. There was no escape; there would be no victory. The Self had won again. She could hate it, but she could not stop it. It would preserve its Self, it would go on taking her with it into binges and purges and ice cream shops and lavatories, always becoming worse, always more shameful, until . . .

Until what? There was no "until." Dawn would never break on this night. Even if she died, Ellen knew in her heart — had known since the answer to a simple prayer had come one Sunday morning when she was only nine — that what awaited her after death was simply more of life. She could not believe that this knowledge had made her happy at one time. She had heard of religious men in India who burned themselves alive. Ellen thought she knew why they must do it. They were trying to get rid of them Selves, to disappear into the air, to scatter them Selves over such a vast territory that they could never possibly reassemble. But the Church was true, Ellen assented bitterly. The Resurrection was real, and extinction was impossible even for the damned. And oh, if ever a soul deserved to be damned, she thought, it was her Self. She would have no escape from it, no victory, no relief from surrender. The Self never slept while Ellen was awake. It never stayed in a room when Ellen left. It never let itself go unsatiated when Ellen was hungry.

With a sudden surge of horror, Ellen realized that she was hungry now. She had rid her Self not an hour ago of everything she'd eaten during her last binge, and her stomach was growling again already. Ellen stared at her Self in the mirror with eyes that widened in terror. Until now after a binge she'd been free from the urge to eat again until at least the next day. Now, it had been only an hour, and the demon was emerging already. What was this thing, Ellen thought, this Self in the mirror? The image was hard for Ellen to see clearly, so great were the hatred and the fear she felt toward it. It was a hideous, slavering, voracious, insatiable monster. She was too weak to fight it anymore. Ellen watched, exhausted, as her Self opened the door and pulled her out of the bathroom with it. She thought dimly that she must stop her Self from going in search of food for another binge. But the very thought of food seemed to feed the Self, and it grew stronger as Ellen headed for the exit. At least the unbearable horror was slowly giving way to blessed numbness. Anything was better than what she had been feeling in the bathroom. As she walked more and more quickly toward the shop where she always bought her ice cream, Ellen felt her Self begin to smile.

Far away, across the wide green field, walked a small company of people just Bill's age. They were chatting and laughing, and Bill thought he could see them getting ready for a picnic. He smiled, watching the expressions on their faces and the comfort they seemed to feel in each other's presence. Their courtesy toward each other was obvious but not stilted, and the whole group seemed to shimmer with a marvelous combination of tranquillity and excitement. Bill wanted more than anything in the world to be invited to the picnic. But it was so far away, such a long way to travel . . . if he didn't hurry, he thought with a sudden pang of anxiety, they would finish and go away before he reached them. Bill began to run forward, forgetting where he had been standing. Suddenly the green field was gone, and he felt the earth vanish beneath him. He was falling—falling, falling, endlessly falling into the blank gray abyss that separated him from the picnickers.

Bill woke up with a gasp and stared at the ceiling, eyes wide, body tense, for almost a full minute before he realized he had been dreaming. It was always the same dream, every couple of months. The same field, the same distance, the same plunge into nothingness that shocked him awake and left him trembling for hours. This time, though, the people at the picnic had been different. He knew them. He'd been out on his first blind double-date with them not—he glanced at the clock—six hours before. Bill didn't know how he'd been talked into something like that in the first place, especially by people in his ward. He hadn't really talked to anyone at church for more than a year, let alone gone out for an evening with ward members. Since he and Jenny broke up, though, life had been pretty lonely, and he'd mentioned the fact to Jeff Bridgeman at church one day, in response to Jeff's simple "How are ya?"

Stupid, Bill told himself, to go telling your life story to someone who probably couldn't care less. But he liked Jeff, thought he could probably trust him, and the stuff about Jenny had just sort of spilled out before he'd had a chance to think. He hadn't been asking for charity. But the next day Jeff had called with a series of statements, not questions — "We're going to a movie Friday night. Dinner first. Your date's name is Tammy. She's terrific; you'll like her a lot. See you at six." Jeff had hung up before Bill could say a word.

He had hardly been able to believe it when Friday at six P.M. he had found himself showered, shaved, dressed, and even a little excited. What was easier to believe was that he was as high as a kite — it would have been unthinkable to meet all these new people, to be with them for a whole evening, without something to help him. He hadn't even felt a twinge of guilt, taking drugs for something like this. No one could be expected to face a blind date without a little extra courage from somewhere. With his ears ringing and his pulse racing from the effects of the uppers, Bill felt confident that he would be able to entertain the others and enjoy himself. Still, he had to admit that he needed a lot more of whatever he was taking to help him perform well these days. It was a struggle simply to feel normal anymore, even when he was high or drunk. It used to be that drugs had made everything seem so extraordinarily vivid. Now Bill needed them just to keep the world from fading out altogether. When he wasn't on something, every stubbed toe and hangnail was excruciating, but at the same time he seemed to feel nothing. The amount of drugs Bill had had to take to get ready for the blind date would have sent him into space a year ago. Now it seemed barely enough to bring him up to the level of everyday life.

Well, Bill thought ruefully, staring at the ceiling, Jeff had been right. Tammy was terrific. So was Jeff's girlfriend Linda, and in fact Jeff himself. Bill was astonished at how

114

cheerful and comfortable the three of them seemed. They didn't talk like Jenny and the friends he'd met through her. They never seemed to say anything bad about anything or anyone. That's all Jenny's friends—and Bill along with them—had ever done. All their conversations had been characterized by a sort of continuous sneer at everyone who wasn't like them, jokes about people who didn't act like they did and were too gauche to know how gauche they were. Bill was used to that kind of humor. He had actually become quite good at it, provided he was stoned. But here were three people, Tammy, Jeff, and Linda, who seemed to accept everyone no matter how they acted. And they kept laughing, like little kids in the middle of a game. Bill was sure for a while that they must be using something. He even asked a few key questions, giving them every opportunity to tell him about their experiences with drugs. "Well, you seem happy tonight," he told Tammy, watching her face, "What's your secret?" and later, to Jeff, "Nice party. Do you *party* a lot?"

Bill shook his head in wonderment. They hadn't shown a flicker of understanding. Tammy had answered that she was happy because it was the weekend, and Jeff had given him a quizzical look and said that he liked parties just fine, but he'd call this just a date—parties had cookies and punch. Either they were both amazingly competent liars, or Tammy and Jeff really hadn't realized that Bill was talking about drugs. Bill couldn't believe anyone was that good a liar. That left only one possibility. Somehow, incredibly, the other three people on his blind date had been having all that fun under their own power.

After this shocking realization, Bill had spent the rest of the evening watching in awe as Linda, Tammy, and Jeff talked and laughed and changed their minds about the movie. As they walked up to the marquee, Tammy had said, "Look, you can go to a movie all alone. As long as we're together, let's do something *together*." Five minutes

115

later they had all been renting shoes at a bowling alley —
and Bill was the only one in the group who'd ever bowled.
A kind of aching warmth began to bother Bill, like heart-
burn, as he remembered teaching the other three the
basics: showing them how to pull back straight and follow
through smoothly, the same way he'd taught his brothers
and sisters to pitch a baseball or clear the high hurdles.
For about five minutes, struggling to make the technique
clear to them, Bill had forgotten all about himself — what
he was and what he did. He didn't remember thinking
anything consciously, there in the bowling alley, but for
those few minutes he'd allowed himself to feel that he was
one of them.

That, Bill thought, had been a mistake. It had brought
on the stupid picnic dream again. What Jeff and Linda and
Tammy were, Bill may once have been, but that was a long
time ago. They were like children, they really were. Care-
free, unspoiled, and above all, innocent. For Bill that part
of life was over. Those people were in good with God, he
reminded himself sternly. Happiness was automatic for
them. They'd get married in the temple and have lots of
little kids, and they would never even dream what it was
like for people like Bill who hadn't made it. What would
it be like, Bill wondered, if he could go back again to when
he was a little boy, to when he'd never done anything
really wrong and he had the chance to make the choice
again? Knowing it was a dangerous and foolish thing to
do, Bill let himself imagine. No drugs, nothing wrong,
everything all fresh . . . Bill put his hands over his face
and began to cry.

It was so stupid to think about it. He needed the drugs
now. He couldn't bear life without them. He just wasn't
a good enough person to handle things alone, or strong
enough to cope with the world as it really was, or something. He didn't know. But he'd tried to stop, he really
had, and it was just no good. The tears that had pooled

116

up by the bridge of Bill's nose overflowed down his cheeks. They ran into his ears, dripped onto his pillow, and soaked the hair at the nape of his neck: more tears than he had believed his body could contain. It was over, it was all over. All happiness, all goodness, all innocence. Innocence was like a crystal vase: it couldn't be glued together once it had shattered. Bill rolled over onto his side, and the tears found new tracks down the sides of his face. Was it any good at all to try to patch up the vase, since the cracks would always be there no matter what? No. There was no reason even to try.

Still, he had to do something. He was running out of money. His savings for his car, his mission, everything was gone. Bill could hardly believe what his life had become. When he was eight and his horse had thrown him and broken his leg, he hadn't cried. When he was twelve and stepped on a rake, almost impaling his foot, he hadn't cried. While the doctor had cleaned the wound and given him a tetanus shot, telling Bill's father that even grown men could hardly stand that kind of pain, Bill had never once really cried. Those wounds had healed. Bones knit, flesh mends, but damaged innocence is damaged forever. Sobbing quietly, amazed that the tears kept coming, Bill thought of ways that he could make himself stop using drugs. He would punish himself, for one thing. He wouldn't watch TV, or eat anything but cereal, or something — anything — until he had been clean for . . . a week. No, a month — well, a week. But even as he made the resolution he knew it wouldn't work. TV and food were insignificant compared to how much Bill needed drugs. He didn't care about anything anymore as long as he had something to get high on. Except, of course . . . that was it. His calls home to his family were the high point of his week. He would abstain from them until he was clean. That would give him enough motivation, he was sure of it. He didn't deserve to call them anyway, really. That was something good people did — talk to their parents and their brothers and sisters. Good people could give their families something worthwhile, and they deserved what their families gave them back. Bill began to cry harder than ever. He was a bad, bad person, he told himself, and he had no right to associate with the Stewarts. He had shamed them. He had brought dishonor to the whole family, and if they knew what he was, they would never speak to him anyway.

Behind his swollen eyelids Bill let himself watch the image of the green field and the happy picnicking group, so far away, beyond the gray chasm. He had been there once. He had been with them; he had been like them. If he could just forget what it had been like to be innocent, he wouldn't feel this way all the time. But only drugs were strong enough to make him forget, and they didn't last long. When their effects faded, as they had done now, the memory of innocence came back to haunt him like the ghost of a dearly loved friend. The sweetness of what he had lost and the yearning for what could never be beckoned beseechingly across the bottomless abyss. Bill pulled the pillow over his face and cried as though the tears would never stop.

Warren was exhausted. He rubbed his fingers over the stubble on his chin and peeled off his coat and tie on the way to his kitchen. He poured himself a glass of orange juice and took a long drink. Hungry, too. He hadn't eaten since lunch, and he'd walked a long way. Warren wondered how much territory he'd covered in five hours of wandering. At four miles an hour (Warren's long legs and athletic stride carried him at least that fast), that would be — good grief, twenty miles! No wonder he was worn out and ravenous. He peered into the refrigerator. Two boxes of Chinese take-out left over from the night before, a very old apple, and the orange juice. Not a very promising assortment. Warren picked up the apple, took a bite, found it mealy, and chucked the rest into the disposal. So he'd go hungry. So who cared. Feeding him was like putting gas in a car that had been hit by a bomb.

He found the remote control to his stereo television and switched it on. Most of the channels had already gone off the air. The all-night news anchorman was recounting the story of a particularly grisly murder in the L.A. area, and on the late movie Humphrey Bogart was kissing Ingrid Bergman. Warren watched for a minute. There was a man's man, he told himself as Humphrey walked into the night. Torn from the woman he loved, facing possible heroic death amid the sands of Casablanca . . . Warren wished that he could trade lives with Humphrey's character. A quick death with honor sounded wonderful. But it was much too late for that. He switched off the TV and ran his hand through his disheveled hair.

Well, he'd done it again. That was all there was to it. Not that it seemed one more time should matter. One more broken promise to himself, one more step away from the life he always thought he would live. It had become so routine he hardly thought he should feel anything about it anymore. But he did. He kept wondering *why*. Why, after all the plans he'd made to keep himself away from it, all the schemes he'd thought through, all the structures he'd put into his schedule so that he wouldn't have time to go wandering, *why* had he done it anyway? That's how it always started, he could see that now. Just wandering, just an innocent little evening walk around town. Just seeing the sights, getting some exercise. And then, of course, he'd been curious. Not tempted, just curious. It was interesting, to see what was happening in "that" part of town. Naturally, when he got to "that" part of town, there were a lot of magazines around. He'd needed to get some cough drops, anyway, and all the convenience stores in "that" part of town carried "that" kind of magazine.

He hadn't really been able to help looking at them once he'd gone into a store, and besides, that pornographic stuff didn't really affect him. It was no big deal.

From the convenience store on, Warren noted concisely, he hadn't been wandering anymore. He had been prowling. And, of course, he knew where and how to prowl. After all these years of "innocent little walks," Warren had picked up all the cues and broken down all the barriers within himself. It was getting easier all the time. The streets seemed to be swarming with people like him, all prowling around, looking for each other. There had been a time when Warren had found this idea tremendously exciting — it meant that he was not alone, that he belonged to a brotherhood of people who felt as he did. That's why he had started talking to these people in the first place, Warren told himself. He had really just wanted to meet someone who was like him. But it seemed that he was different from the people he met in bars and bookstores and on the street, just as he was different from the people he'd met so long ago — it seemed like another lifetime — in church and school and his parents' parties. Yes, Warren had met plenty of people on his "little walks" who shared his inclinations. But most of the men he had met seemed to embrace this identity with defiant pride. He found he couldn't really talk to them. Many of them seemed brittle and shallow and cold and predatory, centered on their bodies, the bodies of others, and the elevation of their sexuality to a total definition of life. Once he had finished a "little walk" and his energy was spent, Warren was always frightened by the memory of the men he had sought out.

The ironic thing, he thought as he rose wearily and went into the bedroom, was that they probably thought the same about him. He remembered what Alice, his office partner at work, had said to him just as he finished canceling his afternoon meetings, telling himself he *had* to get some exercise. "Are you all right?" Alice had asked, her voice concerned. "You look awful. What's wrong? Did somebody die or something?" Warren had realized, right then at that moment, that the expression on his face was the same one he watched for on other men's faces in "that" part of town. It was a kind of intense searching look, driven by desperation and masked in pride, with eyes like the eyes of a captured bird of prey. He felt it on his own face as Alice had spoken, but the recognition had meant nothing to him then. He was becoming just like the men who frightened him, and he would have done anything at that moment to get out of the office and become more like them than ever.

Warren's eyes as he looked back on the evening still had something of the falcon in them. He felt that he could see himself with extraordinary clarity. As his realization of what he had done—what he *was*—grew sharper and more vivid, Warren hated himself with a cold and unsparing hatred. Perhaps, really, he should just give up. After all, there was no way back. If his parents, his friends, his mission president—anyone he had ever truly respected in his life—got the faintest inkling of half of what Warren had done, he would drop lower in their esteem than the most revolting vermin. He knew that. It was an absolute. So why bother to avoid their disgust, when he knew perfectly well he deserved it? Ah, it was just so hard. So hard. Everyone was so proud of him, thought he was so perfect. It would hurt them if they knew. It would reflect on his parents. They would blame themselves and so would other people. Tongues would wag all over the country as one friend passed along to another the little tidbit of news about the Whites' son, Warren, and isn't it a pity, he seemed like such a promising young man . . .

No, he couldn't just accept himself and "come out of the closet." It would hurt too many people. But he was starting to feel that he couldn't really accept those people

121

either, knowing as he did that his real identity was something they rejected and despised. Warren sat down on the edge of his bed and let himself fall backward onto it like a rag doll. He was so tired. He remembered feeling something like this after long days of tracting in Germany. Mile after freezing mile he had trudged through the streets, in his missionary shoes, looking for people who would stop and talk with him. His eyes had scanned faces then just as they did earlier today, looking for someone with the right combination of features, someone who would meet his eyes, someone who was also searching for something. Sometimes those days had been so discouraging that he had almost wept with frustration and fatigue when evening came and he could relax. At those times, Warren remembered, he would open his scriptures and play a little game. It was very simple. All he had to do was find scriptures that described the way the Lord felt about His missionaries and then read them to himself. But instead of reading them just as they were written, Warren would put his own name in the place of all the proper nouns that referred to people. That was it, the whole game. But it had gotten him through some awful evenings.

Warren closed his eyes and smiled, remembering some of the scriptures he'd loved best and the warmth of hearing them, in his mind, addressed specifically to him: "My son [Warren], peace be unto thy soul; thine adversity and thine afflictions shall be but a small moment. And then, if thou endure it well, [Warren], God will exalt thee on high." (D&C 121:7–8.)

"O thou afflicted [Warren], tossed with tempest, and not comforted, behold, [Warren], I will lay thy stones with fair colours, and lay thy foundations with sapphires." (Isaiah 54:11.)

"For God so loved the world [Warren], that he gave his only begotten Son, that whosoever [Warren] believeth in him should not perish, but have everlasting life." (John 3:16.)

A peaceful glow began to spread over Warren's body as the familiar passages flowed through his mind. He was almost asleep, but there was something, some little thing. . . .

Abruptly Warren's bloodshot blue eyes snapped open, and he was back in the real world. He was sickening. How dared he, how *dared* he apply those scriptures to himself after what he had done? There were other scriptures for him and his kind. Head spinning with fatigue, Warren got up and walked to the bookshelf. There were his scriptures, a gift from his parents at the time he left for his mission, gathering dust between his old college textbooks and some cheap paperback novels. Coldly, methodically, Warren pulled the scriptures out of the bookcase and began to leaf through them.

"Woe unto them [Warren] who commit whoredoms, for they [Warren] shall be thrust down to hell." (2 Nephi 9:36.)

"A wicked man [Warren] is loathsome, and cometh to shame." (Proverbs 13:5.)

"Thou [Warren] shalt not commit adultery; and he [Warren] that committeth adultery, and repenteth not, shall be cast out." (D&C 42:24.)

Warren slammed the scriptures shut and threw them against the wall. Repent. Repent. He had sinned, and he was loathsome, and he was about to be totally cast out, unless he repented. What did that mean? That he should never do anything sinful again? What a laugh. The last time he remembered believing that could happen was more than a year ago. He'd averaged a sin a week since then, he estimated, and it was getting worse and more frequent all the time. He was a pervert. That was all there was to it. He was an abomination, a freak, a distortion of nature. He could see how a person could repent of something he'd done, but how was he supposed to repent of what he was? Yes, he believed that the Lord would forgive him, if he sincerely repented, no matter how many times he sinned. But was that to be his life — one constant round of trying, failing, tormenting himself in sackcloth and ashes, and trying and failing again? Other people didn't have to live that way. Other people had "joy and rejoicing in their posterity," and happy homes, and someone to talk to when they were too afraid to sleep. Yes, he believed that God could forgive him, but he wasn't sure he could forgive God. To make a person this way, to give him a flaw over which he had no control, and then condemn him for it — what kind of a God was this? Warren had prayed so hard, so long, so often before he'd finally given up on the whole thing. He'd thought at the time that forgetting this religion, with its whimsical, condemnatory, torturing God, would buy him some relief.

No relief had come. Not then, not since. Warren worked through most of the days now with the thought of night growing more and more intoxicating in his mind. He spent the evenings wandering in a fixed trance, like a hunter among other hunters. He spent the nights alone or with people he feared, watching himself become one of them. And he spent the early mornings coldly, carefully controlling the despair and emptiness that overwhelmed him. Well, Warren thought, God had certainly kept his word about "thrusting the adulterer down to hell." Here was hell, large as life, right here in southern California. Warren considered his options. He could certainly kill himself, but there didn't really seem to be much point in that. It wouldn't change things for him, and it would ruin his parents. He could go on pretending to be normal, live through his entire life in this tumult of hidden deeds and fears of being found out. He thought about it. No. Unendurable. The control he was careful to maintain was wearing thin. He could feel it. Something was going to snap if he went on the way he was. Well, then, he could move away, change his name, never let his parents hear about him, and dive into the world of his own kind. Warren pondered this for a while. Yes, it seemed to be the only possible way to continue his life. He had no choice. It was time to surrender.

Twenty miles. Whew. Warren unbuttoned his shirt and took it off. It was his favorite shirt, a white one. Virgin white, he thought. Warren White. Warren Virgin White. Warren placed the edge of the shirt's collar between his even teeth. With a sudden tug and a twist of his head, he tore the collar off the shirt. Then he carefully placed one hand on each side of the neck and tore the shirt in two down the middle. His strong fingers worked busily, as he ripped the pocket from the breast, yanked the sleeves off the torso, and began to shred the fabric into long ragged strips. When there was nothing left to tear, Warren bunched the cotton he was holding into a compact ball between his fingers and twisted it. He tightened his grip with all the strength he had, until his body shook with the strain. The veins in his neck and forehead stood out like bluish cords. When he opened his hands, the shirt was still there. Warren began to chuckle as he looked at its torn and bedraggled remains. No, there was no getting rid of himself, no matter how hard he tried. Whatever he *did*, he would always have to *be*. It was really very funny. One puny pervert in the broad span of history, struggling to disguise himself from his destiny. The chuckle grew louder, then became an outright laugh. Warren threw the dismembered shirt on the floor and kicked it against the wall. He threw himself on the bed, exhausted, wheezing and coughing with laughter, and his eyes were the eyes of a captured bird of prey.

It is ironic that we often feel that the suffering that comes to sinners as a result of their sin is "fair," that it is

125

less deserving of pity than the suffering of innocents. "Well," we say, watching the news in appalled fascination as an exposed addict's face contorts with shame and anguish, "he brought it on himself." We almost celebrate the addict's humiliation, comforting ourselves with the notion that he is nothing like us nor anyone we care for. Sometimes we think with pity about the wicked one's poor parents, or spouse, or children—but the sinner himself? He deserves whatever he gets, we comment to each other. And those who secretly know that they have committed the same actions and deserve the same punishment nod in agreement, hating themselves more than ever.

How strange it is that the Lord views sinners, including compulsive-cycle addicts, so differently from the way we view them. At times, He almost seems to downplay the suffering of righteous people by comparison. While it seems that He might concentrate harder on preserving the innocent from all the trials and inconveniences of life, the Lord incongruously spends almost all His time worrying about the guilty. Instead of concentrating all His approval on those who resist temptation, the Good Shepherd takes time to "leave the ninety and nine in the wilderness, and go after that which is lost, until he find it." (Luke 15:4.) During His ministry on earth, Jesus spent a good deal of His time with the wicked, forgiving their sins and incurring the wrath of the law-abiding Pharisees. Preposterously, after all the pains we take to be upright, He tells us that "joy shall be in heaven over one sinner that repenteth, more than over ninety and nine just persons, who need no repentance." (Luke 15:7.) How unfair! How infuriating! How could a just God favor the wicked over the righteous?

The answer is, of course, that He does not. He loves us all with an equal and infinite love. The Lord's joy in the sinner that repents, His constant urging that we must all repent and encourage others to repent, comes from His knowledge of what it feels like to suffer the understanding of one's own guilt. That is partly what Gethsemane was for, to let the Savior understand through His own experience what we suffer when we sin. And even He, who walked calmly through persecution and to death, pleaded with His Father that that particular cup might be taken from Him. Christ has felt every depth of horror, every shock of realization, every hopeless yearning that a deed could be undone that all of us combined will ever feel. And so He knows that the pains of the righteous, however unbearable they may seem, are trivial compared to the pains of the guilty. He and His prophets, like Alma, are filled "with great anxiety even unto pain" that we avoid such anguish if at all possible. (Alma 13:27.) The Lord and His servants urge all people to repentance, not because they do not understand how hard it is to repent, but because they do understand. They know the feelings that accompany sin; however, the Lord and His servants also know something that many compulsive-cycle addicts do not: the feelings that accompany righteousness. The feelings of self-hatred we have discussed in this chapter are not among such righteous emotions. They do not lead the guilty addict to reach out to help others or to make restitution for the wrong, as feelings of remorse usually do.

On the contrary, as we have seen in the stories of Ellen, Bill, and Warren, behavioral addicts' hatred, depression, disgust, and despair at their own actions make them withdraw from the company of others. Victims of compulsive cycles are sure that if anyone, particularly the people they love most, knew about the addictive behavior, they would be cast off forever. And so the compulsive-cycle victim who has committed some action of self-indulgence and proceeded on to feelings of self-hatred marches inexorably to the next step on the cycle, actions of self-concealment.

6

THE FOURTH STEP:
ACTIONS OF SELF-CONCEALMENT

....

When we began conducting the research for this book, we immediately encountered some rather shocking statistics. At the time we lived in a city packed to the brim with colleges and universities. Most of the people we knew well were young adult students, as we were ourselves. As we read about the topics raised in our rather unusual Sunday School class, we found that the people we encountered every day—single students with high expectations, a great deal of pressure to perform, few responsibilities to others, and plenty of free time, were precisely the type of people who tend to be extremely susceptible to addictive behaviors. According to the estimates of experts on all sorts of addictions, a high percentage of the people we associated with every day would be expected to suffer from some sort of compulsive behavior. And yet, looking around a classroom or a cafeteria or the crowd at a football game, we could not see anyone we would have suspected of a life-and-death struggle with addiction. Practically all the people we knew seemed bright, confident, attractive, happy, and in perfect control of their lives.

Two years into our research both of us were hired to assist professors in teaching some undergraduate courses. From this new perspective, we began to see in some of our students indications of the pain and frustration that we and all our classmates had hidden from each other when we were undergraduates ourselves. A student whose work came in consistently late and far below the quality of which he was capable yielded to gentle questioning by admitting that he was an alcoholic. A young woman suddenly burst into tears during a meeting to discuss a paper, confiding that she had done a bad job because her fiance, whom she dearly loved, had dumped her after discovering her obsessive relationships with a series of other men. A brilliant young economics major balked when his name and resume were passed on to a prestigious firm who wanted to hire him as a summer intern. He finally confessed that most of the resume was made up of completely unfounded lies — that he seemed to lie uncontrollably even when there was no need to do so. These were humbling and saddening experiences, experiences that motivated us to continue our study of compulsive behaviors in Latter-day Saints. But after the crises had passed, when we saw our students again in a classroom, a cafeteria, or the crowd at a football game, it was almost impossible to believe that we had not dreamed up their problems in our own minds. They seemed as sunny and unperturbed by life as had our own classmates a short time before.

A few more years passed, and every few months unsettling bits of information began to come our way. There, in the alumni magazine, was the obituary of that kid who lived down the hall freshman year, the brilliant one who graduated third in his class and went on to the highest paying job anyone had ever heard of, dead by suicide at the age of twenty-seven. There, across the street, goes the woman who used to argue with the professor in philosophy seminar and who usually brought the professor around to her way of thinking. Now she seems to be living on the steps of the apartment building next door, muttering softly and intensely to her dirty fingers, her hair falling into her eyes. There, on the nightly news, appears the handsome face of the guy who always used to be chosen to go pick up the pizza for the entire group of roommates. It looks like his stellar career on Wall Street might be over — he'll be paying fines and serving prison terms for some time if he's convicted for his illicit financial dealings. What happened to these people in such a short time? Was it happening even back in college, when we knew and admired and envied all of them? Could we have seen it, stopped it, somehow helped? Surely if anything had been really wrong, we would have known. And yet the faces in the classroom and the cafeteria and the crowd at a football game give no hints to tell us who is wounded, or indeed if anyone is. Why not?

After studying addictive cycles with some care and following the stories of many behavioral addicts over several years, we have come to think that one reason many problems are not recognized is that as long as they can, the sufferers will keep their struggles secret. Of course there are many different types of problems that can cause heartache or ruin lives, and many of them have nothing to do with addictive behavior. Nevertheless, people who are caught in compulsive cycles may go longer and suffer more before seeking help than those whose problems are external to their own actions.

The addict has at least two reasons for concealing the increasing pain and sense of losing control that accompany the compulsive cycle. On one hand, there is the pleasure of addictive actions, which come to represent joy for behavioral addicts and thus seem to be the most important thing in their lives. On the other hand, there are the shame and guilt felt by compulsive-cycle victims, which make them fear disclosure on the grounds that once other people know the truth, they will hate the addicts as much as the addicts hate themselves. And so, despite the anguish these people feel every time they reach the third step on the compulsive cycle, they will often go to unbelievable lengths to protect the secret of their "real lives." Furthermore, because the addiction is such a big part of the everyday thinking and behavior of compulsive-cycle victims, they are also forced to hide significant parts of their personalities and inner selves from the people around them. Because we saw so many addicts energetically invested in covering up whole sections of their lives, as well as the addictive behaviors themselves, we call the fourth step on the compulsive cycle "actions of self-concealment."

The number of ways to lie is unlimited. One of Satan's most potent qualities is that he is constantly changing his approach, his tactics, his story. That is not true of the Lord, who is "the same yesterday, today, and forever." "Truth," we are told in the Doctrine and Covenants, "is the knowledge of things as they are, and as they were, and as they are to come." (D&C 93:24.) Truth tells only one story, though in an infinite variety of ways. We may all know the story in our own fashion and by our own experiences, but once our understanding is perfect, the story is always the same. On the other hand, the father of lies is as changeable as a chameleon. There may be only one correct answer to an equation, but there are innumerable incorrect ones. The Lord's message to man has been the same from the creation of Adam until the moment that you are reading these words and will be identical when the curtain finally falls on human history. But Satan's message changes every day, every moment. It makes logical hairpin turns, sneers today at what it celebrated yesterday, and insists on the veracity of two mutually exclusive falsehoods at the same time. It is truly a mass of confusion.

The same kind of confusion came to characterize and surround the Latter-day Saints we interviewed who were caught in the compulsive cycle. Trying to make sense out of the enormous variety of deceptions they had each learned to perpetrate, we thought we could see at least two different categories of actions of self-concealment. The first was self-concealment in the fullest sense of the term:

hiding one's self from one's self. That usually predominated when a person first became involved with an addictive action, before the problem had grown to the point where other people were likely to notice the addict acting strangely. The initial self-deception generally took the form of rationalization.

The addict went beyond rationalization when it became necessary to deceive other people in order to prevent those people from discovering and interfering with the addiction. That is the second stage of the actions of self-concealment. In some cases, compulsive-cycle victims simply try to persuade other people to accept their own rationalizations. But the more disreputable the action of self-indulgence is and the longer it continues, the more likely the victim is to begin telling outright lies to other people. Of course, when a person baldly denies doing something he or she actually did, there is usually little doubt in the liar's mind that the false story is not true. But after many months or years of living in a world at two levels, one the level of actual behavior and one the level of what they pretend to be, long-term compulsive-cycle addicts can become confused. Their minds seem to become so centered on the constant rehearsal of deceitful internal monologues, designed to perfect their lies and ensure successful self-concealment, that they begin to lose track of what they have actually done. At this nearly insane stage of the actions of self-concealment, compulsive-cycle victims may be so utterly attuned to the voice of Satan that they can hardly hear the voice of God. At this stage many addicts begin to deny their testimonies and defy their loved ones. We have come to believe that while an action of self-indulgence may have the power to snag victims into a compulsive cycle, actions of self-concealment have the power to destroy their souls. A description of the components of self-concealment, which we have divided into rationalization and lying, may help to illustrate how this process works.

RATIONALIZATION

To rationalize something is to take something that is unreasonable and bring it within the bounds of reason. We both had a good deal of practice doing that as high school debaters. Adolescence is a time when the intellectual development of the brain and mind first allows young people to deal easily with such abstract concepts as justice, ethics, and logic. It is a great thrill to realize that arguments can be formulated and supported by evidence, and some teenagers become almost too enamored of practicing this skill on every issue they encounter. Overall, high school debaters are perhaps the most enthusiastic arguers in the world. Those who get really good at it will debate at the drop of a hat, composing impressive towers of logic on such subjects as "What Other Parents Let Their Kids Do," "The Uselessness of Math Requirements," and "Why My Sister Veronica Is a Creep."

What high school debaters also come to understand is that virtually any position can be logically rationalized. Every time they compete at a debate tournament, the teams argue different aspects of the same general topic. The teams do not find out until just before the debate whether they are to argue for or against a certain position. Often a good debater will present a brilliant argument in one round, winning the debate on the apparent strength of his conviction, and in the next round turn in an equally brilliant performance debating against the very argument he had supported the round before. In fact, it is those who can argue convincingly on any topic, from any moral position whatever, who eventually take home the trophies. That is rationalization institutionalized. The faithful Latter-day Saint who reads the scriptures, knows the commandments, and has a testimony of the Lord's goodness and power, has no rational grounds for looking "upon sin with the least degree of allowance." (Alma 45:16.) But he can *make* rational grounds for wrongful actions if he is willing to let go, just a tiny bit, of his sensitivity to the Spirit of truth. It is only this Spirit that tells us for certain what is really correct. Reason without the Spirit of truth can make black seem white, and it can do it in any number of ways.

Some of the stories compulsive-cycle addicts told us about their past rationalizations, and some of the rationalizations they offered as an earnest attempt to persuade us to their way of thinking, were so distorted that they would have been laughable if they had not been so terrible. Some of the most common were the "it's only natural" theory, the "my parents didn't raise me right" hypothesis, the "I deserve it" claim, and the "I'm under a lot of stress" defense. Then there was the popular "It wasn't my fault," which had variations, including the claim that the sin was a crime of passion over which the perpetrator had no control, or that he or she had been forced into the action by accomplices. (As we pointed out in our discussion of the action of self-indulgence, there may well be a point at which the actor is truly unable to control addictive actions; however, that point is reached by going into a routine that results in the loss of control, and we believe that entering the routine is a controllable choice.) There were the tried-and-true rationalizations, such as "Everybody does it," "It's not going to hurt anyone," and "Just once won't hurt" — which was almost always followed up by "Just once more won't hurt." There were rationalizations that came from a warped view of the repentance process, such as "Well, now I have to go confess to the bishop anyway, so I might as well live it up for a while," and "I might as well go ahead — I can always repent."

Particularly impressive in an academic sense were the "well, technically speaking" rationalizations. Technically speaking, we discovered to our great enlightenment, there is no explicit injunction in the scriptures against marijuana—as long as you eat it rather than smoke it. Technically speaking, coffee and tea are not forbidden by the Word of Wisdom if they are drunk cold. Technically speaking, it is impossible to break the law of chastity by performing any action that could not result in pregnancy. Technically speaking, stealing is limited to actually lifting property with the hands and removing it illegally from its designated owner—the questionable transfer of someone else's funds to one's own bank account is "just paperwork." The proponents of speaking technically in regard to the laws of the gospel would make phenomenal debaters.

The ultimate in rationalization, however, came from people whose actions were so inconsistent with their own beliefs that they were forced to continually convince themselves that good was evil and vice versa. One man with a sexual addiction spent hours trying to convince a friend that, as believing Christians, they really *should* commit the sin of adultery. Why? Well, he told his friend, because we are here on earth to learn to know good from evil, and that knowledge is gained by experiencing sin, just as Adam and Eve did in the Garden of Eden. The more sin we experience, the more sorrow we experience, and the greater the effect of our repentance. Therefore, the greater the sin, the greater the understanding—and it is to gain understanding that we come to earth. Of course, one didn't want to hurt anyone by committing murder, but the next worst sin on the list of the Ten Commandments was adultery, which wasn't even illegal—technically speaking. Therefore, this addict explained to his friend, the best way for each of them to fulfill their missions on earth and to become more like their Heavenly Father was to have an affair. We never found out whether this man had debated in high school, but if he didn't, he should have.

From the outside, these rationalizations seem so

shoddy and obvious that it is often difficult to take them seriously. But behavioral addicts manage. Their addictions, which are their counterfeits for joy, depend on it. No matter how potent the rationalizations involved, however, a compulsive-cycle victim who is still receptive in any degree to the light of Christ always seems to feel an uneasy suspicion that the compulsive behavior is wrong and should be given up. To silence this still, small voice, most addicts begin to rationalize about their action of self-indulgence almost continually, even when they are not doing anything related to it. Eventually, their constant preoccupation begins to change the way compulsive-cycle victims behave around other people. A person who is generally rather taciturn may suddenly become eloquent and animated in defense of some action toward which others are expressing disapproval. A person who usually appears to enjoy church will, for no obvious reason, spend hours after one meeting explaining to her friends why the speaker was wrong about the need to keep a certain commandment. A casual acquaintance might switch from small talk to vehement defense in response to another's conversational reference to some behavior. Typically, the people around the addict might see this behavior as rather odd, but they soon forget about it and have no idea that the cause for persuasive rationalization might be an addict's attempts to justify compulsive actions to self and others.

The behavior of the chronic rationalizer brings us to the stage of actions of self-concealment that affect the people around compulsive-cycle addicts, as well as the addicts themselves. If addicts can get someone to agree with their rationalizations, they will do so, and they are more likely to behave affectionately toward people who accept their permissive ideas about their actions of self-indulgence. The more the associates of compulsive-cycle victims care for them, the more these associates share the desperate desire to believe that the addict is not really doing anything wrong. Loved ones might eventually begin to rationalize an addict's actions themselves, a step that allows them to associate with the compulsive-cycle victim without risking argument or rejection. Some psychologists call this type of behavior coaddiction or codependency. When it occurs, the victim's associates have themselves entered into the compulsive cycle by engaging in actions of concealment, even though they are concealing the addict's actions rather than their own. Addictions such as alcoholism, sexual perversion, child abuse, and many other cruel sins can often become a "family secret." The wife of the alcoholic, Eric, hid her husband's drunkenness and helped him escape the consequences. The parents of a child who is on drugs may bail her secretly out of jail to avoid a fuss. A small boy, afraid of the abandonment he might experience if people found out about his abusive parents, may keep silent when he has the opportunity to seek help. The bizarre and twisted rationalizations given by the behavioral addict to loved ones whenever he or she is "caught in the act" are accepted by everyone involved as a way to "make it seem all right." One particularly horrendous aspect of the altogether horrendous problem of behavioral addiction is that, having lived with the example of a parent who *rationalizes* a destructive action—or in other words, makes it seem reasonable—the children of addicts often grow up to be addicts themselves. Many researchers have noted the fact that these actions seem to run in families and have suggested a genetic component to addictive behavior. Whether or not such a biological factor exists, many of the compulsive-cycle victims we spoke to mentioned the behavior of a loved person who had set them an example of addiction and provided them with ready-made rationalizations.

LYING

Even if they do not become involved in coaddiction by protecting the addicts and accepting their rationalizations, the close associates and loved ones of compulsive-cycle addicts often become, like the addicts themselves, confused about the truth and unable to feel the spirit of discernment. That is particularly true when the addicts go beyond rationalizations to outright lies. These can be either lies of commission, in which addicts explicitly state that they have not done something that they did do, or lies of omission, in which compulsive-cycle victims simply refuse to talk about themselves or their actions. If a wife returns from an afternoon spent pursuing some addiction and her husband asks where she has been, "It's none of your business" is as effective a lie as some fabricated story about a doctor's appointment or a PTA meeting. Both lies of omission and lies of commission can be tremendously confusing to the person on the receiving end.

Much of the confusion is created by the fact that the loved ones carry with them a certain set of beliefs about the lives of the people they care for. They base these beliefs largely on what the addict tells them and are not likely to spend any time wondering whether this story actually corresponds with reality. Believing that a loved one is telling you the truth about himself or herself is the essence of trust, and the more innocent a person is, the more far-reaching the power of trust to convince. In the case of a compulsive cycle, the loved one's image of the addict's life is based on claims that simply do not correspond to facts. This creates odd little incongruities everywhere in the relationship. Things happen that don't seem to fit with the loved one's picture of the addict. Sometimes they are very small, almost negligible, like a slight pause before an "I love you" or a frown when a smile was expected. Other times the effects are more obvious and often very traumatic to the loved ones being lied to.

One family who had been sensing that their teenage son was withdrawing from them arranged a special Hawaii vacation to coincide with his birthday. They arranged the whole trip around the son's preferences, reserving hotels in places he had always wanted to visit and planning activities he had enjoyed in the past. What they could not know was that their son had arranged to pick up a two weeks' supply of an addictive drug from a pusher on one of the very days they planned to be on vacation. When the excited parents revealed the vacation to the boy at his birthday party, his first thought was that if he went with his parents, he could not obtain the drugs. Added to that thought was the guilt he felt over having betrayed his wonderful parents by turning out to be such a terrible son. He reacted to the surprise by shouting angrily at his parents that they and their generation were disgustingly bourgeois, that he couldn't believe they had wasted money on a trip that could have been used to help the hungry, and that he would have no part of their self-indulgence. Then he stomped out of the house, leaving both himself and his parents with a wound that would never quite heal.

What is so devastating about the compulsive-cycle victim's behavior is that loved ones sincerely believe they know what kind of person the addict is and that they can therefore expect this person to react in more or less predictable ways. Not understanding the subtext to the addict's life, they have no alternative when their predictions fail but to try either to redefine the compulsive-cycle victim in their minds or to figure out what they might have done to cause this unexpected behavior. The more trusting they are, the more they tend to try to figure out how something *they* did precipitated the victim's incongruous actions. It is easy for the addict's closest associates — usually family members — to feel that they are going crazy, that they must be completely unable to interact with other people (children, in general the most innocent and trusting group of humans, are particularly susceptible to this devastating loss of self-confidence). Compulsive-cycle addicts often get to the point where the only way to avoid telling the truth is to reinforce their loved ones' feeling of uncertainty.

An illustration of that tactic is the case of a young man we'll call Andy, a convert to the Church, who had fallen into a pattern of promiscuous sexual behavior during his high school days. After his conversion he abstained from this practice for several months, but he often felt severely tempted and worried that if he ever married, he would not be able to stay faithful to his wife. Not long after joining the Church, Andy met the love of his life. Christine was everything he had ever dreamed of in a companion, and miraculously, she seemed to feel the same way about Andy. They became engaged. But his anxiety about remaining faithful in marriage became more intense when Andy thought that he might lose this wonderful woman, and the anxiety seemed to "push him over the brink." He began to make the rounds of his old girlfriends, first once a week or so, then every other day, and finally every day. He was terrified that Christine would find out about this behavior, because he was sure she would leave him if she knew. That made the problem even worse. Every night Andy would dream up some rather lame excuse to drive his fiancée home early. He told her that he wanted to watch television. When she asked why she couldn't watch with him, he replied that he just liked to watch television alone — that it was something he had to do in order to relax. Puzzled and hurt by his unwillingness to spend time with her, Christine would go back to her apartment and wonder what was so wonderful about watching TV by yourself.

Eventually Christine became really quite disturbed by Andy's refusal to spend the evenings with her. After all, they were engaged. Where was she supposed to go when he wanted to watch television after they were married? She began to call him in the evenings. There was never any answer. She asked Andy about it, and he said he'd disconnected the receiver so he could enjoy his shows. Then one evening the power went out in Andy's section of town. Christine called his apartment. No answer. The next day when she asked Andy what he'd been doing the night before, he responded that she knew perfectly well he'd been watching television.

Christine could not believe what she was beginning to suspect: that Andy had been lying to her all along. She looked into his eyes and asked him about it, and the love and sincerity she saw there could not have been greater. Christine had always found herself to be a very good judge of character. She wondered if she was going crazy. She began to notice other little incongruities in Andy's behavior. When she mentioned them, Andy would respond with anger, telling her he wasn't sure he could marry someone who was so neurotically suspicious. Christine had to agree that she was becoming obsessed with things that probably meant nothing, and she resolved to try to make herself into the kind of wife Andy could love.

One evening Christine looked out her window and saw Andy driving by with his arm around a young woman. Christine could hardly believe it. She tried and tried to think of an explanation for the woman's being there. Maybe Andy had been taking an accident victim to the hospital? But she knew in her heart that the woman had not been injured. Rescuers, in her experience, did not cuddle with emergency room patients. And yet, the idea that Andy could be romantically involved with anyone else was utterly unthinkable. The days Christine had spent with him were so happy, and he so obviously loved her. He was so kind, so understanding, so completely *like* her. They shared everything. He brought her little presents and wrote her poetry. But the combination of circumstantial evidence was so strong that Christine finally came to the conclusion that Andy was having an affair. She confronted him with her suspicions.

Andy could think of no lie convincing enough to explain the woman in the car, so he tried another tack. He told Christine that her lack of trust in him throughout their engagement had driven him into the arms of another. If she simply had enough trust in him, the problem would be solved. Faith, Andy assured Christine, precedes the miracle. His infidelity was her problem. Desperately in love and desperate to believe that there was something *she* could do to preserve their relationship, Christine accepted Andy's explanation. Five years, two children, and one divorce later, Andy was still frantically devoted to his actions of self-concealment, and Christine still felt that if she had been a better wife, Andy would never have strayed.

Andy's addiction was the source of this family's tragedy, but it was lying that did the work of destruction. As part of our research, we spoke with some of the friends and family of compulsive-cycle victims. What they reported, over and over, was the astonishingly convincing way in which an addict could lie. One father told us, "My son was such a delightful child, so truthful, so forthright. Once he got into drugs, he could look you right in the eye and talk like butter wouldn't melt in his mouth, but I finally learned that I simply couldn't believe a word he said. It was devastating." An abused wife related how she had stayed with her husband for years on the strength of his sincerity every time he repented of his actions. "I love him," she told us. "I know him. When he told me that he would never do it again, I believed him. I still believe that at the times he said those things, he was being honest."

The incredible power of an addict's actions of self-concealment seem to come from the most frightening stage of the compulsive cycle. That is the stage when the addicts themselves begin to truly believe in their lies, when the mental monologue and the falsehoods to others have become so pervasive that the victim manages to disengage them altogether from reality. It seems to occur after a prolonged period, usually years or even decades, of continual rationalization and deceit.

Behavioral addicts can lose their ability to distinguish what is actually true and what is false because as they lie to themselves and others, "the heavens withdraw themselves; the Spirit of the Lord is grieved." (D&C 121:37.) The Holy Ghost does not want to leave our hearts, but there is no room for his influence when Satan has been invited in. Once the light of Christ, by which we recognize truth, has been extinguished within the addict's mind and soul, rationalization and lying seem as true as anything else. Or rather, they seem as false as anything else. To a person whose whole life has become a sea of lies, everything bobs and sinks. Nothing is stable. Compulsive-cycle victims we spoke with told us that they spent almost all their time either planning the action of self-indulgence, performing the action, or brooding over having done it in the past. None of this activity could be shared with the people from whom the addicts wished to hide their addictions. As one young woman told us, "After a couple of years, I was lying about everything. I lied about what I did, what I thought, what I dreamt, what I felt. Even a little bit of honesty was likely to clue somebody in to something that could connect me to [my addiction]. And then sometimes I'd lie about things that were totally innocent, like what was my favorite color, just because nothing really seemed any truer than anything else. If I said one thing during the day that *wasn't* a lie, it was amazing."

Often, compulsive-cycle victims at the stage of the actions of self-concealment lose all trust in the people around them, since they know quite well from experience that it is possible for everyone to lie almost perpetually. Realizing, because of their own ability to rationalize, that anything can be defended intellectually, behavioral addicts often adopt a universal sneer toward anything they are told that might be good or true. They can always find fault, always see a flaw, in anyone and anything. They become the ultimate proponents of critical thought — thoroughgoing cynics. Of course, it is quite possible — though perhaps not particularly Christlike — to be cynical without being caught in a compulsive cycle. But the cynicism of people who still feel the light of Christ is based on amusement at something that the Spirit tells them is worthless but that puffs itself up with its own importance. The compulsive-cycle victim who becomes a cynic because of his own familiarity with lying, on the other hand, is critical of everything because he believes in nothing. A very common phenomenon we saw in interviewing victims of compulsive cycles occurred when addicts, having learned to mistrust everything and having lost the Spirit that confirms truth, decided that there were no logical grounds for living the gospel until they could be intellectually persuaded it was true.

When a compulsive-cycle victim has reached this point, the actions of self-concealment have accomplished their purpose in the fullest sense. Such addicts are removed from truth to the point where they no longer feel conflict between their own beliefs and the actions to which they are addicted. They have hidden themselves from themselves; they have hidden the sin from the sinner. Denying that their own actions have robbed them of their faith (and faith is at the root of *any* belief system), compulsive-cycle victims proclaim that they might as well break the laws of God, because no one can prove to them that these laws are correct. A recent Sunday School class in our ward discussed the question of how Latter-day Saints can convince others that the gospel is true. The teacher asked the converts in the class what piece of information they had gained, "what thing somebody told them," that had finally converted them. In every case the answer came back that the final conversion was not based on any single bit of data. It was the confirmation of the Spirit, which revealed to them unmistakably that what they had learned about the Church was good and right, which had led them to accept the gospel. Compulsive-cycle addicts deliberately cut themselves off from the Spirit and therefore lose this source of surety. Having lost it, they are adrift without anchor or oars, spinning helplessly around in a tight little circle, which says that until they are convinced of the truth, they will never believe it; and until they receive spiritual certainty, they will never make themselves ready to receive it.

No wonder the scriptures tell us, "wo unto the liar, for he shall be thrust down to hell"! (2 Nephi 9:34.) It is not the Lord who does the thrusting. His truth shines all around us, always, unchanging, and if we will simply open our eyes, we will see it. It is Satan, the father of lies, who, if we give him the least degree of allowance, will blot out the light. His power will grow in us, if we give it our consent, until we are "walking in darkness at noon-day." (D&C 95:6.)

The stories of Ellen, Bill, and Warren are once again typical of the compulsive-cycle addicts we interviewed in that, despite the intense misery caused by their addictions, each of the three went to extraordinary lengths to conceal their behavior and their experiences from others. The effects of their actions of self-concealment are perhaps best represented from the perspective of the people around them. The characters described in the next section are people we spoke with who were close to these compulsive-cycle victims. We believe that their experiences are typical of, or at least common to, the many people from whom behavioral addicts conceal themselves.

"How was class today, hon?" said Peter Sorenson, kissing his wife Connie and helping her off with her coat. Connie undid the barrette at the nape of her neck and shook her hair down from the tight bun she'd been wearing.

"Oh, I don't know," she said, stretching her slender arms and shaking her head to ease the tension in her neck. "I get nervous. I mean, I've really never taught before, and I'm not sure how they like me. Students, I mean."

"I'm a student, and I like you," said Peter sincerely.

Connie laughed. "But would you like me if I tried to teach you ballet?"

"Are you kidding?" said Peter. "The first time I watched you demonstrate a step I'd probably like you so much I'd faint dead away. I'd just lie there on the floor and like you while you gave me a C minus. Why are you worried about it, anyway? Is somebody giving you flak?"

Connie sighed. "Not really. Most of the kids are really nice—though of course you never know how much of that is genuine. But there's this one girl who's been acting kind of strange. I don't think she likes the class or something."

"How so?" asked Peter, going to the kitchen for plates to set the table.

"Well, she's just—I don't know. She's the most talented beginner in the bunch, there's no doubt of that. I was really impressed with her at the first class. And she seemed so enthusiastic and dedicated—a real hard worker, you know? I thought she'd be a great student."

"So?" said Peter.

"So then she kind of stopped coming. I mean, when she does come, she sort of crouches over by the wall—I mean, she doesn't literally crouch, but she gives the impression of crouching. Like she's trying to sink into the wall or something. Am I making any sense?"

"None whatsoever," said Peter.

"She misses class a lot," Connie went on, not hearing him, "and when she comes she always has these really flimsy excuses—I mean they sound flimsy. I've got no evidence that she's lying, but . . . I don't know. Something just feels wrong."

Peter got out two sets of silverware while Connie ex-

146

amined the steaming pots on the stove. Spaghetti. She fished a noodle out of one pan and tested it between her teeth.

"The thing is," she said, "if she were a lousy student, I would just assume she's lying and let her take the consequences. But she just doesn't seem like the type of person who would make up excuses. I mean, she's more dedicated than I am. I guess I'm kind of worried that she just doesn't consider the class worth her time or that she hates my guts or something, but she's too polite to tell me to my face. It makes me nervous."

Connie got down the crystal glasses they'd gotten for their wedding and put them beside the plastic plates. It was a rather odd combination, but she figured if she just kept encouraging it, the rest of her tableware would eventually catch up to the goblets. She'd seen some china the other day with this beautiful little rose pattern, very subtle . . .

Peter kissed her again, on the top of the head. "I wouldn't worry about it," he said. "If she doesn't like you, it's not your fault. After all, you like her. She's probably just got something weird going on that you don't even know about. Family problems or something."

"What?" said Connie, still thinking about the possibilities for place settings. "Oh, yeah, Ellen Schor. No, I know I shouldn't let it bother me. It's no big deal. But you know, if she's got a problem I wish she'd just tell me. There's just always this feeling that there's something I don't quite understand about her, why she's acting like she does. It's giving me the heebie-jeebies. I don't know, Peter. I was really hoping they'd like me. Maybe I should be trying harder to get through to the class."

Peter put the steaming pot of spaghetti on the table. "Look," he said. "I really don't think it's anything to lose sleep over, but I'll tell you one thing: if someone wants to be sneaky, there's no way you can un-sneak them by working extra hard yourself. If this kid wants to tell you what her problem is, she'll tell you. If she doesn't want to, she won't. That's all there is to it. There's nothing you can do about it."

Connie piled spaghetti on Peter's plate, then on her own. "Okay, point taken," she said. "I'm not in terrible distress over this or anything. It's just that it bothers me to try to understand someone and feel like I don't understand them at all. It makes me feel like I can't understand any of those students, you know? Like I've slipped a cog or something."

"I'm a student," Peter repeated, "and you understand me. You want some salad?"

Connie smiled and picked up the salad tongs. They were sterling silver, a wedding present from Peter's grandmother. Now, she thought, dishing up a large serving, if only we could afford to buy some spoons. Nobody gives you plain old spoons, just sterling silver salad tongs and crystal goblets. With a slight sigh, Connie gave up wondering what was bothering the most promising student in her class.

Mabel Schor peered confusedly into the empty freezer. She could have sworn she had bought some ice cream to go with the pumpkin pie, but there was nothing in the Frigidaire but frost. She and Morris always preferred Vanilla, but she had picked up Burnt Almond Fudge this year in honor of little Ellen coming for Thanksgiving. Burnt Almond Fudge had been Ellen's favorite from the time she was a baby, when Mabel had carefully picked out the almonds so Ellen would be able to eat the ice cream without choking. Funny, she'd never done anything like that for Ellen's father when he was a little boy. But that was the joy of grandchildren, Mabel told herself: you can spoil them rotten without spoiling them rotten. Let their parents deal with discipline and diapers.

Goodness, though, how little Ellen had grown! At least up, that is. She was ever so thin now, like a skeleton almost. Mabel was glad she'd spent extra time cooking and shopping for this year's dinner. Ellen needed a little meat on her bones. That dormitory cooking just wasn't the stuff to tempt a finicky eater. All the Schors were finicky eaters, as Mabel knew all too well. Morris, for example, thought rice was too exotic. So Mabel had learned early in her marriage to notice who ate what and how much. That was why she still remembered about Ellen and Burnt Almond Fudge ice cream. That's why she'd bought it. She *knew* she'd bought it. Mabel looked blankly into the freezer, which looked even more blankly back at her.

Perhaps she was losing her mind. She was only sixty-three, but the old brain might be going. The thing about it was, this had been happening lately. Last Monday she'd made a whole batch of rolls, and the next morning when she went to get them for breakfast, there were only three or four left in the basket. Mabel knew Morris hadn't eaten them; he'd been down at his office almost all day, getting the paper out before deadline. She'd thought for a while that maybe Ellen had taken them to her room — she knew Ellen loved homemade rolls, almost as much as ice cream — but when Mabel had ventured into the guest room, of course there were no rolls there. And naturally Ellen couldn't have eaten that much. No one could have, not in one day. That's what was so bothersome about it. She asked Ellen what could have happened to the rolls, and Ellen had gotten rather angry, or at least very distant. Ellen seemed distant in general lately, and often angry. She'd flared up when Mabel had asked her why she was so thin, and again when Morris had inquired whether she was getting along all right with her roommates. Well, that was adolescence for you. What did they call it nowadays — "finding yourself," or some such nonsense.

Still, Mabel had found herself becoming increasingly

unsettled these last few days. She'd been so looking forward to Ellen's visit and had tried so hard to make her comfortable. It was certainly understandable that Ellen should miss her family at home, Mabel told herself—no youngster wants to spend Thanksgiving alone with two old, boring grandparents. Still, she felt sad and disappointed that she didn't seem able to make Ellen happy, like she'd been when she'd come to visit as a baby. She reminded herself that Ellen hardly knew her, really, that Ellen had not the vaguest memory of Mabel picking the almonds out of the Burnt Almond Fudge ice cream to feed to her when she was eleven months old. Mabel frowned. What had happened to that ice cream? The passing thought that her memory was going returned, and Mabel felt a chill of apprehension. Her holiday was not turning out to be a happy one.

Andrea and Liz moved out of the way politely as Ellen brushed past them on her way out of the dorm. As the door swung closed after her, Liz leaned back against the banister and stretched her long legs across the staircase. Andrea sat on the steps, her elbows on her knees.

"What's with her, anyway?" said Liz, staring after Ellen. "I've had about six classes with her, lived across the hall from her for three years, and I hardly even know her name."

"Ellen," responded Andrea, examining a lock of her long blonde hair for split ends. "Her name's Ellen. She seems kind of mixed up. I worry about her."

Liz looked at Andrea quizzically. "Worry?" she queried. "What's to worry? She's pretty obnoxious, but she gets terrific grades. Competitive as a pit bull. I'm not kidding. And she never talks to anybody. You should see her in class. She just sits and stares at people like she's plotting their assassination or something—unless she's taking notes. I swear, that girl takes more notes during one lecture than I've taken in my whole life, and she's got the grades to prove it. Plus she jogs every morning and dresses for success." Liz sighed, noticing that her toe had begun to protrude through a hole in her Garfield socks. "You see," she explained to Andrea, "that's why it's important that I go on being a lazy slob, to even out the population after Ellen goes by. Somebody has to live on cheese puffs and keep their class attendance down to thirty percent, or everything would get out of balance. It's a dirty job," she confessed somberly, "but I'm proud to do it for my country."

"No, really, Liz," said Andrea, "I mean it. I had this friend in high school like her. At least she was a friend until she got weird on me. The last I heard, she was in the hospital back home."

"The hospital?"

"Yeah. Apparently she was like anorexic or something—she used to throw up a lot, you know make herself do it—and then her heart stopped or something. She almost died."

Liz stared at her friend. "No kidding! How gross! I mean, that's awful!" She looked at the door through which Ellen had disappeared. "And you think she . . . ?"

Andrea scratched her head. "I don't know. I think so. She acts so much like this friend of mine. I mean exactly like her, you know? But I don't have any real reason to go accusing her or anything. It's just a feeling."

"Well, my gosh, have you asked her about it? I mean, I can understand you not wanting to offend her and everything, but what if her heart stopped too? I mean, it's worth a little embarrassment not to find this deceased straight-A student in the room next door, don't you think?"

"I know, I've thought of that," Andrea answered. "Since I moved onto her hall I've been trying really hard to make friends with her. But it seems like it's almost impossible. I used to keep asking her to go out with us for

151

ice cream or to devotionals and stuff, but she always had something else going. What really gets me is that I know a lot of those excuses were made up. I mean, one time she told me she had to go to the dentist at nine P.M. —have you ever heard of a dentist who worked nights? And then, this other time she said she had to study for a final, and then later that night I was sitting in the hall talking to Ruth Seiffert, and Ellen went into the bathroom down the hall, and she stayed there for the whole time we were talking. I mean, it was like an hour or something. That's when I really started getting suspicious."

Liz's eyes widened. "You think she was . . . ?"

Andrea nodded, frowning. "I don't know. At first I thought to myself, look, she has stomach flu. Anyone can have the flu. But then the next day I saw her on the stairs, and I asked her if she was feeling all right, and she gave me the weirdest look. Kind of hostile, almost, but scared, too. Like a stray cat when you come too close to its kittens."

"Well, what did she say?"

"She just said she was fine, absolutely fine. She was almost too definite about it, you know. Defensive. So then I asked her why she was in the bathroom so long—I said I was worried she'd been sick."

"You asked her that?" said Liz, agog. "What'd she say?"

Andrea's frown deepened. "She said I must have made a mistake, that she hadn't been there. But I know it was her, Liz. I mean, how much does it take to recognize someone at about five feet away? But she just lied about it. And about the whole studying thing. And the dentist. And then one time I was at Charlie's Snack Shop, and she was there buying some ice cream, and all of a sudden she came up to me and went into this big explanation of how she was buying it for a party. This is a person who has never smiled back at me in six months. The worst thing was, I couldn't help feeling like she was lying then, too. I don't know what her problem is."

"Bizarre," said Liz. "Truly bizarre. Well, I guess if she doesn't want anyone to know anything about her, it's none of our business. Hey, speaking of anorexia, you want some chocolate chip cookies? My mom sent me some more. Mom is, like, on the Anti-Anorexia Committee. I've got them in my room."

"Yeah, okay," said Andrea, eyebrows still knit. "That sounds great." She threw a last troubled look after Ellen, shrugged her shoulders, and followed Liz upstairs.

Lester Treadwell, of Lester Treadwell's Appliance Emporium, was concerned. He carefully counted the money in the cash register, frowned, licked his thumb, and counted it again. This time his face relaxed into a broad smile. It was all there after all. He must have miscounted the first time. He was really becoming paranoid, absolutely paranoid. There was no reason to worry. A good manager picks good employees, Lester reminded himself, and then he trusts them. It was the only way to run a business. Lester felt pretty pleased with the quality of the people he'd hired. He should let it go at that.

Still, he had to admit his concerns lately were not based altogether on his imagination. Bill Stewart was a good kid, an honest kid, a hard-working kid. He had been the day Lester hired him, and he was now. But there had been some changes. Of course, there was no reason to think the changes meant that Bill wasn't to be trusted. They weren't crimes, these changes, just . . . mistakes. Like this tardiness. Every day Bill seemed to show up a little later. Lester didn't understand it. The kid was clearly trying to get there on time. He'd come into Lester's office every day with a truly contrite expression on his open face. Every day he promised that tomorrow, he'd be early. But he never was. Lester had asked him if he was doing all right, if there was something going on in Bill's personal life, if there was anything Lester could do. He'd meant it, too. Bill had lost weight, his eyes were always bloodshot, and he seemed almost dazed sometimes when he was working on the floor. The other day Lester had overheard Bill telling a customer how many clothes she could wash in one shiny white machine, and the machine had been an automatic dishwasher. It was no big deal—Bill had noticed the mistake immediately and they'd all laughed about it—but it wasn't like Bill. Not like him at all.

Lester shook his head. If the kid was overworked, if he was having trouble keeping up in school, maybe there was something they could work out between them that would help. Bill was a valuable employee and sort of a pal as well. Lester hated to see him keeping all his trouble locked up inside. But when he'd asked what the trouble was, Bill had acted almost angry. Arrogant. He denied that anything was wrong, but from the way he had tightened his lips and turned away, Lester knew he must have hit a raw nerve. There was definitely something different. Maybe it was the kid's girlfriend. Lester knew how stormy that relationship must be—the two were nothing alike, and Lester personally thought the girl was too interested in herself by a long way. Anyway, it was none of Lester's business. It was certainly not a reason for him to be going through the cash drawer like some neurotic old miser.

Just to put the thing to rest, Lester wet his thumb again and flipped through the bills. Twenty, forty, sixty. . . . He reached the end and paused. He counted again. He stacked the bills in several piles of five. The lines between his eyebrows grew deeper. What was going on here? There must have been a mistake made when someone was ringing up a purchase. Yes, that was it. He was sure that was it. Bill would never actually take anything—Lester would hardly even let himself think the thought. But clearly, the boy had been careless with the cash register. They would have to have a talk. Lester stacked the bills back in the cash register and closed the metal clamp. He scowled at them, going over the possibilities in his mind. Then he opened the clamp, removed the money, and walked to his office, jingling the key to his miniature safe, scowling.

Linda and Jeff watched until Bill was safe inside his apartment before they backed out of the driveway. Jeff's battered sports car creaked unhappily as he tugged at the reluctant gear shift.

"Nice guy," Linda commented.

"Yeah, I think so," Jeff responded. "D'you think Tammy liked him?"

"Well, it depends on what you mean by 'like,' " said Linda. "I think she liked him, yes, she thought he was a fine person. As for *liking* him, if you know what I mean — that, I'm not sure about. It's pretty early to tell."

"I suppose so." Jeff braked at a stop sign and adjusted the heat on the car. "I was kind of hoping they'd hit it off. Tammy's a good influence on anybody."

"Oh? Does Bill need a 'good influence?' "

"I think so," said Jeff. "His girlfriend dumped him a while back. He seems pretty broken up about it. I don't really know him that well — I just see him at church and sometimes playing basketball. But he seems pretty unhappy. Doesn't talk much. Just sort of sits in the back. I guess a lot of people in the ward think he's stuck up."

"Hmm," said Linda, thinking. "He doesn't seem that way to me. A little shy, maybe. Shy people can act a little arrogant at first. But he was really nice tonight, especially bowling."

Jeff smiled at her. "Trust you to give everyone the benefit of the doubt. No, I agree with you. I think he is shy. I also think he gets that sort of obnoxious streak from the people he hangs around with. You know when I used to be a waiter at Paganini's?"

Linda nodded.

"Bill used to come in with this whole gang. You know the type. They always wore black, you know? Layers and layers of black. And they'd have hair that was really long in one patch just over the ear or in the center of their foreheads or something, and shaved everywhere else, and they'd keep tossing their heads to get that one strand of hair out of their eyes. And then they'd wear these earrings that looked like they were made for skinning small animals. That type."

"I see," said Linda, nodding. "I can't imagine Bill ever fitting in with that kind of group. He seems so . . . *wholesome*."

"He never really did fit in. I guess he tried. He seemed popular enough, but he always stood out. His girlfriend was right at the center of the group, though. I think that's the main reason they hung out with him. Otherwise he probably would have been too wholesome for them. I mean, those guys are into a lot of bad stuff."

"You think so?"

"Oh," said Jeff, looking over his shoulder and moving into the next lane, "no question. One of the things about being a waiter is, you become like a nonperson. People just go right on talking about anything while you serve them their lasagne. They talked about drugs constantly, these guys."

"Bill, too?" Linda asked.

"When I was around and they talked about it, I noticed Bill kept his mouth shut and seemed really uncomfortable. I asked him about the whole thing later, at church."

"Really?" Linda turned to look at Jeff's profile. "What did he say?"

"Oh, he admitted that a lot of his friends had been into drugs at one point, but he said he never used them. He was very straightforward about it. I don't have any reason not to believe him."

"You think he wasn't involved at all?"

Jeff frowned. "Well, that's what he said. But he seems to think about the subject a lot. The most he's ever talked to me is this one time in church after this girl bore her testimony and said something about resisting temptation to take drugs or something. Bill just came up to me in priesthood class after that and spent the whole meeting whispering to me about how biased this girl was and how stupid and naive people can be about drugs. I guess since he has a lot of friends who are into that stuff, he thinks about it more than most people."

"Certainly more than I do," said Linda.

"I know," said Jeff. "That's what was kind of strange about this conversation I had with Bill. He seemed to think that everyone spends a lot of time thinking about drugs. He also talked as though just about everybody used drugs, which was very strange to me. But like I said, it must be because of his friends. He told me he's never used drugs, and I believe him."

"I believe him, too," said Linda. "We have no right to sit and talk about him behind his back, anyway."

"Absolutely," said Jeff.

"Right," said Linda. They drove on in silence for a few minutes. Jeff fiddled with the radio, managed to locate a dim and static-filled station, then switched the radio back off.

"Still," he said thoughtfully, "maybe it wouldn't hurt to keep an eye on the guy."

"Like a hawk," said Linda. They looked at each other and laughed as Jeff pulled up in front of Linda's house.

Justin sat in the upstairs hall, back against the door to Bill's room, and bounced his new basketball against the opposite wall. Christmas vacation was no fun after Christmas, he decided. There was nothing to do inside, and outside it was too cold for anything fun. That was why

Justin had decided to sit here and wait for Bill, because Bill had said he was going to take Justin over to the gym and show him how to dribble. He'd tried to learn in the house as soon as he'd found the ball under the tree Christmas morning, but Mom said the house wasn't a gymnasium and Dad threatened to take the ball away until spring if Justin didn't settle down.

Bill was acting funny. Justin didn't really remember all that well what Bill was like before he left home. That was a whole two years ago, when Justin wasn't even in school yet. He'd just been a kid, back then. But it did seem as though the Bill he remembered didn't spend all his time in his room. He used to laugh a lot, and give Justin piggyback rides, and tickle him. Now he got mad all the time, and he didn't seem to want to play with Justin. Not at all. Justin threw the basketball against the wall hard, and he heard Marcy's voice yell from the other side, "Justin, cut it out!" He threw the ball again.

Justin felt stupid. He'd gotten all excited about this Christmas because Bill was coming home, and Bill didn't even like him. He even bought Bill a mug that said, "When I grow up, I want to be just like you," which had cost a whole dollar, which meant that he hadn't had enough money left to buy anything for Marcy or Louisa. Bill unwrapped the mug, and everything had gone all wrong, not at all as Justin had imagined it. Bill hadn't even smiled. Well, he had, but in this mean, mad way. Justin guessed he just didn't like it. It was really stupid, to spend all your Christmas money on a brother who doesn't even like you. The basketball hit the wall with a metallic thud, and Marcy shouted, "Justin, if you keep that up, so help me. . . . " Marcy never said what would happen "so help her." She just let you imagine it. Not like Bill. Bill told you everything. He never kept secrets like Marcy and Louisa did between themselves.

Justin picked at a stray little piece of rubber with a dirty fingernail. At least Bill used to be like that, when Justin was a kid. Now they were all much older, and Justin supposed it must be time to start acting more grown up. Bill must be doing very grown-up things, all the time he spent alone in his room. He slept a lot, too, but that's how old people always acted. Justin decided he should get up and find something to do. Bill obviously wasn't going to come out. It was turning into a very boring Christmas. Justin stood up, and thought about knocking on Bill's door, but decided that Bill wouldn't like it. After all, Bill didn't even like Justin any more. He threw the basketball hard against Marcy's wall, and was inwardly pleased when it ricocheted into the door of Bill's bedroom. Marcy poked her head out of the door down the hall.

"Justin, will you CUT IT OUT?" she said angrily. But Justin didn't answer. Just like Bill never answered anybody anymore. He turned on his heel, just like Bill would do, and stalked wordlessly down the hall into his bedroom.

"There he goes!" said Alice urgently, grasping her friend's wrist across the tiny cafe table and pointing out the window toward the street.

"Where? Which one?" Gloria craned her neck, trying to see over the potted plants in the window sill.

"The tall one. Black hair," said Alice. "D'you see him?"

Gloria smiled, still craning. "Yeah, I think so. . . . Whoa, Alice, you weren't kidding!"

"What a hunk, huh?" said Alice triumphantly. "I told you he looks like Tom Cruise."

"Next to him," said Gloria, settling back into her seat, "Tom Cruise is chopped liver."

Alice laughed. "Now, let's not go too far," she cautioned. "We have to keep our priorities in order here." She watched Warren cross the street and disappear into the crowd on the other side. "But speaking strictly as a scientific observer, I would have to admit that he is extremely cute. And incidentally, he also happens to be a very nice person."

"Better than cute," said Gloria. "Gorgeous. And single?"

"I don't even think he has a steady girlfriend."

Gloria feigned a swoon. "My cup runneth over. Why haven't you nabbed him?"

Alice sipped thoughtfully at her lemonade. "I'm not really sure. He doesn't seem nabbable somehow, if you know what I mean."

"I don't," said Gloria.

"Well, let me see. . . . It's kind of hard to describe. He's one of those guys that's just like a brother, you know? I mean, I can really talk to him, about work, school, my dad's phlebitis, whatever. But it just never seems to go any farther than that. There's no . . . I don't know . . . zing, or something. That's it. There's just not any *zing* in our relationship."

"Are you kidding?" exclaimed Gloria, "Alice, I've never been closer than fifty feet from this guy, and he zings me. I mean, I have been zung, right here as we speak. What's your problem with him?"

Alice poked at a piece of ice with her straw, thinking. "Y'know, Gloria," she said. "I've wondered that myself. It's not like I wasn't interested in him when we first started sharing the office—I was. I mean, I do have blood in my veins. But I'm not sure he does."

"Didn't take to you, huh?" asked Gloria sympathetically.

"I guess not," said Alice. "But, no, it was more than that. I mean, even when you're talking to a single guy who doesn't like you, there's a certain feeling, you know? Like a certain way that you respond to each other that's different than you would respond if you were both men or both women. I don't know how to describe it any better than that, but . . . "

"I think I know what you mean," said Gloria. "Zing."

"Exactly!" said Alice. "And with Warren, it's like all the responses are just . . . zingless. In a way, it's great. I can really talk to him because of that, better than I can to most guys. He's a wonderful friend. But when I get a little bit interested in him—you know—there's just nothing coming back. I mean *nothing.*"

"I hate to say this," said Gloria, leaning toward Alice across her seafood salad, "but do you suppose he . . . you know . . . doesn't like women?"

Alice burst into laughter. "Warren?" she said. "No way! Not Warren. Are you kidding? For one thing, he's a Mormon. For another, he happened to tell me that he was engaged once but broke it off. As a matter of fact, he even told me once that's why he doesn't date much. I guess it really shattered him."

"Hmm," said Gloria. "So what's his problem with you? Still nursing his wounds?"

Alice shook her head. "No, I don't think so. I mean, that's a strange thing, too. He told me he'd gone through this big romantic trauma, but then he never mentions the girl's name and he . . . I don't know . . . he just doesn't act like someone whose heart is broken. I mean, there's no rebound dating or anything." She wadded up a bit of her napkin and flicked it into the potted plant. "Oh, heck. I'm probably just rationalizing. He probably has this gorgeous girlfriend waiting for him every day after work, and he's just too kind to tell me I turn his stomach. Ah, well. There are other fish in the sea, I suppose."

"I suppose so," said Gloria, looking ruefully at her seafood salad. She stabbed at it with her fork and took a bite. "Sure is cute, though," she commented.

"Better than cute," said Alice with a sigh. "He's gorgeous."

Susan White climbed out of her rental car and stood

nervously on the sidewalk, looking up at the white brick apartment house. It glowed pale apricot, reflecting the dying sunlight. She thought that window on the right must be Warren's, but she couldn't really remember. The last time she'd been here she'd found out where he lived, but that was after she'd already gone into the building, of course. It wasn't the same, looking at things from the outside. Susan had never been good at those kinds of things, anyway—map things, where you have to figure out the location of one thing from the location of something else. Map things confused her. It must have been some kind of miracle that had gotten her here from Brenda's house over those awful freeways. She'd probably never find her way back.

She walked past the palm trees into the building's entry way. The outside doors were open. Susan went in and tried the inside doors, but they were locked with a heavy electrical bolt. She walked over to the mailboxes and looked for Warren's name. There it was, looking somehow small and dingy next to all the other names on their yellowing paper strips. A bin below the mailboxes held several magazines addressed to Warren, among them a recent edition of a Latter-day Saint periodical. Susan had sent him a subscription for his birthday, along with a card. Since the magazine hadn't been confiscated by the post office or the building manager, it looked like Warren was still at least collecting his mail. He hadn't responded to letters she had written for the last few months—not even the note saying that she'd be in L.A. to see Brenda's new baby and would he mind if she came by to visit for a while? She assumed he'd gotten the note. Anyway, it wasn't here, and it hadn't been returned.

A suave-looking young woman came in from outside, felt in her purse for keys, and unlocked the bolted inner doors. The thought flashed across Susan's mind that she should catch the door before it swung closed and follow

162

the woman in, but she hesitated a moment too long and the woman was gone, leaving the echo of the slamming doors and a faint smell of perfume behind her. Susan stood looking at the messages glued to the inside of the glass door. "Give to the United Way." "No Soliciting." "Please Do Not Open This Door for Strangers." She really had no business sneaking into Warren's apartment building, after all. Susan turned back to the mailboxes and looked at the small intercom buttons next to each name. Honestly, she told herself, she was just being silly. She should simply push the button and Warren would come on the intercom, and he would "buzz" the door open and she would ride the elevator up to his floor and he would let her in and they would have a nice talk. There was no reason to think anything different. Warren had always been a good boy, had never said anything unpleasant or hostile like so many poor mothers' boys. She and Warren had always been close when he was little. She should just push the button.

Instead Susan picked up one of Warren's unopened magazines and began to leaf through it. The fact was that there was something wrong. She had no reason to think so, but she knew it. There was something wrong when a boy didn't write back or even answer his telephone most days. Even to herself, Susan was beginning to sound like one of those awful women who dog their sons' footsteps forever, prying into the poor boys' private life and giving them no room to breathe. She hoped she had kept her worries private enough. When she did get through to Warren on the phone, she never mentioned that she'd been trying to call. She never left any messages on his answering machine, in case he would think she was becoming a nag. He was always very pleasant—no, not pleasant. Civil was the word. He answered all her questions politely, offered no new information, and got off the phone as soon as it was socially proper. He'd never seemed upset at her, and yet, Susan thought again, there was something very wrong. It was as though the voice on the telephone had nothing to do with Warren, as though it were a plastic cutout of his personality. She might as well have been talking to a telephone salesman.

That was why she'd come here, really. Brenda's baby was a good excuse, but it was really her own baby Susan had come to see. And that was why she still couldn't bring herself to touch the buzzer and bring Warren's voice onto the intercom. Some part of her was afraid to hear that disembodied voice so close to its source. What if Warren himself had simply vanished, and only his voice was left now, imitating Warren into phones and intercoms, pretending her boy was still alive? What if the voice answered, and she went up to the apartment, and there was no one there? Susan shook herself, frowning, like a cat flicking something dirty off its paws. She should stop being so silly. There was absolutely no evidence that anything was wrong with Warren. It was just driving on those awful freeways that had gotten her rattled. She pressed the buzzer. No answer.

Well, Susan thought, it stood to reason. Here it was, a Friday night, and of course Warren wouldn't be home. How terribly silly of her. He probably hadn't even gotten her note — really, if someone is going to come see you, you do give them a call just to see when they're going to arrive. Warren was a grown man. He could take care of himself. And a grown man *should* be out on Friday nights — how was he ever going to find a nice girl to marry if she expected him to sit in his apartment all weekend long? She should be ashamed of herself.

Susan pushed open the outer doors. It was almost dark now, and the traffic sounds seemed louder in the dimness. She would give him a call later, from Brenda's. If he didn't answer, she'd leave a message on the machine. He would get back to her. It was no more than common decency, when she'd come all the way to California, and Warren had always been decent if he was nothing else. Susan opened the door to the car and climbed in, fumbling with the unfamiliar mechanisms on the dashboard. She hoped she could find her way back to Brenda's — map things were even more confusing to her in the dark than in the light of day. Susan started the car. She bent her head down almost to the dashboard, looking up at the apartment building to see if she could spot which one was Warren's. It was impossible to tell. Most of the residents of the building seemed to be out at this time on a weekend. From the top floor of the apartment, where Susan knew Warren lived, a row of dark windows gazed out at her in empty symmetry.

"Karen called," Josh called from the other room as Brian walked into the apartment. "The number's on the bulletin board."

"You think I need a note to remember my own fiancée's phone number?" Brian answered, peeling the strip of paper off the board. "Thanks anyway."

"Don't thank me. Thank Jim. You know I never write anything down if I can help it."

"I know it, Josh. We were roommates in college, too, remember? I'll never figure out how you got through Freshman Composition without writing a word."

Josh poked his head into the living room. His hair was tousled and his eyes bleary from a nap. "Great," he said. "Five o'clock, and you're still in your Sunday clothes. They might as well have sewn you into that suit when they made you elders quorum president."

"I know," said Brian. "Actually, I probably would have done better today if I'd left the suit at home."

"Oh, yeah?" Josh climbed onto the seat of the rickety sofa in the living room and sat down on the back. "What were you doing? Working at the cannery or something?"

Brian shook his head. "No. I just went out to see a

165

friend. I didn't even know he was in the ward—I don't think he's ever been to church since I moved here. Anyway, I was looking through the list of elders, and there was his name, big as life. Warren White. Boy, what a blast from the past!"

"Friend from home?" asked Josh, smoothing his rumpled hair with his hand.

"Nope. Mission," said Brian. "He was my senior companion when I was a green missionary in Germany. He was a great guy."

"Yeah," said Josh. "I think you told me about him."

"Did I ever tell you," Brian went on, "about the time this woman told us if we came back to her house to see her husband, she'd sic the dog on us? The very next day old Elder White tells me that's exactly what we're going to do—go back and see this guy. I thought he was crazy. In fact, I still think he was a little crazy. But Elder White said he felt that this guy was praying for us to come back and talk to him, so we had to go."

"So did you?" asked Josh.

"Oh, yeah, we went right back to the house. And as soon as we get there, the lady comes out with this huge dog. I mean, this was more like a horse with fangs. I thought I was going to faint."

"So what happened?" Josh slid down the back of the sofa into the seat.

"Well," said Brian, "she sicked the dog on us, and it came running over, but it didn't act upset at all. It just started kind of wagging its tail and smiling at us. You know how dogs do. Kind of cute, for a four-hundred-pound man-eater."

"You probably smelled like a friendly Saint Bernard," Josh commented. "You usually do."

"Right. Thanks. Anyway, the lady was so impressed by the dog liking us—I guess any friend of the dog's was

166

a friend of hers—that she let us in and sat in on the discussions. She ended up joining before her husband did."

"Elder White sounds like a real S. G.," said Josh. Brian looked at him quizzically. "Spiritual Giant," he explained.

Brian grinned. "Yeah, he really was, back then."

"Back then?" said Josh, raising his eyebrows. "Isn't he still?"

The grin faded. "Well, that's why I went to see him today," said Brian. "I just couldn't believe it was the same guy I knew then, and that now he'd gone inactive. Elder White is the very last person I would ever expect to stop coming to church. I thought it must be someone else with the same name, or maybe he'd been bedridden, or lived in an iron lung, or something."

Josh found a comb in the crack between the chair and the cushions and began to use it on his hair. "So, what's the story? Did you talk to him?" he asked.

"Yes. Yes, I did. I think."

"You think? What d'you mean? Did you talk to him or not?"

Brian loosened his tie and shook his head. "I don't know. It's the same Elder White, all right. I mean, it looks like him. But just about everything else is different."

"Different how?" asked Josh.

"Different like not good different. Josh, this guy used to be so . . . sweet. There's no other word for it. He was the sweetest guy, and he really had a spirit about him, you know what I mean?"

Josh nodded and Brian went on. "But he's changed. I don't understand it at all. When I first got there, he seemed really happy to see me, but when I said I'd seen his name on the ward list, he just froze up like an iceberg. He's really down on the church, really negative about it. I just can't believe it's the same guy."

"Well, did you ask him about it?" Josh put the comb in his pocket.

167

"Of course I did. I mean, I was there in a suit and everything, so there was no use pretending I wasn't coming for church stuff. I asked him why he wasn't coming to sacrament meetings."

"What'd he say?"

"He said he was too busy. I believe he's busy. I've never seen anybody look that tired. He looked like he hadn't had a good night's sleep in about a year. But Elder White, too busy for church? In the old days he would have quit his job before he skipped church. I just wonder what's happened to him."

"Is he married?" said Josh. "Maybe he married a non-member."

Brian shook his head again. "No. I think he lives alone. I told him I was engaged, and he was kind of nasty about it. He said congratulations and then asked me if I was making divorce plans yet or something. I mean, this is not like Elder White. It was really strange."

Josh picked a few hairs off his shirt and walked over to put them in the wastebasket. "What are you going to do about him?" he asked.

"I don't know. I asked him if I could pick him up for church next Sunday, and he said he had to work. So I asked him if he could make it to the fireside on two weeks from Friday. You know, the old 'don't-give-'em-any-out' trick. He got this weird look on his face and said, 'Fridays are dead.' Just like that. No checking the calendar, no explanation. Just, 'Fridays are dead.' It gave me a nasty feeling. I don't know what's going on with the guy."

"Well," said Josh, "it sounds like he doesn't much want you to know."

Brian hung his tie on a wall rack, considered changing into jeans, and then remembered another meeting later on that day. "You're right," he said. "I should leave him alone. It's just so funny — Elder White is the guy who taught me to go back when someone's been rude and nasty to you. But I feel like if he'd had a dog, he would have sicked it on me today. It kind of makes me reluctant to try again."

Josh put his feet up on the sofa, laid his head against the raveled arm, and closed his eyes. "Well," he said. "If you do go back, just make sure you smell like a Saint Bernard."

Some of the people who were puzzled by the self-concealing actions of Ellen, Bill, and Warren knew them very well and were hurt by their loved ones' unfathomable behavior. Others were only slightly acquainted with these three compulsive-cycle victims or didn't know them at all. These people tended to wonder why they found themselves unable to understand the behavior of their acquaintances and finally decided that they should remain aloof since the addicts did not want them to become friends. All these people wondered if some flaw in their own personalities or interactions with the compulsive-cycle victims might be causing the strange behavior. But whether or not they identified the problem for what it was, all of these people finally decided that since there was no way to deal comfortably with the addict, they would simply forget about the relationship and turn their attention elsewhere.

This reaction is typical, understandably so because behavioral addicts keep everyone around them at a distance in order to disguise and protect their addictions. As a result of the actions of self-concealment, people in advanced stages of addictive behavior find themselves becoming increasingly isolated from the people around them. Even if they could become such effective liars that no one noticed any odd behavior, most of these addicts' inner lives would still be focused on actions, and feelings about those actions, which are not shared with others. Thus, even if compulsive-cycle victims are surrounded by friends and family who try hard to love and understand them, the behavioral addicts are constantly aware that other people do not "really" know them and never will. The result of this feature of the actions of self-concealment is, of course, that the victim is more and more profoundly subject to the feelings of isolation, which constitute the first step on the compulsive cycle.

We have come full circle. Every time loneliness leads the addict to attempt to fill the void of isolation by committing some action of self-indulgence, every time the action leaves the victim desolate and sick with feelings of self-hatred, and every time actions of self-concealment are performed to protect the addict from the supposed condemnation of others, the compulsive cycle strengthens its hold on the individual's mind, body, and soul. And the stronger the cycle becomes, the harder it is for the victim to believe that it can be broken. For many who have suffered from addiction to some behavior for years and even decades, there seems to be no hope for escape.

Ellen, Bill, and Warren all reached that point. So did many of the other people we interviewed. Some of them, at this writing, appear to have given up trying to break the cycle, and others are locked into what seems to them an eternal pattern of trying and failing. Some, however, have managed to break out of the pattern they thought would dominate them for the rest of their lives and into eternity. The three people whose cases we have been following are among this third group, but they are not the only ones. One of the ironic things we have found about people who successfully break the compulsive cycle is that the stories of their addictions are rarely if ever told. When a Latter-day Saint succumbs to an addiction, the story often seems to spread like wildfire. But when an addiction is conquered, the victim's past is soon forgotten in the progress of a happy and productive life. We noticed, however, that the people we spoke with who broke out of the compulsive cycle, like those who fell into it in the first place, shared many commonalities of experience. We believe that their experience in overcoming behavioral addictions can be of use to others who may be searching for some way out of an addictive behavior. Breaking the compulsive cycle, as we observed this process in our interviews, is the subject of the next chapter.

7

BREAKING THE COMPULSIVE CYCLE
. . . .

It is very cold. The fog that has been settling around you is becoming thicker and thicker; your breath steams and blends with the tendrils of mist as you trudge across the broken rocky landscape. You have no way of knowing how long it has been since you lost track of the other members of your expedition. Nor do you know—within a hundred miles—where you are, since your party set out in the first place to explore uncharted territory. All that you are sure of is that you are very far from the food, and warmth, and company of civilization. You may also be far from the cove where the expedition's ship is anchored—you are so disoriented from cold, fatigue, hunger, and the fog that everything and nothing around you looks familiar.

You are trying to follow the coastline, hoping it will take you back to the ship. It is a rocky, precipitous shore, with sheer cliffs dropping to the ocean hundreds of feet below you. The rocks are dank and slippery under your feet, and every so often you lose your balance and have to scramble for a foothold, sending pebbles and bits of mud tumbling into the black water. You are afraid of falling, especially in the fog, but more afraid of turning inland to become irrevocably lost without the sea to guide you.

Both those fears are trivial, however, compared to the knowledge that if you do not find the others soon, they will be forced to give you up for lost and continue their journey. You know, but do not acknowledge to yourself, that night is falling. The cold is growing more bitter, and the fog even more dense. You force yourself to speed up, not knowing whether your last reserves of energy are taking you closer to safety or farther from it.

Suddenly, you feel the earth crumble under one foot. Your stomach seems to leap into your throat as you feel yourself falling and skidding, in a shower of rock, down the face of a steep cliff. Just as you understand, in a flash, that you are about to die, you come to a thumping halt on a narrow shelf of stone far down the cliff face. It is now almost completely dark and you can see very little, but once you have managed to calm down a bit, you discover that the ledge is just big enough for you to sit on. Feeling the rock above and below you with bruised and freezing hands, you determine that there is no way to climb up or down from this precarious perch. You can hear the waves below you in the darkness, but you do not know how far you are from the water.

The thought passes through your mind that you may as well drop into the blackness and end it all, because there seems to be no hope that you will ever come out of this situation alive. A quick end to your suffering sounds better, on the whole, than slow death by starvation and exposure on this miserable piece of rock; however, the thought that you may actually survive the fall to the ocean (as well as the strange persistence that leads people to cling to life in the face of certain death) makes you stay where you are. You feel a jolt as a piece of the ledge breaks away and skitters down the cliff out of sight, and you press yourself up against the damp stone as you realize that the ledge is beginning to disintegrate under your weight.

You sit on the crumbling precipice for what seems like, and may well be, hours. For a while you try to cast your thoughts back to happier times, to Christmases and summers and peaceful afternoons spent in comfort and warmth, with family and friends around you. You soon

173

realize, however, that the memories are making your situation seem even more unbearable than it is, and you do your best to stop thinking about them. The night is now utterly black, and fear and despair begin to get the better of you. Although some irrational part of you is still yearning for rescue, you intellectually acknowledge that there is no hope, that you must reconcile yourself to death.

You are trying not to anticipate what death will be like when, suddenly, you notice a tiny speck of light piercing the fog below you. It disappears, then reappears again. You can barely see it. You think you must be imagining things and try to forget about the light, but there it is again, bobbing through the fog for an instant and then vanishing. It seems to be almost directly below you now, but you can't tell how far away. Your heart begins to pound in your chest, and all your suppressed hopes rise up into consciousness, as you begin to let yourself believe that somehow, someone has come to your rescue. Faintly, over the crash of water and the grinding of stone, you hear a thin, wavering voice calling your name. You shriek back, desperate to be found and saved. You shout until your lungs ache and your throat is hoarse, "I'm here! Help!"

The answer comes back almost inaudibly through the mist, "I've got you! I'll save you! Hang on!" You are overcome with relief, as you sit huddled on the disintegrating ledge. You break into sobs of joy, knowing that very soon strong hands will be pulling you to safety. You even begin to relax.

And then the voice says something that sends fear stabbing through you again, as strong as it ever was. You are alone, in total darkness, not knowing how far it may be to the water or what is around you in any direction. You are not even sure that the voice is not a desperate hallucination. All you are sure of is the wretched ledge that is keeping you from tumbling into the freezing sea.

And the voice is saying one thing, over and over: "Jump! Jump! Jump!"

You are determined to procure a lifeboat, to set out on a rescue mission, which the captain says is a waste of time, too much trouble, and a terrible risk. You know the odds all too well, but you refuse to give up just because success is improbable. Out there, somewhere, in the freezing darkness, is your friend. You know how difficult and frightening the overland trek was this morning, even with a team of seasoned explorers and all your navigational instruments to guide you. You had been so worried about finding your own way that you didn't notice your friend had broken away from the group. By the time you thought to look for him, as the team stopped for a brief rest, he was already out of earshot. You don't know what happened to him or where he is, except that he couldn't be more than several hours' march from any point along your exploratory route. But you can imagine very vividly what he must be going through, now that the weather has worsened, night is coming on, and — above all — he is by himself. Even more vivid is your image of how you would feel if you sailed blithely away and left your friend to stumble in the darkness until he died. You would almost rather die yourself.

The rest of the crew berates you for delaying the journey on account of one foolish person. After all, they point out, your friend was quite able to keep up with the group. He was always the kind of person who went a little too far, explored a little too much, refused by too large a margin to conform to the team's directives. Good riddance to him, they say. Let him take the consequences of his actions. You know your shipmates are speaking from their own fear, fear of delaying their arrival at some more hospitable place, and fear of going back into the fog along the treacherous shoreline. Their fears are justified. If a rescue party

175

does set out in a small boat, it is more likely that they will all die than that they will rescue your friend. At heart, though, most of them are uncomfortable with the notion of leaving anyone alone and hopeless in this awful spot. Finally, you make them a deal. You will go out in a small boat, alone, for an hour. If you do not find your friend before the hour is up, you will return, and the ship can continue its voyage. If you do not return before the hour has passed, the others should go on without you. After all, you explain to the explorers, there is more chance that two can survive in the wilderness than one by himself. They nod, expressions of disbelief on their faces. You all know that no matter how many people set off together into this particular wilderness, every one of them is likely to be overcome.

As your little boat pushes away from the ship, you wave good-bye to the other sailors. They do not wave back. You realize that although you can see them vaguely by the light of your torch, they cannot see anything but the torch itself. You hear them talking about you, mournfully, as you row toward the shore. They seem to think of you as already dead. You try not to let this bother you, shrugging it off by reminding yourself that you have made this trek before, you know the coastline fairly well, you are the strongest oarsman in the bunch, and you have all the motivation anyone could hope for.

A few long pulls on the oars take you close to the sandy stretch of beach where the search party went ashore. Instead of getting out of the boat, you turn and head along the coastline. This is terribly dangerous, since the waves are likely to smash the tiny craft into a rock at any time. But you know your friend. The two of you have learned the same strategies, and you think alike. You know that he is likely to be looking along the coastline for the inlet and the ship. You stay far enough out to avoid the breakers. The fog is dense a few yards above the water, and you

176

feel as if you are rowing under a soft, undulating ceiling as you strain your eyes and ears for any trace of your friend.

Suddenly, incredibly, you spot a flash of white, flapping in the cold breeze. It looks and moves like a piece of cloth. As you move closer into the shore, you see that it is hanging from a small ledge of rock just above the water. Closer still, and you discern what is holding the cloth in place. The dim figure of your friend sits huddled on the ledge. The piece of cloth you noticed is dangling from his torn clothes. His head is down, pressed against his knees. A patch of fog rolls between you and you lose sight of your friend, but you continue to guide your boat toward him. There is not time for any elaborate rescue. You are both in danger if you cannot get back to the ship in time. Acutely aware of the risk and nearly bursting your muscles to pull the boat near your friend without letting it shatter against the rocks, you begin to yell his name.

After a few shouts, you hear your friend's voice, hoarse and strained but full of hope, calling back to you. "I'm here! Help!" You scream back, "I've got you! I'll save you! Hang on!" You hope that you sound confident, since you are by no means sure that you have the strength left to save yourself now, let alone your friend. With all your might, you bring the boat into position directly under your friend's body. You wait for a swell to bring the boat up to its highest level, just ten or twelve feet below the rock ledge. You can see your friend's dangling shirt below the level of the fog, but you know that he probably cannot see you. There is only one way that he might possibly be saved. "Jump!" you shout as the boat rises toward him. There is no response. "Jump!" you shout again, knowing that you cannot hold this position much longer. Nothing.

The whole situation is driving you almost mad with anxiety and anger. You have risked everything to save him, this friend who wandered away out of stupidity or willfulness or both, and now you are both about to die because

177

he refuses to take the last little step toward his rescuer. If only he would look more carefully, see how close rescue really is! If only he would take stock of his situation and realize that the ledge is not security but death! If only he would be brave, just for the moment it would take to leave the ledge and risk a dousing in the water, to get to the safety of your boat! You cannot see clearly what he is doing or understand why he is pausing so long. There seems to be no reason for it. "Jump!" you scream furiously, losing hope and energy. "Jump! Jump! Jump!"

This metaphor is meant to illustrate some of the emotions and conflicts experienced by both the addict and the addict's loved ones who are trying to help the addict break a compulsive cycle. It is also meant to show how the process can be both extremely straightforward and extremely difficult. Our discussions with people who have conquered addictive behaviors, and our observations of those who have been less successful, have convinced us that breaking a compulsive cycle can be very simple; however, it is almost never easy.

One of the central themes of this book is our belief that a person who is caught in a compulsive cycle has accepted the action of self-indulgence as a counterfeit for joy, and that this counterfeit ironically cuts the person off from the experience of true joy, which comes from healthy interaction with loved ones and, above all, from the presence of the Lord's spirit. Anyone who has become thoroughly addicted to some behavior—who has accepted the counterfeit for joy as joy itself—is bound to have an exceedingly difficult time giving up that action. The compulsive-cycle victim may never have experienced, or may not remember, what true joy feels like or how to obtain it. The closest such a person may come to joy is the pleasure of the addictive action, and addicts are not sure any other source of fulfillment exists to ease the ache of the void within them. To voluntarily eschew the action of self-indulgence without the assurance of finding anything else to fill this void is extraordinarily frightening. The addictive behavior is the ledge to which addicts cling, knowing it is not improving their lives but preferring it to the unknown fate they would meet if they jumped.

To the family member, church adviser, or friend, the addict's tenacious grip on the behavior that is destroying him or her seems absurd and incredibly frustrating. The loved one faces not only the problem of the victim's compulsive behavior but the problem of personal energy. We are all struggling, in this difficult world, to make our way as best we can toward shelter and safety. It requires a great deal of energy to stop and carry someone else, especially when that someone seems unwilling to help by coming even one step toward rescue. It is an agonizing feeling to stand in a relatively secure place and watch a loved one cling to his or her own destruction. It tears would-be rescuers in conflicting directions. Should they go on, forgetting about the stubborn addict, and save themselves? Should they try to enter the world of the compulsive cycle to drag the victim back, and perhaps be lost themselves in the process? It often seems that there is no energy left to simply wait for the addict to come around, because the storms, waves, and darkness of this world can soon destroy even the strongest who stop rather than working every minute to move toward safety.

Parents are perhaps the group of mortals who are most familiar with the terrible decisions involved in trying to help a compulsive-cycle victim who seems to resist help. But ultimately it is our heavenly parents who feel the anguish most acutely. Their love and understanding of the problem goes deeper than any earthly version of it, and their knowledge of the consequences of sin and waste is more acute. The Lord could, if He were willing to violate our free agency, pluck us out of the most desperate circumstances, and He knows how close salvation is to each of us. He longs for us to take advantage of His atonement. He urges us in every possible way to take that one blind step toward him in faith that He will support us. But unlike Satan, Christ has covenanted that He will "never force the human mind." (*Hymns of The Church of Jesus Christ of Latter-day Saints,* 1985, no. 240.) He will not push us off our various precipices. We must be willing to jump. Too often, our fear pins us to the cliffs, until they finally crumble beneath us and we fall to the very death we hoped to avoid by refusing the offer of help. The Lord's sorrow at this terrible result of our own trepidation echoes the feeling of every person who has ever watched a loved one succumb to a compulsive cycle. "O ye people . . . which have fallen," Christ mourned at the destruction of the wicked on the American continent before His appearance there, "how oft have I gathered you as a hen gathereth her chickens under her wings, and have nourished you. . . . yea, how oft would I have gathered you as a hen gathereth her chickens, and ye would not." (3 Nephi 10:4–5.)

Both the individuals who fall into compulsive cycles and the people who love them must believe that the Lord understands each of them perfectly. He knows how difficult it is to face up to the consequences of erroneous actions, and He knows the stress and anguish of trying to rescue those who will not be saved. Since these are different phenomena, although they may overlap, we will divide this chapter into three parts. First, we will discuss some misconceptions that we believe can be particularly damaging to the process of breaking the compulsive cycle. These are beliefs commonly held by both behavioral addicts and their loved ones. Second, we will speak directly to those individuals who struggle with addictive behavior in their own life. Finally, we will address the significant other who hopes to assist the victim in overcoming addictive behavior.

MISCONCEPTIONS ABOUT
BREAKING THE COMPULSIVE CYCLE

Two of the most pernicious and pervasive myths about compulsive cycles are actually different sides of the same coin. They come from a common tendency to see people and their behavior as static in time, when in fact every aspect of human mortality is in constant flux. For example, when we speak of what someone looks like, we generally assume that we are speaking of one distinct visual image. Actually, however, what establishes the person's identity is the continuity between an infinite variety of images — does a person "really" look like a baby, a child, a teenager, a middle-aged person, or an elderly person? Identity comprises the unique way in which an individual undergoes the process of aging, not any step along the way. The same logic applies to both sin and repentance. Each is a continuous process that we often mistake for an isolated event.

This error in perception leads to a kind of once-and-for-all mentality in dealing with compulsive cycles. A confession to the bishop may be seen by both a behavioral addict and the addict's anxious loved ones as The Repentance that will change everything. The victim of the compulsive cycle may go along for some time after such a repentant act, thinking that he or she is "over it." After the repentance, conversely, if temptation arises again and the addictive action is repeated, both the addict and the loved ones may conclude that this particular surrender to temptation is the watershed event that seals up the addict as a hopeless case. One of the most common themes in our interviews was the discouragement of someone who had "given it up for good" only to find that "it" was still a temptation too powerful to resist. Once they had succumbed to the temptation, many addicts concluded that they would never escape, that they were condemned to wrestle with their addictions for the rest of their lives. For

181

many people we spoke with, the agonizing rollercoaster of determined repentance and devastating defeat had continued for years.

The title of this chapter, breaking the compulsive cycle, may imply that there is some dramatic action that can shatter the entrapment of addiction in one fell swoop, freeing the victim quickly and permanently from the cycle. That seems to be an impossible goal. There are, we believe, actions that can and do break the compulsive cycle. But they must be used in a continual process, not as a grand one-time effort. One point we would most like to impress on both compulsive-cycle victims and their loved ones is that neither success nor failure in breaking the cycle is ever final. Every repentant act works into the process of growth that can finally free the addict from the addiction, and every return to error can teach new lessons about the factors that have bound the addict to it. The Lord will forgive an infinite number of sins and accept an infinite number of repentances. Whether or not we are involved in serious compulsive behaviors, continual repentance is the only mechanism by which any of us may hope to achieve perfection.

The shame, hurt, and fatigue of forsaking an addictive action again and again, only to return to it with a vengeance each time, may lead the behavioral addict to the conclusion that it would be best to give up trying. Loved ones may also decide that the sinner is a hopeless case and abandon any effort to assist in breaking the compulsive cycle.

But it is the belief that escape is impossible, not the addictive action itself, that makes the case hopeless. Satan may have power to tempt us in ways that we do not fully understand, and in the case of the compulsive cycle, he does. But the basic attributes of godliness in each of us—faith, hope, and charity—are beyond his grasp. Addicts who abandon hope of escape from the cycle of compulsive behavior, even though hope itself may be painful in the face of repeated failure, have made a choice that cements them to the addiction. Satan can mar our happiness, but he cannot reach our hope. He can take it from us only if we give it to him.

In our interviews and research, we heard and read many firmly stated claims that an addict can never really be free from the addiction—that in the final analysis, the desire for the addictive action will always gnaw at its victim's spirits, no matter how long the addict might abstain from it. And yet, we heard well-meaning Church members say over and over again that a single, "true" repentance would blot out sin forever, that if the addict would simply repent honestly enough, the addict would instantly and permanently be freed from temptation.

As far as we can judge from the experiences of people who actually have broken compulsive cycles, neither of these opinions is true, and both work to convince the addict that he or she is condemned. On the one hand, if the addiction is permanent, there is obviously no escape from it, and the addict might as well give up. On the other hand, most addicts have repented deeply and sincerely, only to find that they still suffer overwhelming temptations— which seems to mean that their repentance was ineffective and that, again, they should simply stop trying. The danger of these fallacies becomes clear if we consider that although sin may slow our progress toward happiness, giving up the effort to become perfected will stop us dead in our tracks.

The people we talked with who had broken compulsive cycles spoke of both sin and repentance as processes, not events, and thereby escaped the twin myths of the irrevocable sin and the irrevocable repentance. They assured us of their confidence that if they continued in the lifelong process of spiritual growth, they could be completely free from their addictions. As one woman put it, "it's like being totally healed after a long sickness; it's like flying, . . . this marvelous freedom."

Breaking the compulsive cycle had not, in any case we encountered, been a one-time event. It had happened over and over and over until it became virtually continuous, and none of the recovering addicts we spoke with felt that their repentance was completed or indeed ever could be in this probationary period on earth. The lifelong process of repentance these people described—what we call the "joy cycle"—is discussed more fully in the next chapter. In this chapter, however, where we are considering the initial, difficult efforts to stop the process of sin and embark on the process of repentance, suffice it to say that breaking the cycle of compulsive behavior is almost never a one-time ordeal. The road to freedom is liberally dotted with instances of apparent failure. Neither the victim nor the loved one should ever allow despair to stop the journey.

A second common misconception we saw in people who could not overcome addictions was the belief that the compulsive cycle could be broken by force. Many addicts and their loved ones tried physical, structural means to eliminate the addictive behavior. We spoke to two bulimic women who had had their jaws wired shut with the willing help of their concerned parents and spouses. A missionary tried to overcome compulsive masturbation by sleeping only four hours every night, spending the rest of the night pacing in an effort to "burn off the excess energy" that he believed led him into temptation. An addictive shopper chopped up her credit cards and threw them away in an elaborate ceremony designed to end her addiction at last. A sexually promiscuous man took a job in a Middle Eastern country where, as he understood it, extramarital liaisons were illegal. He believed that fear of legal reprisal would keep him from his addiction. These were all valiant efforts at repentance. They clearly demonstrated the sincere commitment of the addicts to give up their various actions of self-indulgence. But as far as we were able to discern, such measures simply do not work.

For one thing, there always comes a time when structural barriers to the action of self-indulgence are removed.

A compulsive-cycle victim who does not wish to spend life chained to the wall in a padded cell cannot rely forever on structural constraints. (That statement is not necessarily meant to be humorous. Some, though not many, addictions are so menacing to society that the addict is justifiably kept imprisoned, away from the opportunity to commit the sin.) When the chance to sin arises, a behavioral addict whose repentance depends on lack of such chances will succumb to the action of self-indulgence with hardly a struggle. What is even more alarming is the tendency of almost all addicts to escape from structural barriers deliberately once the pressures created by the compulsive cycle become unbearable. When the compulsive-cycle victim reaches that point, the only function of the barriers is to intensify the addict's self-concealment, isolation, and self-hatred.

It is truly frightening, in such cases, to see how far some behavioral addicts may go to obtain the addictive action. In fact, the effort to overcome barriers to the addiction might lead the compulsive-cycle victim into more extreme behavior than he or she has ever engaged in before. A teenager who was addicted to marijuana agreed with his parents to have them watch his every move until the addiction was broken "once and for all." When the need for the action of self-indulgence became too strong for him to bear, this normally kind and loving young man threatened his parents with physical violence and eventually beat his mother to escape from the house. The woman who cut up her credit cards went for a while without shopping, and then she began stealing items from stores—which became a new stage of her addiction. The missionary whose pacing was designed to keep him from masturbating eventually took to wandering the streets at night, alone, and finally fell into a much more serious sexual sin, which led to his excommunication. Building structural barriers between the compulsive-cycle victim and the action of self-indulgence is like nailing a lid on a geyser. Because the pressure leading to the action comes from within the person, not from the environment, either the lid will eventually be blasted off or the pressure will be released through other channels.

Another, less obvious reason that the structural-barriers approach to breaking a compulsive cycle does not constitute effective repentance is that the Lord cares less about our actions than about our motivations. He does not want us to simply find a way to grit our teeth and clench our knuckles against our desires for the rest of existence. He does not want us to strain against self-imposed bonds, longing for delights we have deliberately set out of our reach like Ulysses sailing past the song of the sirens. Many honest Latter-day Saints are discouraged by the Lord's doctrine that "whosoever looketh on a woman to lust after her hath committed adultery with her already in his heart." (Matthew 5:28.) They take this scripture to mean that they must *forcefully* control not only every action but every thought. Compulsive-cycle victims see that as practically impossible, because a large portion of their inner life is spent thinking about the action of self-indulgence and be-cause the compulsion to think about the action is even more pervasive than the compulsion to perform it. As one young man put it, "I could conceivably manage to force myself to abstain from [this addictive behavior] for the rest of my life. But I haven't been able to control my thoughts. And if thinking about it is the same thing as doing it, I might as well do it. I can't stop thinking about it. I don't have that kind of self-control." This man's perspective as-sumes a coercive approach to breaking the compulsive cycle. Temptation is overcome by "control," which pits the individual's spirit against his carnal mind in a constant battle. The stronger impulse wins and maintains the vic-tory, by force, against the weaker.

This image of coercive control over one's own impulses

is more reminiscent of Satan's plan for salvation by decree than it is of Christ's plan for the repentance of free will. Are we given individual agency only so that we can exercise against ourselves the contention and force that the adversary would have used to control us? Compare the perspective of the young man who said he didn't have the "self-control" to master his thoughts to the imagery Christ uses when speaking to Joseph Smith on a similar topic:

"Let thy bowels also be full of charity towards all men, and to the household of faith, and let virtue garnish thy thoughts unceasingly; then shall thy confidence wax strong in the presence of God; and the doctrine of the priesthood shall distil upon thy soul as the dews from heaven. . . . thy dominion shall be an everlasting dominion, and without compulsory means it shall flow unto thee forever and ever." (D&C 121:45–46.)

Where is the coercive righteousness here? Where is the self-control, the police action against wicked and misguided thoughts? Every image in this passage is one of submission, rather than struggle. We are told to *let,* not *force,* our bowels to be full of charity and virtue to garnish our thoughts. The doctrine of the priesthood is not something won by conquest in battle. Rather, it is something that settles on the soul like "the dews from heaven." The reward of the righteous is not a prize we grasp after slashing our way through our evil impulses. It "flows" to those who receive it, "without compulsory means." A glance at Christ's mortal ministry shows that the Lord practiced on earth what He preached to Joseph Smith from heaven. His actions in mortality and His advice to Joseph show the same infinite meekness, the same willingness to yield, the same unlimited power arising from the absence, not the presence, of force.

Those who berate themselves or others for not forcing themselves out of an addiction thus come closer to Satan's method of directing behavior than they do to Christ's.

Those who nobly consign themselves to a lifetime of struggle against their own desires are condemned to both heartache and ultimate failure, for even if they can control their thoughts and actions by strength of will, the thoughts and actions will forever fight back, and few are strong enough to subdue the rebellion indefinitely. Repentance is not a military victory. It is a process of continual surrender to our Heavenly Father. One man who had broken a particularly vicious compulsive cycle some years before we interviewed him told us, "I have learned that the only time my addiction seems tempting to me is when I let pride move me away from listening to Heavenly Father. If I start to think I can control myself, I lose control." The idea that the compulsive cycle can be broken by force is often honestly come by, but it is wrong. The very common phenomenon of berating an addict for not having enough willpower is therefore both incorrect and very destructive, for willpower is a coercive agent. As such, it intensifies the conflict within the victim of the compulsive cycle without freeing him or her from the addiction.

One last crucial misconception we would like to dispel is the idea that the addictive behavior is a simple cause-and-effect event, rather than a self-reinforcing cycle. This mistake is a very easy one to make, because the process of the addictive cycle is often buried very deeply beneath apparently uncomplicated temptations. In our thinking and language, we tend not to differentiate among various types of error according to the motivations that underlie them. That makes it very difficult for both compulsive-cycle victims and their loved ones to understand the addict's actions. To explain why it is so misleading to classify all identical behaviors as similar, despite the motivations behind them, we will briefly consider an example of the same illicit behavior in light of various underlying motivations. The sin we will consider, in this illustration, is as follows:

One fine day, June Albrecht is wheeling a shopping cart through her favorite supermarket. As she passes a bin full of candy, June grabs a handful, pops several pieces into her mouth, puts the rest in her pocket, and continues to munch somewhat furtively as she shops. June does not pay for the candy when she leaves the store.

Those are the facts of June's case, and they do not alter according to her motivations. From the point of view of the law, which considers only our actions, June has committed a crime for which she should duly make restitution. But as we have said, the Lord, who "looketh on the heart" (1 Samuel 16:7), sees the incident as involving not only June's actions but also her motivations.

Consider how you might evaluate her actions if you knew that June had simply been walking happily through the store, noticed that she had means and opportunity to take some of her favorite candy, and decided that it wouldn't hurt anyone if she nabbed a few pieces. That is what we might call a "simple" sin, motivated by circumstances outside the sinner. The availability of a tasty treat would then be a "simple" temptation. It follows that this would be the kind of sin that is easily corrected by "simple" guilt—June might remember the theft, feel remorseful about it, pay for the candy on a later shopping trip, and forget the whole affair. Many of us committed this kind of sin as children. Usually we overcome the urge to indulge ourselves after we realize the necessity of honesty for our own integrity and the good of those around us. By the time we reach adulthood, most of us have little trouble resisting simple temptations to sin. We no longer take things that look attractive to us merely because the opportunity presents itself.

Now take another case. Suppose that June's husband has recently abandoned her, leaving her to raise several small children. She has no job, no money, and no family to help her. She has gone without food for some time to let the children have what she can afford to buy. She knows that she should stick to basic foods and not waste her few remaining dollars on candy, but when she sees the bin of sweets she can't help but think of how happy the children would be to have a little treat. Against her better judgment, she finds herself purloining the candy. Once she has it, she succumbs to her own hunger by sneaking a few bites as she walks. June feels terrible about the theft but doesn't have the money to pay for both the candy and the milk for the baby.

This maudlin example would be enough to soften most hearts in regard to the wickedness of June's sin. (Generations of readers have placed themselves squarely in the camp of Victor Hugo's fictional hero Jean Valjean, who committed a similar crime.) The reason for our inclination to accept June's theft in these circumstances is that we realize that hers was not a simple sin arising from the mere presence of temptation. The motivation for her crime in this context is a very real need that comes from within June, not from her external situation. We sympathize with June because we understand such internal needs — indeed, in circumstances like the ones we have just described, it is the hunger of June and her children, not the theft of a handful of candy, that strikes us as the greater injustice. We almost all feel that there is a difference between a sin motivated by simple temptation and one motivated by need.

Now consider the case of June Albrecht as it actually happened to a woman we interviewed (the name, of course, is invented). The crime we have described was, for June, part of a repetitive pattern of small thefts that almost always involved food. June did not consider her shoplifting a great problem, because she had often seen her mother take tidbits of food from the grocery store when June was a child. What did bother her was her increasing tendency to overeat candy, which had led to an unwelcome weight gain. June swore off sweets several times, but whenever she passed candies in a store she found herself not only eating them but stealing them. When she tried to stop, she found herself becoming nervous, irritable, and tense, and she always finally went back to take some candy.

June did not connect this behavior with the habit she had developed as a child of sharing bags of candy with her twin sister and best friend, Beth. As children, Beth and June had often taken candy or cookies from the pantry shelves and sneaked into the backyard to share a forbidden treat. This behavior had disappeared as the girls grew up, and June rarely ate sweets as an adult. She and Beth remained very close until Beth had begun to date a young man who belonged to The Church of Jesus Christ of Latter-day Saints. June had never heard of the Church. All she knew was that Beth was becoming "a religious fanatic," and that the two were drifting apart. When Beth joined the Church and married the young man, June's overeating and shoplifting began. As she put it, "It was as though since I had lost Beth, I was trying to replace her with something I remembered sharing with her." The addiction disappeared spontaneously when June began to investigate the Church, then joined it, and became even closer to her sister than before. It wasn't until then that she realized that her actions had been motivated by her desire to replace her relationship with Beth.

This oversimplification of the complex problem of one person's addiction brings out some important distinguishing characteristics of the compulsive cycle. In the first place, June clearly was not experiencing the trauma of physical need. She had plenty of cash to buy candy if she wanted it, and she was not only well fed but overfed. It is therefore quite likely that if we were observing June's situation, we would assume that she was committing what we have called a "simple" sin. Such sins, as we have seen, have at least two characteristics with which we are all familiar: they are motivated chiefly by irresponsibility and lack of resistance to temptation, and they are easily prevented or overcome by an active conscience.

But June's was not a simple sin. In fact, she was responding to a deeply felt need—the need to replace the closeness she had once felt with her twin sister. In the case of a hungry person stealing food, the need is apparent both to the sinner and to the observer. It is clear to everyone that if the hunger is satisfied by some other source of nourishment, the need for the sin, and therefore the temptation arising from need, will be eliminated. In the case of the compulsive cycle, the connection between the addictive behavior and the need is usually unclear to everyone, including the sinner. The sin is therefore assumed to be a simple sin, and everyone involved condemns the addict for not overcoming temptation in the relatively easy way that a child learns basic honesty. The victim, meanwhile, has no idea why the behavior is continuing, and experiences the terrifying feeling of being unable to control his or her own actions.

Confusing an addictive behavior with a simple temptation leads to one of the most destructive reactions to the compulsive cycle for both sinners and those who would help them repent. We call this problem "misdirected focus." By this phrase we mean that virtually every person involved in the problem of an addiction tends to concentrate on some *part* of the compulsive cycle, rather than seeing the cycle as an integrated whole. To begin with, everyone usually agrees that if the addictive action ceased, there would be no problem. That is the reason addicts and their loved ones erect the kind of structural barriers we have described, in an attempt to block the action from occurring. This approach is often worse than useless because it stymies the addict's misguided attempts to fulfill a need, but it leaves the need still present and unsatisfied.

The problem of misdirected focus tends to take a somewhat different form in compulsive-cycle victims themselves and in loved ones who wish to help but who do not share the addiction. As the previous chapters have pointed out, we see the compulsive cycle as being divided along two different axes. On one axis are the subjective emotions *felt* by the addict: the feelings of isolation and the feelings of self-hatred. On the other axis are *actions* through which the victim attempts to cope with these feelings: the actions of self-indulgence and the actions of self-concealment. Of these two different types of phenomena, it is the feelings that create the need within the addict that lead to undesirable actions. They are painful feelings, and like all suffering beings, addicts find it hard to remove their attention from the pain and from the effort to escape that pain. If you have ever stepped solidly on the sharp end of a needle, you know how effective pain is in making you forget everything but your suffering and the need for immediate relief. Therefore, although the pain of the compulsive cycle is emotional rather than physical, behavioral addicts are likely to spend virtually all their attention on their need to feel better. There may be times, especially just after the commission of the sin, when they solemnly swear that they will control their actions, but in general behavioral addicts tend to focus on their feelings of longing and discontent.

The counselor, observer, or loved one, on the other hand, does not feel and often cannot understand the subjective needs of behavioral addicts, mostly because the need does not relate logically to the addictive action. Most of us, for example, could understand June's sorrow at her loss of her sister's companionship. The connection between that loss and the stealing of candy, however, is very obscure, buried in June's past. Not even she recognized it for many months. It is hard for anyone, watching a behavioral addiction in full bloom, to understand why the addict should feel so compelled to perform this behavior, and the extent of the victim's pain in the absence of the action of self-indulgence is almost impossible for the non-addict to comprehend. All the observer sees is the actions on the compulsive cycle: the action of self-indulgence, whatever that may be, and the lies and deceit that stem from it. It is these actions that cause the pain for the addicts' loved ones, and so it is toward them that the loved ones direct all their attention. What the addict is *doing* seems to be the paramount question from the observer's point of view. The addict, conversely, is preoccupied with what he or she is *feeling*.

The most common situation when addicts and their loved ones are trying to break the compulsive cycle, then, is one in which the addicts focus most of their attention on the feelings involved and the people around the addict focus most of theirs on the actions. The victim is like a person who has stepped on a needle and feels the pain but does not recognize where the pain is coming from. He pursues the addictive behavior like the wounded man turning to morphine for relief, while the sharp point of his unfulfilled need festers, unaddressed, within him. The loved ones desperately strive to keep him from the sin, thinking that they can break the compulsive cycle by refusing the addict his morphine, not seeing the needle or understanding the pain that drives the addiction.

In cases we saw where the compulsive cycle had been broken, the focus of the victims and their associates had been switched — in other words, in these cases, the addicts had begun to focus on their actions rather than on their feelings, and the loved ones had focused on the addicts' feelings rather than on their actions. We never saw a case where the compulsive cycle was broken by focusing only on one, two, or even three of the steps we have described. The reason we have formulated the cycle as we have is that the four steps we have described were *all* recognized and described to us, in one way or another, by the people we spoke with who managed to free themselves from addictions. The realization that they were caught in a cycle that involved an interplay of feelings and actions, and was not simply a cause-and-effect relationship between temptation and lack of willpower, seemed to be an essential step in breaking the compulsive cycle.

Many other misconceptions might interfere with the process of overcoming addictive behavior. Some of them are most prevalent among compulsive-cycle addicts themselves; others are more common to loved ones who are not involved in addictions but who want to help addicts free themselves. Both these groups of people need to "unlearn" certain ideas that prevent them from helping to break the compulsive cycle. The converse of eliminating these erroneous ideas is the adoption of new perspectives, which in turn can lead to constructive actions by both behavioral addicts and their loved ones. Neither the new perspectives nor the constructive actions will surprise anyone who is familiar with Latter-day Saint doctrine or the standard works of the Church. The Lord has never kept them a secret. Nevertheless, we believe that the experience of people we spoke with who have broken the compulsive cycle helps clarify ways in which well-known doctrines apply to the special problems of behavioral addiction.

The advice that follows, which is directed first to victims of the compulsive cycle and then to loved ones who desire to help them, is based on interviews with such recovering addicts. As we followed the stories of all our interview subjects over a period of five years, we noticed dramatic changes for the better in the lives of some, whereas others proceeded predictably along the compulsive cycle without any show of improvement. We interviewed those who seemed to have broken out of behavioral addictions, as well their loved ones, to determine how that process occurred and what these people would say to others who were struggling to break addictive patterns. Although the recommendations we drew from their accounts are divided into two sections, one of which is addressed primarily to compulsive-cycle victims and one to those who wish to help them, we believe that the advice will be far more helpful if both parties read both sections.

BREAKING THE COMPULSIVE CYCLE: ADVICE TO THE ADDICT

If you are an addict who has not yet acknowledged your addiction or who still clings to the action of self-indulgence as the source of all good things, this book will make you angry. Every page may infuriate you because of the open and intended opposition we have against things you hold dear. You may see yourself here but feel that we have got it all wrong, that we are presenting a narrow-minded and distorted picture that makes your life seem evil when in fact you are working hard to be a moral person. To you, we apologize: we have no desire to force our beliefs on anyone and no wish to impose them on you.

On the other hand, you may be a victim of the compulsive cycle who feels that your addiction is hurting both you and those around you: that it is skewing the course of your daily life and that the days are adding up to months and years of unproductive or truly destructive fantasies and actions. If you have seen your addiction as clearly wrong, you may want to change but feel powerless to do so. You may have repented a thousand times, and gone back to your addiction a thousand and one. This advice is written to you, to reassure you that there is hope and to tell you how people very much like you have realized that hope.

Understanding the compulsive cycle might be seen as the first step in breaking it. That is the reason we have devoted most of this book to a description of addictive patterns. Seeing more clearly the interaction of feelings and actions that makes the cycle so difficult to break might help you realize that you cannot escape an addiction by focusing all your attention on trying to abstain from the activity to which you are addicted. Those who have broken the cycle report that it must be attacked at all four steps simultaneously. *The compulsive cycle can only be broken when every step on it is replaced by something that leads to the joy for which we were created.* We believe that you have been indulging in the action of self-indulgence as part of your need for joy. The resulting loss of self-esteem and the self-concealment that follows are driving you further away from that joy. Until the emotional needs expressed in this cycle are fulfilled (your need for a sense of belonging and your need for self-respect), the search will continue to manifest itself in your behavior. But until your behavior changes (indulgence in the addiction, and lying to conceal both your actions and your thoughts), these needs cannot be fulfilled.

The first step in unraveling this dilemma is to search your mind and heart for the connection between the addictive behavior and your need for happiness. Take as a hypothesis the possibility that when you think you need to perform this addictive action, you may really need something else. What is the real need? The answer may be too painful for you to think about. Thinking about it may send you scurrying back to the action of self-indulgence with more desperate enthusiasm than ever. Our guess, judging from the testimony of all our interview subjects, is that you need to feel loved and worthwhile. That guess is certainly not wildly original. The need to feel loved is the most basic emotional need of the human spirit. What may come as a surprise to you is how deeply you feel that you are unlovable or unworthy of love and how much pain that feeling carries with it. If you have become very much involved in a compulsive cycle, we urge you to examine your soul for the feelings of isolation we encountered in every addict we interviewed. If you find such feelings there, think of how they may have become linked, in your life, with the activity to which you are addicted. The links are different in every case, and they are often hard to see, but when you think of them, you will know them. No one, not even the most highly trained psychiatrist, can tell you which links are significant as well as you can yourself.

To realize the link between a real need for love and the action that provides a false fulfillment of that need is to weaken the link dramatically. As you discover more and more ways in which links have been formed in your life, you can find authentic ways to fulfill needs that have been blunted but left unsatisfied by your addiction.

The comment about psychiatrists, by the way, may feed into a favorite misconception held by virtually all addicts: that is, that you can escape from your addiction without the help of other people. Some of the individuals we spoke with who had broken the compulsive cycle had done so with the assistance of psychiatrists or psychologists and assured us that their therapy had been crucial to their recovery. Others had joined groups, such as Alcoholics Anonymous, which had proved pivotal in breaking their addictions. A few had managed the escape with intensive help from friends, roommates, or family members. No one had broken the compulsive cycle without help. Our point in saying that you are the one who ultimately recognizes the links between your needs and your addiction is not that you can think your way out of a compulsive cycle on your own but that the final burden of learning and realization rests upon the addict, not with the counselors.

This advice—that you should address the problem of feelings by looking within yourself—might be very welcome to you. Many addicts spend a great deal of time thinking about their addiction, the reasons for it, the crises in their lives that "justify" it. In our interviews, we heard many intricate self-analyses that excused the addicts' actions in their own mind. But you must realize that pondering the workings of your own life is not enough to free you from the compulsive cycle, for your analysis, if it comes only from yourself, is subject to the same misconceptions and biases that led you to the addiction in the first place.

For that reason, we recommend that the first priority for the addict who wishes to break the cycle of compulsive behavior is to focus on replacing the two actions on the cycle: the actions of self-indulgence and the actions of self-concealment. Understanding the process of the compulsive cycle is not enough to break it. In order for the victim to be free of the sin, every step on the cycle must be replaced with the element of righteousness of which the addictive cycle is a counterfeit. The feelings of isolation in the cycle lead the addict to the action of self-indulgence, the actions produce feelings of self-hatred, which lead to actions of self-concealment, and these actions in turn produce feelings of isolation. The reasons behind your original isolation, and the links between those feelings and the action of self-indulgence in your life, are particular to you. Discovering those links is a vital internal step to breaking the compulsive cycle.

But you cannot change your feelings simply by willing them to change. You may know intellectually that your addiction is not equivalent to happiness, but you cannot simply eliminate your desire for it any more than you can fall out of love deliberately. However you got started on the compulsive cycle, you are perpetuating your addiction by enacting behaviors that create feelings that lead you back to the behaviors. *You cannot change your feelings without changing your actions.*

But aren't we contradicting ourselves here? Haven't we spent pages describing how impossible it is to simply stop an addictive behavior? Not exactly. What we have tried to point out is the futility of trying to change only the isolated action that is considered sinful and destructive, while leaving the rest of the compulsive cycle in place. As we have already said, the way to break a compulsive pattern is to replace the actions and feelings on the cycle with actions and feelings that produce righteous joy. But if you will examine the cycle, you will notice that the feelings it includes are a product of the addict's interaction with, and view of himself in relation to, other people. The feelings are essentially social phenomena. The sinner cannot change them alone because they involve the actions and opinions of the people around him. By contrast, the actions on the cycle are things addicts act out on their own volition. It is here, therefore, that we believe addicts should focus their attention and efforts. Understanding the compulsive cycle gives new meaning to the beautifully simple and profound summary of repentance revealed to Joseph Smith in the Doctrine and Covenants:

"By this ye may know if a man repenteth of his sins — behold, he will confess them and forsake them." (D&C 58:43.)

These two criteria address the two action steps on the compulsive cycle and show that neither confessing (replacing the actions of self-concealment with actions of self-disclosure) nor forsaking (substituting fulfilling, righteous actions for the addictive action of self-indulgence) can stand alone as true repentance. Both must be done simultaneously if the compulsive cycle is to be broken.

Most behavioral addicts who honestly wish to escape their addictions have tried hard to forsake the action of self-indulgence, whatever that may be. We believe that one flaw that is common in these attempts is the addicts' belief that they need to eliminate only the very worst part of the addictive action. In the chapter on actions of self-indulgence, we described the extensive routines that addicts go through before they perform the actual addictive behavior. An example is a compulsive shopper who spends hours window shopping before making any purchases or a sexual addict who wanders through the red-light district of a city for a long time before hiring a prostitute. Repentant addicts often think that they can "blow off some steam" by indulging in part of this routine without "going all the way." "I'll just go window shopping from now on," the addict resolves, or "I'll just walk around 'that' part of town for a while to see what's going on." As we have pointed out, the addict loses control after making the choice to enter the addictive routine. *Truly forsaking the action means forsaking the whole routine, even things that may seem quite innocent.* Taking a stroll through town might seem to be an admirably healthy undertaking, but for a person who always ends such constitutionals in a liquor store indulging alcohol addiction, it may be a serious mistake. Even people who claim to be desperate to give up their addictions often balk when they think of giving up the whole addictive routine, including deliberately constructed fantasies, which may feed into the problem.

If you are strong enough to eliminate every trace of your addictive action from your life, you will probably find yourself with a tremendous amount of spare time, time that you are used to spending on your addiction. As we have pointed out elsewhere, the action of self-indulgence can often grow to occupy a huge proportion of the addict's schedule. Simply removing the action of self-indulgence without substituting any other activity is not only difficult but unproductive.

Breaking the compulsive cycle is a process of substitution, not of abstinence. Some addicts attempt to replace one addictive behavior with another which they consider more acceptable. For example, a smoker might turn to overeating as an alternative addiction, or a drug addict might use prescribed medications as substitutes for illegal ones. According to our observations, the opinions of people we interviewed who had broken addictive patterns, and the advice to be found in the gospel, replacing one worldly addiction with another is not an effective repentance. It does not resolve the addict's needs in any productive way; it simply attempts to contain damage, which has come to be accepted as inevitable.

The actions we believe can work as effective substitutes for the actions of self-indulgence that make up part of the compulsive cycle are actions that accord with the divine nature of human beings. We call these "actions of progression." The word *progression* has a particular place in Latter-day Saint doctrine in that we believe progression is an attribute of godhood, one that continues throughout eternity. Progression is the essence of salvation. It is what our Heavenly Father does, and it is what we must do if we are to become like Him. The Latter-day Saints' image of heaven is not a place where angels sit on fluffy clouds, playing harps and enjoying an eternal stasis. It is a dynamic place, where work, learning, and relationships continue with perpetual and fascinating newness. It is an exciting place, and so far as we can discern from the scriptures, there are at least two characteristics of the activities we can perform there that make it exciting: all of them increase our capacity to love and our capacity to understand. People who have gone through after-death experiences typically have two central objectives when they find themselves with a second chance at life. They want to learn more, and they want to love more. Any activity that moves you closer to these two objectives qualifies as an action of progression.

If you are deeply engrossed in an addiction, you may truly be unable to remember anything that is interesting enough to you to replace the action of self-indulgence. One thing we heard repeatedly in accounts of people who had broken the compulsive cycle was that they had, for one reason or another, begun to replace their addictive actions with actions they had enjoyed when they were children. Think back to when you were very small, and try to remember something that you enjoyed doing and would do for some time *whether or not anyone else was with you.* These activities typically signal the existence of interests that are not likely to have disappeared with maturity, even if the activities themselves have ceased. The recovering addicts we spoke with often mentioned having rediscovered interests and talents that had been dormant or ill-attended during the years of addiction. One man who, as a boy, had always loved to disassemble and reassemble electrical gadgets in his parents' home (something they did not always appreciate), later found that working with computers and other high-tech gadgets was so interesting to him that he could often successfully replace his addictive action by "playing" with his electronic "toys." A woman who had always loved drawing decided to learn sculpture as part of overcoming a problem with compulsive overeating. When she felt the urge to eat, she would first spend five minutes working on a clay sculpture. If, at the end of five minutes, she still felt hungry, she would have a snack, but eventually, she told us, "It got so I was more interested in the sculpture than in eating, even when I was really quite hungry, and I lost weight."

The exercise of our talents in a way that enhances understanding—in other words, learning—appears to have a very powerful effect on many people, in some cases as strong as an addictive action. We believe that is because this exercise of talents is an action of progression, intrinsic to the divine nature in each of us, and so it has the power to bring us closer to our Heavenly Father and to others. Doctrine and Covenants 130:18 makes it clear that what we learn in this life will "rise with us in the resurrection," and thus, many learning activities can be classified as actions of progression. Nevertheless, the mere increase of understanding is not enough to make an action qualify for that distinction. We are told many times in the scriptures that great knowledge and talent can be developed merely to obtain the honors of men. In that sense, exercising our talents can in itself become a compulsive activity. We have all known very talented people who place the exercise of their talents above their loving relationships in the same way that an addict values the action of self-indulgence above friends and relatives. We have all known people who left husbands and wives, children, parents, or friends, because their work and the fame or status they gained from it were more important to them.

For an activity to qualify as an action of progression, then, it must fulfill another criterion besides increasing our capacity to learn. It must also increase our capacity to love — to love God, ourselves, and others. The scriptures portray our Heavenly Father as engaging in two types of activities: He creates, through the manipulation of material substance and the origination of ideas, and He works to bring human beings back into His presence. Both of these activities are essential aspects of godhood, but the second is apparently the most important. "For behold, this is my work and my glory," the Lord tells Moses in the Pearl of Great Price, "to bring to pass the immortality and eternal life of man." (Moses 1:39.) Since "eternal life" is defined by the Lord as knowing Him and being with Him, we may broadly put it that to our Heavenly Father, obtaining and enjoying our company is His "work and glory," His "action of progression." That assertion might come as a stunning proposition to anyone; to a person engrossed in the self-hatred of a compulsive cycle, it is almost incomprehensible. But there is no way around it: the Lord loves us, wants us with Him, and spends His efforts working to bring us into the embrace of His love. Every action He performs partakes of that objective.

The actions of progression with which you might attempt to replace an addictive action of self-indulgence are infinite. Nonetheless, "by their fruits ye shall know them," as Christ told His disciples, and "the fruit of the Spirit is love, joy, peace, longsuffering, gentleness, goodness, faith, meekness, temperance." (Matthew 7:20; Galatians 5:22–23.) If an activity increases your closeness to your Heavenly Father and to other people, makes you more likely to serve others rather than yourself, and decreases your desire to perform actions contrary to what you feel is right, you may be sure it is an action of progression.

Along with the activities for which you showed an affinity as a child, direct acts of open communication are also actions of progression. Conversation, working or playing with others, and willing service of all kinds are effective replacements for addictive actions. The idea in forsaking the addiction is to substitute such actions of progression for the whole action of self-indulgence, including every routinized behavior contributing to the undesirable activity.

For the person who is in the power of a compulsive cycle, the most effective action of progression that can help break the cycle is sincere, open confession to a respected confidant. This statement should make it obvious why we believe that both the types of action on the compulsive cycle — the actions of self-indulgence and the actions of self-concealment — have to be replaced simultaneously if the cycle is to be broken. You cannot perform many true actions of progression, which bring you closer to mutual understanding with God and other people, if you are keeping a large part of yourself a deadly secret. *Forsaking* the sin, or replacing the actions of self-indulgence with actions of love, cannot be effective or successful without *confessing* it — replacing the actions of self-concealment with actions of self-disclosure. The most crucial error made by individuals who could not break the compulsive cycle was that they clung to their secrecy, thinking that they could get over the problem without anyone finding out. Over and over we heard, "I've figured out my problem and prayed about it, and I will work it out between myself and God. I don't think anyone else ever needs to know." The actions of self-concealment went on unabated in these cases. It followed that the addicts were never able to feel that the people around them knew them, accepted them, and loved them as they were. The feelings of isolation were never fully relieved, and as a result, the actions of self-indulgence continued to be powerfully tempting.

No one we spoke to who wanted to break the compulsive cycle questioned the idea that they should forsake the addictive action. On the other hand, most of them fought strenuously against the idea that they should tell anyone about all of their addictive activities. The underlying reason for that, although they all gave many reasons, appeared to be their fear that the hatred they felt for themselves because of their actions would be reflected back to them by others who discovered how imperfect they really were. Confession was most repugnant to those addicts whose behavior was serious enough to require confession to their bishops or other Church authorities. We would like to consider some of the misconceptions and problems that recovering addicts told us had temporarily blocked their ability to take this step in replacing self-concealment with self-disclosure.

Many compulsive-cycle victims we spoke to saw the Church policy of requiring official confession of some sins to be punitive and humiliating. They thought of it as a means by which God instills pain in sinners as a retribution for wicked actions. Some seemed to feel that the process of confession was like a prison term or a flogging, that it was meant to create such intense misery that the sinner would not dare return to the sin. Some saw it as more similar to the stocks, where wrongdoers are publicly paraded around to receive the mockery and abuse of the self-righteous. These addicts felt angry and fearful toward a God who they believed would "write all their sins on a scroll for everyone to read at the final judgment," or who would "shout their sins from the housetops" in an effort to hurt and shame them. We even spoke to some people who had gone to priesthood leaders to confess and had received treatment that seemed to indicate that the leaders themselves thought of confession as this sort of punitive retribution. Most of the people we spoke to about this issue, however, admitted that they had never fully confessed the extent of their addictive behaviors to an official of the Church.

If they had done so, they might have discovered what we found in our interviews with people who had confessed to Church leaders, including some addicts who were excommunicated, and with Church authorities ranging from General Authorities to bishops: if you have sinned, no matter in what fashion, the process of confession to Church leaders is not meant to use shame as a weapon against you. On the contrary, it is to teach you "by your own experience," and not just in theory, that you are valuable and acceptable to the Lord and to His servants, in spite of your imperfections. It is to let you know that there are many people who possess both the desire and the authority to assist you in escaping the bonds that keep you from progressing toward happiness. One stake president told us, "I have felt as much love in the room during the excommunication of someone who was truly repentant as I ever felt performing a baptism — more, I think."

Many people we spoke with were unable to face the humiliation of confessing serious sins to Church authorities. Even the gentlest and most skillful treatment from a priesthood leader could not obfuscate this humiliation, for the sin was indeed a sin, and the sinner had indeed committed it. One of the most powerful insights that was reaffirmed by the testimony of those who had broken compulsive cycles was that the only thing that can free anyone from humiliation is humility. Humiliation is the sting pride sends up when it has been injured. In the absence of pride, there is no source for humiliation.

One man—we'll call him Jim—told us how he had struggled for years with an addictive pattern of sexual behavior, feeling that he should confess his sin to his bishop but unable to overcome the humiliation he felt at the thought of revealing his "true" nature to a man who happened to be his subordinate at work and his next-door neighbor, as well as his priesthood leader. When Jim was involved in an automobile accident that nearly took his life and left him physically helpless for months, he began to develop a humility he had never felt before. As he learned to accept the cheerful help of nurses who bathed him, dressed him, and soothed him when he wept with pain, Jim came to realize his innate dependence on others and the absurdity of demanding perfection in them before he let them see his imperfections. During his recovery, Jim invited the bishop over and confessed his sins. As he did so, he felt sorrow but not humiliation, because, as he told us, "my humiliation went away when I gave up my pride." As it happened, Jim's bishop reacted to his confession with an understanding born of spiritual sensitivity—"more than I thought he had in him," as Jim told us with a grin—and the two of them set to work on a recovery program, including a Church disciplinary council, which helped Jim break his addiction. Jim had not expected the overwhelming warmth he felt from his bishop and later in the council, but he told us that even if he had received much harsher treatment, he did not think he would have felt humiliated. "Humility is my magic weapon against humiliation," he told us.

Perhaps the greatest illustration of this principle is the humility exhibited by Christ at the trial that preceded his crucifixion. The Savior no doubt felt great pain, emotionally and spiritually as well as physically, when his beloved people spat at him and demanded his execution. But no matter how the mob attempted to humiliate Jesus—by dressing him in foolish clothes, writing mocking epitaphs above his head, and battering him with words and weapons—his dignity seemed to grow stronger as his circumstances grew worse, until Pilate "marvelled greatly" at his composure. (Matthew 27:14.) Remember that Jesus had no sins of His own when He endured this trial, but He was bearing all of our sins, and all of yours, and all those of the most despicable evildoers who ever walked on earth. If his own soul had contained so much as a whisper of pride, surely the humiliation would have destroyed him. But in Jesus there was no vanity to be hurt.

As always, the Savior's example presents us all with a standard to emulate in the pursuit of our own happiness. If the fear of humiliation is locking you into actions of self-concealment by keeping you from confessing your sins to others, understand that you are listening to the defensive bargaining of your own pride—a pride that belongs to Satan's world, not God's, and that will not make you happy. Consider that refusing to confess or waiting for a wiser Church leader to show up might help you avoid some humiliation temporarily but that relinquishing your pride can protect you from humiliation permanently and entirely. Few people have obtained the kind of humility it takes to confess serious sins without humiliation, but those who have confessed benefit in every aspect of their lives.

In summary, then, here are the procedures that we believe will allow you, the victim of the compulsive cycle, to break the cycle effectively. First, make every effort to understand the pattern and causal links in your addiction. Second, learn to recognize the entire routine surrounding the action so that you can forsake actions that might lead you to the loss of control that results, finally, in sin. Resolve to replace the addictive routine with actions that lead to progression, especially interaction with other people. This resolution overlaps with the third step, which is to stop concealing your actions and your thoughts, and begin to

209

disclose the real facts of your life to people who can help you overcome your problem.

The "people who can help you" fall into three groups, and we believe that to break the compulsive cycle, you must disclose the whole truth about yourself to all three. The first person is yourself. If you are like most addicts, you have covered your problems with such a network of rationalizations and outright lies that you no longer consciously think about the real facts of your case. That may be keeping you, among other things, from being able to recognize the links between your actions and the real needs that motivate them, thus preventing you from breaking those links. If you can ask yourself what you did and why, and answer honestly, you will begin to unravel the complex chain of circumstances that might have predisposed you to your addiction. The first step to replacing actions of self-concealment with actions of self-disclosure, then, is to admit to yourself, calmly and without hysterical self-recrimination, exactly what your life is like. It is an amazing thing to realize that it is possible to lie to oneself and believe the lies, but almost all behavioral addicts do it. Tell yourself the truth, the whole truth, and nothing but the truth, without either trying to justify your actions or indulging in self-hatred.

The second person to whom you must confess your addiction is our Heavenly Father. If it is surprising to think that we can successfully deceive ourselves, it is absurd to believe that we can also deceive God. But the fact that He knows your actions and your motivations better than you do yourself does not mean that going to Him in honest repentance is superfluous. Because of the Lord's respect for our free agency, He can only help us with our problems when we invite Him to. After you have reached a clear realization of your doings, of the fact that you are caught in a cycle of feelings and actions that are limiting your happiness, discuss the problem openly with the Lord in prayer and ask Him for help. Believe that He can help you, and that He will, no matter what kind of a person you may be, no matter how deeply you are involved in error. The prophet Moroni tells us: "Behold, I say unto you that whoso believeth in Christ, doubting nothing, whatsoever he shall ask the Father in the name of Christ it shall be granted him; and this promise is unto all, even unto the ends of the earth." (Mormon 9:20.)

This astonishing passage of scripture contains no conditions, no qualifications, no caveats for people whose problems are too heavy or sins too deep. Moroni continues: "O then despise not, and wonder not, but hearken unto the words of the Lord, and ask the Father in the name of Jesus for what things soever ye shall stand in need. Doubt not, but be believing, and begin as in times of old, and come unto the Lord with all your heart, and work out your own salvation with fear and trembling before him." (V. 27.)

The power of prayer was attested to by every person we interviewed who had managed to break the compulsive cycle. If you have tried and failed again and again to free yourself from a temptation, you may have concluded that no power on earth is strong enough to conquer your addiction. You are right. In our research on secular treatments for addictive behaviors, we never found any treatment to be as successful as those which advise the addict to turn to God for help. Alcoholics Anonymous is a good example, as are a number of similar "Anonymous" organizations for people whose addictions range from gambling to sexual deviance. These are not Latter-day Saint organizations, nor need they be to take advantage of Moroni's promise. The important feature they share is that their members voluntarily ask the Lord to take control of lives that are out of control. One striking similarity between all the stories we heard of people who had escaped behavioral addictions—not only the Latter-day Saints we spoke with but also nonmembers whose stories we heard or read—was the spiritual rebirth that accompanied their surrender to their Heavenly Father, a surrender that occurred through prayerful confession.

The third party to whom you must confess, in order to break the compulsive cycle, consists of those people around you who love you and on whose love you depend for your emotional nourishment. In the case of sins that should be confessed to Church authorities, these authorities must be included among this group of people. This step in confession is typically the most difficult barrier for a behavioral addict to overcome. The fear of being cast out from the people you know best is so intense that it alone may serve to lock the addict in the compulsive cycle for years and years. Often, the fear may be justified. Those who love you the most are also those who can hurt you the most by their rejection, and they are the very people most likely to be hurt by your addiction. The alcoholic who fears that his friends will think less of him once his addiction is made public may find that some of them do. The teenager with a drug problem is probably correct in assuming that his parents will be shocked and horrified to hear about his addiction. The promiscuous husband who is terrified that his wife will leave him if she finds out about the problem may be right. The risk of rejection does exist, because your loved ones are not perfect, but we believe it is much, much smaller than most compulsive-cycle victims fear. We also believe it is a risk that must be taken, because you can never overcome feelings of isolation until you are convinced that the people who are closest to you know you completely and love you as you are.

The flaws in others' ability to cope with your addiction make confessing it to them extraordinarily frightening. But in our research we found far fewer cases of loved ones rejecting addicts because of a repentant confession than we would have expected. We were also surprised to find how carefully each confession to a Church leader or disciplinary council is handled, how much real revelation is experienced by the people who judge these confessions, and how different the outcomes of confessions may be, depending on the Lord's directives for individual cases. We found that *the dissolution of loving relationships, including fellowship in the Church, is almost always a product of continuing sin, not of a struggle to repent.* One reason loved ones might be tempted to give up in despair when they discover your addiction is that they may misunderstand the problem, by assuming that there is no hope for change. Explaining the workings of the compulsive cycle and reaffirming that it can be overcome often enable significant others to deal with the discovery that someone they love is involved in a behavioral addiction.

A good illustration of this point is the change in attitudes of the general public toward specific addictions when information on the problem is made available. Not many years ago, alcoholism was considered so shameful and inescapable that many sufferers and their loved ones hid a drinking problem long after they should have gone for help. Even more recently, drug abuse was subject to the same stigma; however, the growing public understanding of these problems that has been accomplished through government action and educational media coverage has recently begun to change these perceptions. Now it is possible for sports figures, political personalities, and performing artists to come forward, practically in droves, and publicly acknowledge that they are working to overcome some substance addiction. As the public has become more educated to what addiction is and that it is neither a product of innate evil nor an inescapable trap, the general reaction to celebrities who confess to an addiction has been an increase of love and support, rather than horror and rejection.

Part of the reason substance abuse is now less scandalous than it once was is that the addiction is usually blamed on the power of the chemicals involved. We believe chemical addiction is powerful, but often only ancillary to the cycle of needs and actions we have described. There are still some forms of addiction—most notably sexual behaviors—that are not recognized as being addictive, partly because there is no addictive chemical involved and partly because repetitive sexual activity is seen by our culture as a sign of virility and freedom. The very fact that sexual addictions are not recognized for what they are is part of the reason we found, in our research and in our interviews, that sexual addictions seemed harder to break than chemical dependencies. The sexual addict's problem is more likely to be mistaken for a simple sin than is the substance abuser's, and therefore the people around the addict are more likely either to respond to his or her confession with horror or to celebrate the obsessive activity as a sign of prowess. When we began our research in 1984, there was practically no popular literature available that suggested that sexual behavior could be addictive. Since then, the terrible blight of AIDS has become an everyday feature of life. Researchers who study the disease have begun to wake up to the fact that there are people who are unable to control their sexual behavior even at the risk of their lives and that these people are as lost in their addiction as any alcoholic or drug addict.

The way in which you confess your addiction to your loved ones is crucial to their reaction. If you simply stride into your parents, proclaim, "I am a homosexual; what are you going to do about it?" and walk out, you are very likely to meet with the devastating reaction you might be dreading. Arrange a time when you can talk to your loved ones without interruption or disturbance for a considerable length of time—at least a couple of hours. One husband we interviewed made his first break with the compulsive cycle by arranging a week's vacation alone with his wife, during which he told her about his drug abuse and answered all of her questions. As of this writing, the drug problem is not present, and the marriage is thriving.

Describe what you understand about addictive cycles, and tell your loved ones that you need their help to overcome an addiction from which you have been suffering. Ask humbly for this help. Describe the addiction and answer any questions honestly. You do not need to recount every little instance of addictive behavior. A guide to knowing whether you have fully confessed is this: after your confession, you will be impervious to blackmail. In other words, there will be no action in your past that you are afraid will be discovered by the persons to whom you have confessed. There might be certain events they do not know about, but there will be nothing hidden away because it is "even worse than the other stuff." If it is easier for you to write down your confession in a letter, it should always be followed up by face-to-face conversation.

As you might expect, your loved one may be overwhelmed by your confession. There may indeed be tears, recriminations, and anger. These will not surprise you. What will surprise you, if you ask for help in complete humility, is the power of the love for you that exists in the other person. You may not believe it until you actually go through the confession (that is what confession is for), but many of these people around you can and will love you, even when they know all your imperfections. If your confession elicits sorrow and anger, remember that no one feels sorrow or anger over a sin because of indifference to the sinner. It may take some time for your loved ones to comprehend the extent of your problem, or to learn that you really do need their help to break the compulsive cycle. Be as understanding of your loved ones as you hope they will be of you. Accept their imperfections as you hope they will accept yours.

You might also be surprised to find that your loved

ones are intensely relieved by your confession. Usually, loved ones are sensitive enough to realize that they have not been in touch with what a secretive addict is really thinking and experiencing. Your loved ones may have been living in a state of continual confusion and alarm because of the feelings of unreality and uncertainty produced by your actions of self-concealment. You may think that you have been protecting them by hiding your addiction, but in the end, the deceptions hurt much more than the truth. In our research, we heard and read of many relationships that had been brutally severed by deception. We saw love die in the absence of truth much more quickly than in the presence of weakness. We have also heard of people whose relationships did not survive the shock of an addict's confession, but we personally spoke to many recovering addicts and their loved ones who had achieved an unusual degree of emotional and spiritual intimacy through working together toward repentance.

The actions of self-disclosure involved in your confession and in talking continually with loved ones and counselors about feelings, thoughts, and experiences are the activities for which your actions of self-concealment were Satan's counterfeit. If you perform these actions, along with actions of progression, you will see how the other quadrants on the compulsive cycle — the feelings of isolation and the feelings of self-hatred — begin to disintegrate by themselves. They are pushed out of their positions by the feelings of self-respect that follow a constructive or creative action, such as honest work or loving interaction with others, and the feelings of belonging that result when someone you care for knows the whole truth about you and loves you anyway. At this point, you will have begun to live in accordance with what we call the joy cycle, rather than the compulsive cycle. The new feelings that result from righteous actions help perpetuate those actions, and make them easier the next time around. For there will probably be a next time.

Remember that a compulsive cycle is never broken once and for all and that your old habits are likely to die hard. But if you stick to the principles of confessing and forsaking your sins, every slip will be less devastating and every temptation weaker, until one day you realize that while you will never be immune to your addiction, you are free of it.

BREAKING THE COMPULSIVE CYCLE: ADVICE TO THE LOVED ONE

If you suspect or know that someone you love is caught in a version of the compulsive cycle, you have been spared the formidable test of an easy road in your effort to achieve joy and personal perfection. If you have been to college, you may have spent thousands of dollars to have others educate you, often by making you do things that were so tedious or difficult that you never would have done them on your own. The experience of dealing with a loved one who is trapped in an addiction will offer you experiences that are more difficult than any college assignment and potentially more educational—and they won't cost you a cent. A few tears, yes. Some lonely, difficult hours, perhaps. A great deal of thinking, praying, and new understanding, yes—if you let the experience motivate you to learn, instead of suffering it without effort like a mule standing miserably under the lash rather than moving forward to get away.

You may be overwhelmed by the injustice of your situation. You may feel that you do not deserve to be forced to suffer because of someone else's mistakes. We agree. You do not deserve the pain of dealing with someone else's addiction. On the other hand, you do not deserve the joy that can come from being pushed to new understandings by the same difficulty. Both of these experiences go beyond the limits of what anyone "deserves." Christ suffered more because of your loved one's sins than you are able to, and He certainly did not deserve it. On the other hand, His work and His glory consists of helping sinners learn to overcome their errors and achieve their potential. In confronting the sin and error of someone you love, you will be emulating a role Christ assumed when the plan of salvation was first put into action. You may never have a better opportunity to become like Him.

The first section of this chapter pointed out some misconceptions about the compulsive cycle that are common to almost everyone. The second section considered other erroneous ideas that we believe are most common in victims of the cycle themselves. We would like to begin this section by discussing some beliefs that are often expressed by those who would counsel victims of compulsive cycles and that we feel are inaccurate and destructive.

The first of these misconceptions is the idea that you can change another person. That is simply not true. You can lock behavioral addicts up, you can reason with them for hours, you can pray for them until you are blue in the face, and still, you *cannot* change them if they choose not to be changed. The law of God protects the right and power of every individual to determine his or her own choices, to work out a personal salvation. As we have already pointed out, physically restraining an addict from indulging in the action of self-indulgence only makes the problem worse. The most eloquent persuasion means nothing to people who have made up their minds not to listen. Alma the Elder, in a great act of faith, procured the services of an angel to help convince his wayward son to repent— but Nephi obtained the same blessing for his brothers Laman and Lemuel, and they persisted in their unrighteous actions nevertheless. The ultimate power to change always rests with the individuals themselves, and there is no way you can commandeer that right.

That does not mean, however, that you should resign yourself to simply watching a loved one succumb to a compulsive cycle. It does not mean that you can abnegate your responsibility to help the addict change. What it does mean is that in your response to your situation, you should not waste your energy trying to improve the compulsive-cycle victim like a sculptor hammering away at a malformed statue. It is worse than useless to spend time brooding about the addict's problem and devising strategies for making the addict change. That is Satan's technique. It is wrong, and it doesn't work. The fact that there is no way you can alter an intolerable situation by changing the source of the problem may lead you to the conclusion that you are powerless to do anything but endure the unendurable, but that is not the case. You have great power to change your circumstances because you, like the addict, have the power to change yourself. The first and last thing you must do if you wish to help a loved one break the compulsive cycle is to strive in every way to repent of your own shortcomings and become more Christlike in your own actions. Take advantage of the fact that pain is a great motivator to faith. Let every hurt feeling, every confused moment, every worry lead *you* to loving actions that might eventually rescue the compulsive-cycle victim from *his* pain, rather than to a self-righteous or self-pitying attack on the addict.

Since Christ has spent most of history trying to help His loved ones overcome their temptations, the record of His action in the scriptures is practically a how-to guide for dealing with this difficult situation. The best thing you can do for both yourself and your addicted loved one is to follow the Savior's well-documented example. Consider a few of the ways in which Christ has dealt with the kinds of emotions and situations that now confront you. Jesus' behaviors and attitudes in relation to the sinners He encountered in His mortal life were nothing less than shocking to His contemporaries. For one thing, He associated freely with people He knew were imperfect and even wicked. He treated them with unconditional kindness, took pains to comfort and heal them, and held no grudges even when they condemned, scourged, and crucified Him. At the final day, Jesus will be responsible for judging us according to our actions in life, but during His mortal ministry the love He expressed for all sinners was utterly unconditional.

When you discover that someone you love is struggling with an addiction, that perhaps you have been lied to and your trust betrayed, the temptation to lash out at the sinner can be very strong. You have been unjustly injured, and you may feel that justice should be served by returning hurt for hurt. There are at least two reasons you should resist the temptation to accuse and punish a loved one who has hurt you by falling into a compulsive cycle. In the first place, the thought that an innocent bystander should offer love and support rather than retribution to a wrongdoer, which is almost unthinkable to many people, was clearly not unthinkable to Christ. Because the Lord's actions mark the way to happiness, we can assume that revenge, which he eschewed, does not lie along that road. In the second place, you are not an innocent bystander. To the Jews who would have stoned the woman taken in adultery, Jesus said, "He that is without sin among you, let him first cast a stone." (John 8:7.) He did not say, "Let him whose sins are pretty tame in comparison to hers cast the first stone." In the Sermon on the Mount, the Savior queried, "Why beholdest thou the mote that is in thy brother's eye, but considerest not the beam that is in thine own eye?" (Matthew 7:3.) He was speaking to you as much as to your addicted loved one when he used that analogy.

How could Jesus have been sure of the sweeping implications of this statement—that is, in every case, one who condemns a sinner is more in error than the sinner himself?

The Lord provided the answer when he said that "with what judgment ye judge, ye shall be judged; and with what measure ye mete, it shall be measured to you again." (Matthew 7:2.) This sentence not only implies but unambiguously states that we ourselves set the standards by which our mortal actions will be judged. The standard by which you will be judged is specific to you, because it is taken from the record of your own judgments toward the actions of others. Your opinions of other people's sins are based both on what you know they have done and on what you suspect motivated their actions, as we illustrated with the story of June, the candy thief. But you cannot fully understand the situations and feelings that motivate the actions of others, and that is what makes the act of judgment so terribly dangerous.

When you condemn someone else's actions, you are in effect setting up a rule—*by which you will yourself be judged*—that states that given the particular set of circumstances this person is facing, anyone should be condemned for perpetrating similar actions. Because you do not comprehend the extent or power of the motivating forces in anyone else's life, however, you have no idea how you would respond in the same circumstances. It may well be that you are weaker than the sinner but have never borne such heavy burdens—in which case you are damned by your own judgment even if you have not committed the sin. The act of judging others is therefore more likely to rob us of salvation than many more obvious sins. Christ alone understands not only our sins but the pressures that lead us to commit them. Thus, when He tells us, "I the Lord will forgive whom I will forgive, but of you it is required to forgive all men" (D&C 64:10), He is not protecting some kind of egoistic divine privilege. He is preserving us from transforming our ignorance into rules of judgment by which we will condemn ourselves. When He commands us not to judge each other, He is not stripping us of power but giving us an instruction that will save us from our own sins. If you refrain from judging others harshly, you will not be judged harshly yourself.

Those who have discovered their own weakness are wary of making judgments, for they know that some kinds of duress can make human resolve shake like a reed in the wind. Paula Johnson, a woman we interviewed whose husband Ted was involved in a compulsive cycle, told us how she learned this lesson during the prolonged and difficult birth of their first child. The Johnsons had decided on a "natural" childbirth, and according to plan, Ted gently rebuked Paula when she asked for an anesthetic after many hours of labor. He reminded her of what they had read during her pregnancy — that the sensation of labor was "not really pain, just pressure." After a succinct but colorful response to Ted's well-researched explanation of what she was going through, Paula demanded and got an anesthetic from her obstetrician. Looking back on the experience, she realized, "I had been doing the same thing to Ted about his problem that he did to me during labor — I just didn't know what he was going through to make him turn to [his addiction], so I kept telling him it should be easy to give it up." Paula's response to this new understanding was to stop assuming that Ted had "no good excuse" for becoming involved in an addiction. As she gradually turned her attention to learning more about the experiences that led him into a compulsive cycle, she found her anger and vindictiveness toward him dissolving in empathy — an empathy that did much to help Ted overcome his addiction.

The temptation to judge can lead a behavioral addict's loved one to accentuate the problem by rejecting the sinner and increasing the feelings of isolation. It can also lead to the dissolution of priceless relationships. But in our research we encountered this phenomenon much less often than a problem at the opposite side of the scale. We mentioned this problem in the chapter on actions of self-concealment, when we discussed the ways in which loved ones can come to accept and even share in the addict's pattern of hidden activities. Some researchers call this phenomenon "coaddiction." It occurs when, because loved ones do care so deeply for the addict and because they are ashamed of the victim's actions, they enter the cycle of deception, leading to isolation, leading to desperate attempts at happiness, leading to a profound loss of self-esteem, leading back to deception. An example would be the family members of an alcoholic who join in the addictive pattern by lying to friends, neighbors, or employers about the problem, by protecting the alcoholic from the consequences of drunken behavior, and by increasingly cutting themselves off from people who might find out. Coaddiction is almost always a product of loving "not wisely, but too well." The loved one's affection for the addict and the desire not to be judgmental, precisely the qualities we have just encouraged, often lie at the root of this multiple tragedy.

Again, following the example of Christ can help you avoid the pitfalls of being too accepting of an addiction. Jesus' unconditional love, meekness, and refusal to offer violence even when it was being used against him are qualities we hear discussed over and over again by faithful Christians. There is often an implied message that all unpleasant emotions must be swallowed or suppressed if we are to become Christlike. But an unbiased reading of the standard works shows a Jehovah who told Enoch, Moses, and most of His other prophets that His anger often "waxed hot" against the disobedient children of Israel. We see the mortal Jesus uncompromisingly cleansing the temple of defilers. We hear Him express the deep pain of shattered intimacy with the words, "Judas, betrayest thou the Son of Man with a kiss?" (Luke 22:47.) We hear Him instruct the Latter-day Saints, through Joseph Smith, that we should speak out against evil—"not with railing accusation, that ye be not overcome" (D&C 50:33) but "with sharpness, when moved upon by the Holy Ghost"(D&C 121:43). In short, we see a God who possesses a full range of human emotional reactions to being hurt, as you may have been hurt, by the sin of a loved one. These emotions are part of our divine heritage. It does not seem to be either possible or wise to eliminate or stifle feelings such as anger, hurt, and sorrow. Like all our passions, they are to be bridled and directed, not squelched. A loved one's refusal to acknowledge the feelings that arise in response to an addict's behavior is often the beginning of self-deception, which leads to coaddiction.

Christ gave simple and effective instructions for dealing with these painful feelings in Doctrine and Covenants 121. He tells us that we should maintain a constant spirit of kindness that will enable us to know when we have been "moved upon by the Holy Ghost" to express anger, frustration, or hurt. But that should be followed, the Lord tells us, by "then showing forth afterwards an increase of love toward him whom thou hast reproved, lest he esteem thee to be his enemy; that he may know that thy faithfulness is stronger than the cords of death." (Vv. 43–44.)

This type of interaction is not the judgment that rejects and isolates the victim of a compulsive cycle. It is an account of your own hurt feelings, which stem from your love for the addict, followed by an honest expression of that love. If you never express the deep conflicts you feel over the addict's actions, you are liable to find yourself becoming tremendously resentful. In the end, your resentment may all but bury the love that caused the hurt — and cause you to hide that love along with the resentment. Furthermore, swallowing your anger and grief is one form of shielding an addict from the natural consequences of inadvisable actions, which is a key element in coaddiction.

Many of us do not learn from our secular culture how to differentiate and deal with different types of angry emotions. In our research, we found an interesting tendency toward gender differences in the ways loved ones reacted to an addict's problem. Men seemed more prone to believe that judgment and revenge are justifiable elements of righteous anger. This belief made them more prone to reject persons caught in a compulsive cycle outright. Many women we spoke to, on the other hand, seemed so averse to passing judgments that they swallowed their hurt and anger and became coaddicts. It is quite a trick to sort out the types of anger, which our culture tends, one way or another, to lump together.

Fortunately, Christ's example is again available for us to study and emulate. Perhaps the surest guideline in this divine example, one that can serve you well through all the unprecedented and very difficult situations you may confront in helping a loved one break the compulsive cycle, is the simple fact that Christ never performed any action that would interfere with His own progression. He freely forgave sin, but He never participated in it, excused it, ignored it, or facilitated it. In short, He did nothing that might have jeopardized His salvation. A woman we interviewed quoted the story of a pioneer sister who went to the Prophet Brigham Young to complain about her marriage. "Brother Brigham," she fretted, "my husband just told me to go to Hell!" President Young promptly replied, "Well, Sister, don't go." Christ invites us all to come where He is by repenting of our sins and our errors. He will accept repentance as many times as it is offered. But if we fail to repent, He will not compromise Himself by coming down to the place where we have chosen to remain. Although He loves us infinitely, He will not go with us to hell.

The reason Jesus was able to go through mortality without ever becoming confused about the proper response to conflicts between forgiveness and uprightness is that He remained in constant contact with His Father in Heaven.

225

The accounts of people we spoke with who had seen the compulsive cycle operating in the lives of loved ones were remarkably similar in their emphasis on the need for counselors, Church leaders, and family members to remain sensitive to spiritual promptings. Paula Johnson, the woman who realized during childbirth that she was judging her husband too harshly, began to give up this tendency to be judgmental because of one particular experience — labor and delivery. But she reported that after she had done that, she began to experience spiritual guidance in dealing with Ted's addiction to an extent she had never felt before. She began to avoid harshness, half-truths, and many other errors typical of addicts' loved ones simply because "when *I* was doing my best to repent instead of wishing Ted would shape up, I always had that wonderful feeling and I was prompted about how I could help him change."

Bishops, stake presidents, and other Church officials as well as the family members we interviewed reported receiving the same high level of spiritual help in their dealings with compulsive-cycle victims. The uplifting experience of feeling the Lord work through them to redeem His "lost sheep" was a wonderful and unexpected recompense for the pain they suffered as a result of the addict's behavior. *That was true as long as the loved one was trying to live righteously, whether or not the compulsive-cycle addict was willing to change.* The pain caused by the addict's actions was still present, but the joy brought by the Spirit made life not only bearable but happy for the loved ones. Joy and sorrow are not mutually exclusive, as we are often inclined to believe. God told Enoch, "Among all the workmanship of mine hands there has not been so great wickedness as among thy brethren . . . wherefore should not the heavens weep, seeing these shall suffer?" (Moses 7:36–37.) Yet we also know that the Lord is the source of all joy and feels infinite joy. The two feelings are paradoxical only in an earthly sense. The Spirit can offer great, intense joy when the world contains only misery.

This brings us back to where we started — the proposition that your own righteousness, and not that of your loved ones, ultimately determines your happiness. If you are in perfect tune with the Lord's Spirit, you will hardly need this book to tell you how to help your loved one break a compulsive cycle. The Holy Ghost will communicate advice tailor-made for the specific instances you encounter, whereas we can only offer some generalized suggestions; however, some of the ideas we ran across in our research might help you orient your behavior as you strive to perfect your lines of communication with the Spirit.

We have said that victims of addictive cycles tend to focus their efforts on eliminating bad feelings, whereas loved ones tend to focus theirs on eliminating bad actions. To break the compulsive cycle most effectively, this situation must be reversed. Before the birth of her baby, Paula Johnson had focused almost all her attention on her husband's actions, assuming that she knew all she needed to know about his subjective experiences and feelings. After she switched her approach to trying to understand Ted's perspective, her concern began to diminish his feelings of isolation — and with them, the addictive actions he was trying to forsake. It may seem repugnant to try to comprehend and even empathize with the feelings of a long-term behavioral addict. The urge to accuse is much stronger and much simpler than the effort to understand. Resist that urge, however, and you will find yourself learning much not only about the sinner but about yourself.

We have recommended that victims of the compulsive cycle who wish to break their addiction should go to their loved ones and Church authorities to confess. If you find yourself in the role of confessor, put yourself in the addict's shoes. Understand that whatever weaknesses led the addict to the compulsive cycle, that person is showing tre-

227

mendous strength in coming forward to confess. Even if you abhor the sin, allow yourself to continue loving the sinner. Realize that an addictive pattern is the result of someone taking a wrong turn in the effort to arrive at happiness. The need for that happiness is something we can all understand. Always remember that God is stronger than Satan. Acknowledge, along with the victim, that there is abundant hope for the repentant.

So far, we have been discussing your role in helping your loved one conquer addiction almost exclusively in terms of your attitudes and perspectives. But, many would-be rescuers asked us in our interviews, what can one actually *do* to help another person break the compulsive cycle? Some of the ways that you can help are implied in the diagram of the cycle itself. Just as the addict must replace the actions of self-indulgence with actions of progression and the actions of self-concealment with the actions of self-disclosure, you must do everything in your power to replace the feelings of isolation with feelings of belonging and the feelings of self-hatred with feelings of self-acceptance. Although all of these replacements must be made simultaneously if the compulsive cycle is to be broken, we believe that it is perhaps most crucial for you to focus on helping the addict to eliminate feelings of isolation.

Remember that much of the isolation addicts feel is caused by their own self-concealment. Your loved one believes you could not possibly love him or her if you knew what kind of a person he or she really is. To dispel that misconception, you must find out what kind of a person your loved one really is, make sure the addict "knows you know," and continue to show love and support. It will do you little good to storm, philosophize, argue, bribe, threaten, or speak words of wisdom. To break down the terrible walls that trap a compulsive-cycle victim in feelings of isolation, there is one thing that you should do more than anything else: *listen.* If and when a loved one comes to you to confess any misdeed, listen. If a compulsive-cycle addict refuses to confess and wants only to defend the virtues of a thoroughly destructive habit, listen. If the addict doesn't talk to you at all about the action — even if you don't know but only suspect there is a problem — listen, listen, listen. Listen to your loved one's silences as well as any outbursts of talking. Listen quietly to the statements that make you want to fight back with your own opinions or stop the painful words with words of your own. Listen without pouring out expressions of affection that the unbelieving addict might view with suspicion and recalcitrance. *Listen with the sincere intention of learning to understand.*

Some honest Latter-day Saints feel frustrated that the Lord does not speak to them more often, that they do not hear voices speaking out of silent air or burning bushes. They feel that a God who does not speak — a silent God — must not care. But the Lord's silences are never the silence of indifference. They are the silence of listening. The Lord has extended an open invitation to every one of us to go to Him any time and tell Him about our problems, our fears, our temptations, and our mistakes. He is that rarest of things, a friend who really wants to listen to us talk about ourselves. He has told us through virtually every prophet that He is waiting eagerly to listen to us if we simply speak to Him in faith. It is when we have made the first move to communicate that He can and does respond. All of the people we interviewed who had broken the compulsive cycle felt that their sincere repentance had been rewarded by the ability to truly feel that they were receiving answers to their prayers — not always immediately but eventually.

To help a loved one who is trapped in a compulsive cycle, then, you must sometimes follow the Lord's example of attentive silence even when you are tempted to vent your mortal spleen. Extend invitations to the sinner, as the Lord does, by really listening to *whatever* the addict says, without sending back a rebuttal, changing the subject, or ignoring what you have heard. Listen to your daughter talk about the new makeup styles you detest. Listen to your husband fussing over a problem in his work that bores you. Listen to a friend mourning a breakup with a sweetheart you never liked in the first place. The fact that you are listening will make the compulsive-cycle victim increasingly likely to disclose more and more of the thoughts that have been hidden under actions of self-concealment. As these thoughts begin to emerge, timidly, piece by piece, just continue to listen. Even if what you hear stings, you should try not to react too strongly to information that has been hidden precisely because the addict is so afraid it might shock you.

Simple attentive silence is unbelievably effective in tearing down the walls that keep the compulsive-cycle addict from feeling your love. But of course, *total* silence hardly constitutes a normal human response to another person's conversation. Besides, you may become confused and need some kind of clarification to follow what your loved one is saying. If you feel the need to ask questions or make comments, remember that when you are dealing with the problem of your loved one's addiction, you should be focusing your attention on the addict's feelings and not on the addict's actions. Any questions you ask will be most effective in breaking through the victim's isolation if they have to do with those feelings. "Why did you do that?" is usually not a helpful question in such a conversation. Behavioral addicts usually do not know why they did it, or they simply put their actions down to the belief that they are just naturally terrible people. But the question, "What were you feeling that led you to do that?" may lead addicts to look into their own motivations for their action, which will help them realize just a bit more about the connections between their feelings and their actions in the compulsive cycle.

As you question your loved one, then, ask about the feelings associated with the behavior rather than about the behavior itself. And as you listen, listen to the feelings being expressed more than to the descriptions of action. Listen to the tone of voice, the halt in speech, the struggle to bring out words that your loved one wishes desperately did not have to be spoken. Especially if a long-term addict comes to you with a confession, you may hear an account of actions that you hate. But if you listen, you will hear sorrow, and loss, and confusion, and grief, and loneliness—and these you can love. You do not need to think of "the right thing to say" in the midst of a discussion about the loved one's addiction. Victims of a compulsive cycle have locked themselves into their isolation and made it impervious to intruders from without. There is no right thing to say. You must wait for the addict's true feelings to leave their isolation slowly, timidly, like a frightened wild animal emerging from its burrow to take food from your hand. If you keep your hand extended by listening without any strong reactions, the addict will probably master the fear of self-disclosure and eventually make contact.

One reason we can make these bold assertions with some degree of confidence is that we saw the power of listening and calm questioning in the course of our research. On several occasions, we interviewed compulsive-cycle victims who had just been introduced to us by friends who knew about our project. We did not know these people before the interviews. We spoke very little to them about their problems. Since all we wanted to do was gather information, we simply let them talk, and when we became confused, we asked simple questions motivated by a desire to understand the person's subjective feelings, not by any personal investment in the problem. This very uncomplicated procedure often produced three reactions in the addicts we interviewed, which at first came as a complete surprise to us but later became so familiar we came to

231

expect them. First, the compulsive-cycle victims would almost invariably say to us, not too long into the interview, "I've never told anyone about this before." Second, the interview subjects seemed eager to get in touch with us again and talk more about their struggles with their addictions. Third, we would often receive the completely undeserved compliment, "You really understand me." Of course, we often felt we didn't understand these people at all—but *they* felt we did, and that was a chink in the wall that separated them from other people. And all that we had done was listen quietly and ask simple questions about the *feelings* that accompanied addictive behaviors!

Of course, you should not think that you have to develop a sort of therapist-patient relationship with the compulsive-cycle victim who needs your help. You have feelings, too, and if you never express them, you will begin to feel as isolated from the addict as the addict once felt from you. You are equals, partners in the enterprise of trying to break the compulsive cycle, and equals share things in relatively equal measures. There are two feeling steps on the compulsive cycle. The feelings of isolation can be demolished by quietly listening to the victim's feelings, but to replace feelings of self-hatred with feelings of self-esteem, the addict needs to learn that the two of you can communicate on the same level. There should be times, especially at the point of a confession, when all your attention must be on the behavioral addict's feelings. It is a terrible waste to cut off a confession in midstream by breaking into a tirade about your own feelings on the matter. But there will be other times, times when the addict has talked himself out and really wants to hear what you think, times when *you* will be the one to ask for a chance to talk over your feelings.

Breaking the compulsive cycle requires communication between the addict and the loved ones, and communication must be a two-way street if the addict is to feel the self-respect of dealing honorably and fairly with others.

The addict who has been listened to needs to hear what you feel about the problem. Any prevarication or dishonesty on your part will probably be sensed, and the addict will know that you are still somehow "different" from him because you seem to find it necessary to lie about your feelings toward him.

When you feel it is appropriate to bring up some of your own feelings, then, you should do so. But you must be extremely careful not to adopt an accusatory, self-pitying, or selfish tone in your discussion of your feelings. One helpful technique, mentioned frequently in Church magazine articles on family relations, is to make sure every sentence is phrased in terms of your own experience and feelings rather than your assessment of the addict by using the phrase "I feel . . . " whenever you are discussing your reactions to the compulsive cycle. Rather than saying, "You must not care at all about what this is doing to me," you might say, "This all makes me feel as though you must not care . . . " Instead of shouting, "How could you do this to me?" you might say, "I feel really hurt by what you've done." Be careful that you truly are expressing feelings, not judgments, in these sentences. Statements like, "I feel that you are a miserable clod," or "I feel that you just did this because you have no self-control" are not descriptions of your own emotional state; they are descriptions of judgments you are making because of your feelings. An interesting bit of trivia relating to this type of communication is that in the Japanese culture, where strong personal relationships are the norm and almost any kind of isolation is anathema, it is linguistically improper to describe someone else's feelings without qualifying the statement to show that you are in fact only surmising what the other person feels. For example, simply saying "He's tired" is incorrect in Japanese. The correct phrase would be translated, "I think he is tired." The Japanese thus have a linguistic reminder of something you must remember on your own: when you discuss your feelings about an addiction with the addict, don't claim to know all about the problem. Just describe the feelings in you as they arise. Christ expressed pain, anger, and grief during His mortal ministry, but He never attacked others for causing these painful feelings.

In summary, then, as a person who wishes to help a loved one break the compulsive cycle, you should be concentrating on the addict's feelings, not on his or her actions. You should try to help the addict change those feelings by, first, establishing a tradition of listening attentively to the sinner. If your loved one confesses unacceptable actions to you, do not react with harshness. Continue to listen as calmly as you can, asking questions about the addict's feelings in relation to the actions rather than about the actions themselves. Focus on gathering information, not on devising and advising strategies to change the compulsive-cycle victim. Then, after your loved one has had a full opportunity to tell you everything that is weighing on him or her, respond by honestly describing your own feelings, *always including your feelings of love toward the addict.* Continue to express your love to the victim by listening, sharing your feelings, and performing normal daily actions of friendship and service that will show the addict that you still value the relationship, that things are not unalterably changed, and that this is a problem the two of you will work on together. Avoid falling into judgmental attitudes or becoming a coaddict by lying to others about the problem. Above all, strive in every way to increase the level of your own righteousness, so that you will be able to find joy in living despite the difficulties and pains of helping a loved one overcome an addiction.

As you can see, breaking the compulsive cycle requires the cooperation of the addict and at least one other person. Neither party can accomplish it alone. Whereas the compulsive cycle necessarily drives people apart, breaking the cycle necessarily brings them together. Nor can the process be accomplished without turning to the Lord for help, and the same thing is true for mortal-and-God that is true for mortal-and-mortal: the compulsive cycle separates, and breaking the cycle reunites. You may be amazed to hear that the people we spoke with who had broken addictive cycles were profoundly grateful for the opportunity of wrestling with the terrible problem of addiction. Their loved ones and counselors shared this gratitude. The three case studies we have followed throughout this book may serve to illustrate some of the means by which real people broke the compulsive cycle. Here, as in the accounts of the actions of self-indulgence, we will record the subjects' experiences in their own words.

It's hard for me to pin down any one specific time when I "turned around" my obsession with eating and dieting. It was a lot of times, all strung out together, that brought about the real lasting change. I guess the thing that started me thinking in different ways about the problem was a conversation I had with my ballet teacher in college—or rather, a conversation she had with me. Apparently she had attended some kind of workshop on teaching dance, and they had had a panel on eating disorders, which are a problem for a lot of dancers. I guess she had started to suspect that I was having the same kind of trouble. One day she asked me to stay after class, and she just simply asked me if I thought a lot about my weight and if I dieted a lot. I was really hostile to her, but inside I remember being very relieved to have someone talking to me about this thing that took up so much of my time and energy. I felt as though she understood me. That teacher probably doesn't remember me at all—I'm sure she has no idea how grateful I still am to her. She suggested that I get in touch with a group on campus where people with eating disorders could go for help. I was very sullen about the whole thing, but I took the phone number she gave me.

I kept the number of the counseling group for several weeks. I don't know what kept me from calling right away—pride, maybe. I kept trying to convince myself that I didn't really have a problem. The thought of asking for help was really humiliating for me. Also, part of me was afraid that if I went for help, I would get it—you know, that I would stop bingeing and purging. I depended so much on the whole process emotionally, even though it was making me suicidally depressed, that I was afraid to give it up. Does that make sense? No, but it's the way I felt. Anyway, things finally got so bad that one night I picked up the phone and called the center. The woman on the other end was really sweet to me. She kept asking me questions and seemed really interested in my thoughts and experiences. I was amazed at how good it felt to talk to someone. I started to cry almost as soon as I got on the phone, which was really embarrassing for me because I had never let anybody see me cry, but she didn't seem to mind at all. She invited me to join in a sort of therapy group that met on campus one night a week.

I was kind of afraid to show up at this group, but I did it anyway. It was a real watershed experience for me. All of a sudden I had this whole group of people to talk to who would listen to me and who had similar feelings and problems. I remember one night, after I'd been going to the group for a few months, when I looked around at all those people and thought, "Why are you all sitting around talking about eating? Don't you ever do anything else? Nobody here is boring, but this obsession with food is! It's such a waste of interesting people!" That was a real shock to my system, because all of a sudden I could see that this thing I had thought was so important was really very trivial. When I could hear other people talking and see how their obsession was holding them back as people, I could apply those insights to myself. It was really good for me.

I was surprised to find that one of the student volunteer workers at the eating disorders group was a girl named Andrea who lived just down the hall from me in my dorm. At first I was horrified when I saw her at the center. I thought, Now she knows about me — she'll tell everybody! I expected her to treat me like a really sick person. But she didn't. She came up to me when she saw me, and gave me a big smile and said, "Oh, Ellen, I'm so glad you're here." I didn't even know she knew my name, let alone that she'd been worried about me! It seemed incredible. Andrea and I became good friends, because I knew that I didn't have to hide anything from her. She had a lot of other friends, and she started inviting me along when they went places together.

It made me feel strange, a little nervous, but warm, when I would spend an evening talking to other girls in the dorm instead of doing my homework. I always felt like saying no and staying away from people, because I'm really a very shy person, but the eating disorders group kept encouraging me to do things with other people, so I did. It got easier as time went on. When one of my dormmates heard that her father was having a cancer operation, I remember for the first time in a long, long time that I started spending more time thinking about someone else than I thought about myself. The rest of us in the dorm got together and had a bake sale to raise money so this girl could go home to help her mother with the younger kids while her father recovered. I realized after the sale was over that I had spent the whole day thinking about the people around me, instead of the food. For me, that was incredible.

Another event that stands out in my mind as a real turning point was the time I went to visit my grandparents after I had been involved with the therapy group for about six months. I'd gotten to the point before that where I kind of went to see my grandparents as a duty. I couldn't figure out why they would want me there, because it never even crossed my mind that someone might actually like me. I thought they were just taking advantage of their authority or something. I couldn't imagine any reason that anyone would want to associate with me if they weren't getting something out of it. But the experiences with the group and the friendships I was making apparently had made some kind of a dent in my thinking, because this time when I went to see my grandma and grandpa I approached them as friends, instead of as a diligent granddaughter. I remember them sitting there and asking me questions about myself, and I started to think, My gosh, they're actually interested! I was so startled by this idea that before I knew it I had mentioned the group where I was still going to talk about eating disorders. They started asking me questions about that. At first I was terribly embarrassed, but I couldn't just lie to them, so I told them I'd been having some problems with food and dieting and stuff. I expected them to just come unglued, but I'll never forget the expression on their faces. They looked *relieved!* Grandma said, "Oh, so that's what's been wrong, and you're getting help. We've been so worried."

Something about that moment somehow convinced me once and for all that these people actually cared about me. I can't really describe the feeling. It was like I had been locked inside a steel safe, and all of a sudden the steel just disintegrated into dust around me and I was outside on a sunny day for the first time in my life. It was the most amazing feeling. I started to bawl like a baby, which upset my grandparents a lot. They kept asking, "What's wrong? What did we say?" and I kept trying to answer, but I really couldn't tell them why I was crying. My grandpa came over and put his arms around me, and that really did it! I was crying so hard I could hardly breathe. I kept trying to tell them that there was nothing wrong, but all I could get out was, "No, it's all right, I'm happy, I'm happy!" Actually, I was just flooded with all kinds of emotions. I was sad for all the times I had been lonely and afraid. It wasn't like self-pity, because I was looking at the Ellen in the gray steel safe, who wasn't me anymore. It was sympathy for that person that was making me cry, because all of a sudden I understood that she never had to go through all that. I realized that there is so much happiness in letting yourself feel things for others that it makes up for the sadness you can also feel. I hadn't been sad for all those years. I had been trying not to feel *anything* rather than risk feeling anything bad. That's what the obsession with food really was. It was a way to keep myself from feeling. That day with my grandparents I realized how ironic that was, because not feeling is the worst feeling of all.

Even after that day, I still definitely had my problems. Getting over all my habits was a long, slow process. I remember the first time I felt really lonely and went to the convenience store, as I always did, to buy some ice cream to make myself feel better. I picked up the carton, and then suddenly I thought, "This is ridiculous. You're lonely, not hungry. Ice cream's not going to help, so think of something that will!" I put the carton back and walked home and helped a friend with her homework, and after that I never had as much of a compulsion to binge when I was under stress. I remember the first time I realized that I couldn't remember what I'd eaten that day and that I didn't care. I remember the day my sister said, "When did you stop measuring all your food?" and I couldn't remember that, either. This all happened over a period of several years. Gradually, my friends, school, church, and other activities just started to push my obsession out of the way.

The gospel was very important in this process. It showed me what was important in life and kept me working toward those things. I started studying the scriptures and realizing, for the first time, that God wasn't a terrible person who stands up in heaven demanding that you control your life. The feeling I got when I read the scriptures was the same as the "sunny day" feeling I first felt in my grandparents' living room. My favorite quotation from Joseph Smith is, "Happiness is the object and design of our existence; and will be the end thereof, if we pursue the path that leads to it." (*Teachings of the Prophet Joseph Smith,* sel. Joseph Fielding Smith [Salt Lake City: Deseret Book, 1938], p. 255.)

I really believe that. I've experienced it. I am experiencing it. If you can follow the first two commandments — loving God and loving human beings — I believe that you can get over almost any problem. Now, whenever I feel the things that used to make me binge or obsess about my weight, I think about those two commandments, and then I find some way that I can live by them. I suppose if I stopped doing that I could go back into my old ways, but honestly, it seems so unlikely I hardly ever even think about it. I've tried dealing with life by controlling everything through control of my own body, and it doesn't work, I promise. The first two commandments work. They have for me, and I believe they would for anybody.

I guess the way I got into drugs was so gradual I didn't really even know how deep in I was. I kept thinking I had it all under control. When my roommate found out about it and threatened to go to my parents, that was the first time I started to see it as a problem and realized I'd better stop. From that time on I was at least always trying to quit, you know; at least I didn't believe that taking drugs was cool or anything. So maybe that was the real turning point. But really, I didn't make much progress in my actual behavior. I felt guilty about the drugs, but when I felt like I needed them, it just didn't matter. So the problem went on for about two years after I'd already realized it was a bad thing. In fact, it got worse. It seemed like the harder

I tried to quit, the worse I felt; and the worse I felt, the harder it was to quit. But at least I was trying.

It was about a year after the incident with my roommate that I got a letter from my sister saying she was worried about my little brother Justin. He was only about nine at the time. She said he'd started hanging around with some tough older kids at his school and that one of the kids used to steal beer from his father and they'd drink it after school. Marcy—my sister—had seen my brother doing that. She said she didn't know whether or not to tell our parents because she knew how mad our dad would get. She'd tried to talk to Justin herself, but he wouldn't let her. I guess he'd become kind of different, really hostile and sarcastic compared to how he used to be. He wasn't doing great in school, the whole bit. And he was only nine! So this letter said that she wished I was home, because I would know what to do and Justin always copied me in everything, so she was sure I could talk some sense into him.

Boy, you can imagine how I felt! My first reaction was, I was just totally stunned by this. I mean, to me Justin was only a tiny little kid. I used to give him piggy-back rides. I couldn't believe that he could get into anything wrong like this. My next reaction was, I was angry. I wanted to go out and smash anything that might hurt my little brother. Because, you see, I knew what he was getting into. Maybe if I'd just been somebody who never did anything wrong myself, I would have thought it was just some kind of phase or something. I don't know—maybe that's all it was. But I knew what it could lead into. I was furious at those kids who gave Justin this beer and stuff. If I could have reached them right then, I probably would have pounded them flat. I was really mad. And then I started to feel responsible. Marcy was right—Justin always had copied me a lot. I started wondering if I had ever let him see me drinking or doing drugs or maybe let him smell something on my breath or been obviously high in front of him. I couldn't get that off my mind. I started feeling really sick about it. In the middle of this whole thing, I went to take whatever it was I was hooked on at the time. Then I realized something. I was setting an example for Justin even if he couldn't see me. It didn't matter that I'd kept everything a secret. It comes through no matter how well you hide it. Somehow, it comes through.

A couple of days later I decided I just had to quit. I'd been trying on my own for so long I knew I couldn't manage it by myself. For a while after I got Marcy's letter I thought, you know, that would give me enough motivation so that for sure I'd be able to quit. But right away I could see I was just kidding myself. In fact, I got really honest with myself for the first time in a long, long time. I used to sort of kick myself after I'd use the drugs, sort of to pay up for it or something. But this time was different. I felt like I didn't have time for playing around. I had to stop because of Justin as well as myself. So I just thought out logically, "How do I do this thing and make it work?" I knew the local hospital had a rehabilitation program, because my friends and I used to crack rude jokes about it all the time. So one day I just drove myself over to the hospital and went looking for this program. It was weird. I was kind of like a passenger in the car. A big part of me didn't want to go in for help, but the part that did took over and sort of carried the rest of me along with it.

I guess I expected a medal or something for turning myself in, but no one at the hospital treated me that way. They were nice, but they were real no-nonsense people, I can tell you! One of the first things they had us do was write down our whole history of drug and alcohol abuse. They wanted everything, including times we might have broken the law to get drugs or sell them or anything. I guess I should have been scared that they'd have me arrested, but for some reason that never even occurred to me. I'm a lousy writer, but I really got into this confession

242

thing. I wrote down every last detail—stayed up all night and didn't even notice it. I guess I'd really been wanting to tell someone about it for a long time.

We had to read our confessions in a group session. I thought that was going to be really humiliating, but it turned out other people had problems just as bad as mine, and I could see the counselors weren't acting like it was the end of the world, so pretty soon I relaxed. The whole thing was so different from talking about drugs with my friends. My friends and I used to always pretend like what we were doing was so cool, but down deep we knew we weren't doing the right thing. Here, everyone was being totally honest. It really felt good. I can't describe it. It was like fresh air or something. Just honesty. When I read my story everyone listened very quietly and asked a few questions at the end. I was still a little afraid somebody would get mad, but no one did. It was great! I felt mostly relieved. I remember I looked over at one of the counselors who I thought was the smartest one, and I said, "So, do you think I'm a hopeless case?" You know, kind of joking, but really serious. He just looked back at me and said, "Nope." It was the first happy thing I'd heard for a long time. That program got me through a lot.

One of the things we had to do was to try to make restitution for anything we'd done wrong because of our drug abuse. There are only so many things you *can* make restitution for, you know, but what we could, we were supposed to make up for. My big thing was, I had been stealing money from the store where I worked. Every day I would take the money for a few purchases without ringing up the sale into the cash register. Sometimes, if I needed money fast, I would actually take a little from the cash register and try to make it look like an adding mistake— you know, take exactly a hundred dollars so I could say I'd just hit the wrong key on the register or something. My boss was a nice man, and he suspected something, but he always gave me the benefit of the doubt. I really hated the thought of going in there and telling him I'd been taking his money. I mean, I *hated* it! That was the hardest thing I had to do. Before I went in, I worked out a plan where I would work full-time for part-time pay so I could pay him back the money I'd stolen. I didn't even know how much it was.

Mr. Treadwell was really mad at me, I can tell you. I thought he was going to hit me. He turned bright red when I told him about the money. Then he said, "I didn't think you were that kind of a young man, Bill." It just about killed me. I wanted to get mad back, but we'd talked about this whole thing in my group, and I knew I didn't have much right to feel angry at him just for feeling angry at me. I told Mr. Treadwell about my plan to pay him back. He looked at me for a long time and then he said, "Why should I trust you?" I thought about that for a little while, and then I said, "I guess you shouldn't." Boy, that was a real killer. I realized I had to rebuild my reputation from scratch. I started seeing how drugs could wreck your whole life. But Mr. Treadwell is really a good man, and he let me have one more chance. I slipped and took drugs a couple of times after that, but I never stole from him again. We're good friends now.

The other thing I did was to write to my parents and tell them what was going on. I had almost lost contact with them. I thought my father was going to kill me, but I figured he couldn't do it long distance. I told them I was worried about my little brother and said we needed to all work together so he wouldn't do what I'd done. My mother called me the day after she got the letter. I guess she and my dad had been up all night talking. She said, "You know we love you" and a bunch of other stuff. It was pretty sentimental. I started calling back regularly. I used to worry a lot about the expense of calling long distance, but my mom specifically said that I should call any time, so I took her up on it. I still felt a little guilty costing them so much, but they didn't seem to mind. My dad got on the phone and sort of talked about the weather for a minute, and then he started kind of choking up. It was awful, but at the same time I could see he really wasn't this big tower of strength like I'd always thought he was. He had a heart. That was a pretty great surprise to me, even though it hurt.

One of the things I realized was that when I was with my old group of friends they put a lot of pressure on me to take drugs. I know you're supposed to "Just Say No," but I'd already said yes so many times it was too hard for me to just stop. Once I got in those circumstances, the temptation was too much. So I stopped hanging out with them so much. I would stay home alone instead of going out with them on a Friday night. But then I started getting really lonely, and that made me want drugs again. I talked about that in my program, and everyone told me what I should do was make more friends who didn't take drugs. At first I said I didn't know anyone who didn't, but then I remembered that I'd been out on a blind double-date with some people from my ward, Jeff and Linda and Tammy. Tammy had been my date. They were really nice. I felt unbelievably stupid and awkward, like I was begging for somebody to be my friend, but I called Jeff and asked if we could double again. He said, "Sure." Then I asked him if he'd call Tammy for me again, and he said, "Call her yourself! I bet she felt bad you never got back in touch with her!" That was incredible to me, of course, but Jeff had me on the spot, so I promised I'd do it. I was so nervous! Here I was, this drug addict, calling up this nice Mormon girl to ask her out! I was so amazed when she said she'd like to go, I just about passed out.

We went out a couple of times, the four of us together, and then we started hanging around each other on campus and at church. Yes, I started going to church again. Mostly it was because Jeff and Linda, and of course Tammy, were there every Sunday. But it wasn't just a Sunday thing for them. They talked a lot about the Church even on dates, which I could hardly believe. They were very casual about it, but it came into the conversation quite a bit. I remember one night we were having some ice cream after a movie, and Jeff and Linda were talking about an exam they had taken in a chemistry class they had together. All of a sudden it hit me that they were talking about the Church in the same way my old friends and I used to talk about drugs! We used to talk about how much easier things were to understand when you had this "expanded consciousness" from drugs, and we'd talk about how we'd do better in school because of them, how we studied better, how we understood things faster. That was exactly what Jeff and Linda were saying about prayer getting them through their exams! They were kind of joking, but I could tell that underneath they really believed it.

After that I started kind of praying that I would get the help I needed to get by without drugs. I think it really helped. Tammy and I started dating pretty regularly, and after a while I started to feel like she was the one for me. I knew she was a strict Mormon, but that didn't worry me because I was pretty much off the drugs and I was going to church and praying. I was actually more religious than I'd ever been before. Finally I started hinting around about how the two of us might get married. One day, Tammy came out and said to me, "Look, Bill, you're twenty-one years old." I said, "Yeah, so what?" And she said, "If you're going to go on a mission, you'd better do it soon. The older you get, the harder it is to make the decision." I almost dropped dead. Tammy knew about my drug problem, and she knew I'd never even thought about a mission since I was nineteen. But every time I would try to talk to her about our future together, she would say, "Well, let's wait to see whether or not you decide to go on a mission."

One day I decided that since I really believed the

Church was true, because it was helping me get over my drug problem, I owed it to God to go. I realized that one of the reasons I didn't want to do a mission was that I knew once I went I wouldn't be able to get drugs or alcohol easily. Even though I was trying my best not to take anything—and doing better at it all the time—the thought of not being *able* to get drugs if I "needed" them was pretty scary. Also, I knew I would have to confess to the bishop, and I didn't want to do that. I still felt like no one had the right to judge me. I was pretty proud. But one morning, when I realized that I *should* go on a mission, I finally said this little prayer, sort of like, "Oh, all right, get off my back. I'll go, I'll go!" It was a really moving prayer, you can tell.

The funny thing was, from that time on there was a real difference in my life. All of a sudden I seemed to need a lot less Dutch courage to get through things. I felt like I was kind of being carried along. It was strange. I went to the bishop, and he put me on probation and asked me how long it would take me to earn the money for my mission. I said about six months. The bishop said, "Well, then, let's work together during that time and get you all ready to go!" It felt good. He was really nice, not at all like I expected.

Anyway, I worked for six months and kept going to my hospital group and dating Tammy and calling home and checking in with the bishop, and the drug problem just sort of lost its hold on me somehow. Best of all, that summer I went home and spent a week fishing with my dad and brothers in Idaho. We had the best time! I had kind of forgotten what a great time I used to have with my family, being outdoors and playing games and stuff. One day Justin and I went out on the lake in the boat and had a long talk about his problems at school and everything. I think he needed to talk. He's a good kid—he just needed someone to talk to him who could understand what he was going through. I love my family so much. I can't believe I ever let drugs get between me and them. After we got back from the fishing trip, Tammy drove up to meet my family. My mom liked her a lot. What shocked me was that one day I came into the kitchen and found my mom and Tammy talking about me and drugs! I still thought it had to be some big secret, even though everybody knew about it, but there they were, just talking about it like they were discussing canned peaches or something. Tammy is a real no-nonsense person, just like my mom. We all ended up talking, and I felt like I finally didn't have to hide anything from anyone anymore.

The six months went by, and I got my mission call to the Southern California Spanish-Speaking mission. If you'd told me two years ago that I could learn another language, I wouldn't have believed you. If you'd put me in a class and told me I had to learn Spanish in two months, I would have stoked myself up on so many drugs you would have had to prop me up with two-by-fours just to keep me from slithering off my chair. But my mission has been a great experience. I've learned even more about the power of prayer and service to others and what they can do in your life. I feel like my family and Tammy are proud of me, and I want to make them even prouder. I don't know whether or not I was right about not being able to get drugs on my mission, because I've never tried. I'm just too busy to think about it! Now I can see that the drugs were a substitute for the Spirit and for service to other people. And those things are free. You can't beat that.

There were a couple of people who really helped me change my life. One was a former mission companion who moved into my ward, and one was a woman who worked at my company. I had been inactive in the Church and very active in my "alternative life-style" for quite a while before Brian joined my ward and became elders quorum president. He saw my name on the ward records one day soon after he moved in, and he came out to see why I hadn't been at church. I was as rude to him as I could be, not because I didn't like him but because I did. I wanted him to be so offended that he would go away forever and not find out about me. It was like that with everyone I knew in the Church. The more I respected them, the harder I tried to drive them away. Most of the time it worked, but not with Brian. He asked to be assigned as my home teacher, and he used to come over regularly just to chat. He never pressured me about the Church. I used to feel terribly depressed after these visits. Brian's life seemed to be everything I kept telling myself I didn't need or want — he loved his Church callings, he had just married a beautiful woman, and they were planning a family. Some of the worst things I ever did, I did to block the feeling of loss and loneliness that would come over me when I thought about what it would be like to be Brian. I just thought there was no hope of that for me. I can't describe the anger and the hopelessness that made me feel.

After a couple of years, Brian was called to be the bishop of our ward. Another man was assigned to be my home teacher. The first time he showed up, one Saturday morning, he really gave me the hard sell about coming back to Church. He used these little cardboard puppets to act out a story about reactivation, and then he said, "Shall we go to sacrament meeting together tomorrow? I know you can do it. " The whole thing just made me furious — I felt he was being incredibly patronizing. So I said to this poor guy, calmly, "Did you know that I'm gay? And I have no intention of changing. Why don't you go home and make up a little story about that?" His reaction was just what I'd expected. He looked totally disgusted and sort of edged away from me as though he thought I might attack him or maybe it was contagious. He left immediately, and I never saw him again. In a way, I felt like I'd won some sort of victory, but at the same time it was an incredibly depressing experience. It was like I had finally proven for myself that the way I expected Church members to react to me was exactly the way they would react. I was like some sort of leper.

At six o'clock the next morning my doorbell buzzed, and there was Brian in his shirt and tie. I was angry at him for having woken me up, but he just breezed in and sat down on the couch. Apparently he'd called my home teacher to see how I was doing, and the home teacher told him what I'd said. He said, "Warren, is it true?" I felt so sick, because I really liked Brian, and I knew what a good man he was, and now he knew about me, and he would hate me, too. So I just got very cold toward him and said, "Yes. Now you can leave."

His reaction took me completely aback. His face kind of fell, and he said, "Oh, Warren, how awful for you!" Well, he might as well have pulled out a knife and stabbed me in the heart. I was all ready for whatever angry or disgusted thing he might say, but I just wasn't ready for sympathy. As if it wasn't bad enough that this guy now knew my worst secrets, I started to cry right in front of him! I thought I would die from embarrassment. I sat there and thought, Great, now he's going to think I cry all the time because I'm effeminate or something. But I couldn't stop. Brian just sat there with this sympathetic look on his face. Finally I kind of got hold of myself and said, "Look, there's nothing you can do about it. That's just the way I am, and that's that. So you see, that's why I can't come back to Church."

Once again, I expected that that would be the end of it, that he would just leave or get mad or something. Instead, he sat there for a long time, and then he said, "Warren, remember that lady we baptized in Frankfurt?" I knew right away what he was talking about. When we were companions, one day we had practically been pulled off a bus and over to a little house by some power we couldn't understand. It wasn't really physical, but it might as well have been. We both felt it. There was a lady living in the house whose son had just been killed in a train accident. She let us right in and told us that her dead son had appeared to her in a dream the night before and told her that he would send some people with the keys to seal the family together so that their separation would only be for a little while. She said her son told her what we looked like and promised that he would make sure we got there. It was the most incredible experience to baptize this woman and then her husband and daughters. Obviously, it really strengthened my testimony.

Anyway, there was Brian sitting in my apartment ten years later talking about this incident I'd almost forgotten. We started discussing other experiences we'd had on our missions where we'd really felt how true and good the gospel was. Without even realizing it, I started enjoying all this reminiscing. Brian is a fun person to talk to, and we'd always gotten along really well. We ended up talking for over an hour. I'm sure he missed some kind of bishopric meeting, but he never mentioned it. After we'd gone through all our experiences as companions, we talked about what happened the rest of our missions. Then we talked about the people we'd baptized. Brian had kept track of them, though I of course hadn't. It was good to hear news. I really cared about those people. So then, after we'd about talked ourselves out, Brian looked at me and said, "The Church is true, Elder White." I looked back at him and said, "I know." And I did. I always had. Then Brian said to me, "Well, how can you believe there's no place in it for you?" I started to cry again, of course. While we had been talking, I had felt all warm and relaxed again, the way I had on my mission, but as soon as he brought me back to the present, everything seemed to go wrong all over again. I knew he'd gotten to me, though, because

I got really mad. I usually have very good control over my temper, but I almost yelled at him. I told him he didn't understand me, he had no idea what he was talking about, he was a bigot, and he should get out of my sight. So he left. Since then I've often felt bad about my reaction that day, but Brian never said anything about it. I guess he understood the kind of strain I was feeling.

That night, I prayed for the first time in years. I really poured out my guts. I told God how lonely I was, how angry I was at Him for making me this way, and how confused everything seemed to be. I prayed for a long time, lying in bed. When I finally fell asleep, I had a very powerful dream. It wasn't like the lady in Frankfurt—no people from beyond the veil or anything. In the dream I was walking along a road with Brian, and there was this terrible earthquake going on. He was laughing and talking, and suddenly I said to him, "Brian, don't you see everything's falling down around us? It's awful! Everything's going to be destroyed!" He answered calmly, "Oh, yes, I know, but there's nothing to worry about. Look, there's your brother." And he pointed behind me. In the dream, I got very excited because I had always wanted a brother, and I had never had one. So I turned around to look where Brian was pointing. Then I woke up.

I don't remember what I saw in the dream when I turned around, but I seemed to remember seeing something, or somebody. All I know is that I woke up with the most overwhelming feeling of peace and love and happiness. I just lay there sort of floating around in this wonderful feeling. I was so happy I really thought I would die, and if I had died I don't think I would have minded. I also realized who the brother was. It wasn't just my brother, it was my Brother, with a capital B. All of a sudden I knew what I had to do, and I wasn't even worried about it. The only thing I wanted was to keep that feeling with me forever and ever. I called Brian and woke him up, and said, "Listen, I want to come in and confess." He said, "Warren, are you all right?" He told me later that I sounded so thrilled about this whole thing he thought I must be drunk. The happiness I felt in that dream stayed with me through almost everything that followed for about a year.

Well, we set up an appointment, and I went in to talk to him. He had me go to the stake president after I spoke with him. They considered having a Church disciplinary council but decided just to put me on probation. That really blew me away. I expected that I'd be right out on my ear if anyone ever heard about me. Instead of excommunicating me or even disfellowshipping me, they put me on a pretty strict probation—and then they called me to be a greeter at church, which meant I had to show up on Sundays. I couldn't believe it. Brian said frankly he couldn't believe it either, but that's what the Spirit told them to do. The response I got from the stake president and Brian gave me a lot of hope. They seemed to really sincerely want to work with me, they thought I could live the gospel and be happy, and they told me to call them anytime.

At first, I called them a lot more often than I wanted to. Old habits die hard, especially the kind of habits I'd gotten into. I can't believe they never gave up on me, considering how often I slipped. I hated having to disappoint them, but they always approached it as a learning experience. They'd say, "Well, try to figure out why you did it. Don't just beat yourself up for having done it." They were wonderful. The only time things really got bad was one time when I decided that I just couldn't bear to disappoint them again, so I started lying to them and saying I wasn't having any trouble with temptation. As soon as I started lying, that feeling I had received in the dream was suddenly gone. It was horrible. I felt as bad as I had ever felt. The more I lied, the more it was like I might as well go ahead and do whatever came to mind, since I'd have to confess eventually anyway. When I finally went back to the stake president, it was even harder than the first time I confessed. But that warm feeling came back to me after I'd done it, and I learned a lot from the experience. I learned that lying about my problem was the biggest thing that would stop me from changing.

One thing I realized was that I used to do things that had nothing to do with sexual temptation but that when I'd do them I'd always end up in the wrong places. I used to take long walks, and I'd always drift toward the wrong part of town. So I bought a bicycle and started riding it for exercise instead of taking walks. Another trouble spot was driving home from work at night—I almost always ended up driving to "dangerous" places I used to go to, "just to see what was happening." Once I got there, it was all over. I didn't have the willpower to resist at that point. I prayed hard for a way to solve this problem, and a short time later a woman at my office asked if I would like to carpool with her, because we lived in the same neighborhood. Alice wasn't a Latter-day Saint, but she was very religious, and we used to talk about our different beliefs on our daily commutes. She was—is—an amazing person. She seems so interested in other people, and she really listened to the things I said. We became very close friends.

One day, for no real reason, I told her about my struggle with homosexuality, my confusion about God's laws and homosexuality, and my efforts to repent. She seemed absorbed, listening to me go on and on about myself. She asked really thoughtful, intelligent questions and seemed to be thinking very hard about my answers. I remember when I told her about my past, she said, "Gee, that surprises me," but she didn't sound shocked at all. She hardly said anything that whole trip; she just listened to me talk. I felt as though a huge knot inside my chest was beginning to loosen up as I talked to her. I remember thinking something very childish as we went into the office building that day. I didn't say it, but I thought it. I thought, Alice is my

254

best friend. I felt like a six-year-old, thinking that, but I was so happy I didn't care.

Seeing how well Alice reacted to my problems and negative feelings got me started thinking about a lot of things. In my family, my father always used to try to protect my mother from any bad feelings or news. If there was something about a disaster in the paper, he would tuck it away somewhere that she wouldn't find it. He taught me to protect her from bad things. The problem with that was, I started thinking that women just couldn't handle knowing about everything that was going on inside me. It's hard to really feel love for someone if you're always trying to protect them from the bad things in yourself. But here was Alice, dealing with all my "bad things" without even batting an eye! One day I called my mother—she about dropped dead from surprise, because I had never called her in almost four years—and I actually started talking about the way Dad used to shield her from bad things. She started laughing and saying how silly he was, that he was so sweet always trying to make her world perfect, and that she avoided letting him know that she was aware of bad things because he got so worried about her. The whole thing really shook me up. This wasn't my mom! This was some kind of *real person!* It was a long time before I felt ready to tell my parents what I had been through in my life, but that day was the beginning of a real change in me and my whole family.

One day when we were driving to work, Alice told me her boyfriend had proposed to her and she had accepted. It came as a total shock to me. I had known she had a boyfriend, which was fine because I didn't "like" women anyway, right? I thought, This shouldn't bother me, but it did bother me. A lot. I thought, She can't marry him! She's *my* best friend! The emphasis was on the word *my*, and that came as another surprise to me. Suddenly I saw Alice and her fiancé—a husband and wife—as best friends.

I had always thought that marital relationships were like the relationships I had had with men: in other words, very physical. There might be other elements of the relationship, but the *primary* element was sexuality. Now all of a sudden I was seeing Alice and her fiancé adding sexuality as an element of their friendship, instead of the other way around. It was an incredible revelation to me, because suddenly I realized that I wanted that kind of relationship with Alice! All at once, everything I knew about life and love seemed to be fitting together in new ways. It was very bewildering to me, but very exciting.

Because she was my best friend, and I had always been completely honest with her, I told Alice all of it. She made it clear to me that she was sorry, that she was in love with her fiance. But—it was a very strange conversation—as we both sat there and talked on and on about what it felt like to be in love and I realized more and more that I had been in love with her since the day I had decided she was my best friend, we both kept congratulating me on how I was seeing love and intimacy in this new way. It took me quite a while to deal with having realized I had fallen in love with someone after she had gotten engaged to someone else, but from that conversation I got my first real glimpse of hope that I could be happy in this life. The progress toward breaking my old habits took a giant leap forward that day. Since then, I've found out that my hope was justified. I have been happy, very happy, and I have changed. I know not everyone thinks I *should* have changed, and a lot of my gay friends see me as a traitor and a fool for "knuckling under to the establishment," but my happiness means more to me than their approval. I owe a lot of that happiness to Brian and Alice, and I'll never be able to repay them.

Ellen, Bill, and Warren all "broke" their compulsive cycles by substituting useful and productive actions and

feelings for destructive ones at each step. Actions of progression replaced actions of self-indulgence. Feelings of
self-esteem arose from those actions and were reinforced
by people around them, replacing feelings of self-hatred
that had become habitual. Actions of self-disclosure were
substituted for actions of self-concealment, and feelings
of belonging emerged from a combination of this self-
disclosure and the supportive response of friends, family,
and Church leaders. In each case, the subjects claim that
the cycle of compulsive behavior was broken. But let us
reiterate that this was not an event, but a process. The
compulsive cycle is not simply obliterated by repentance:
it is transformed. Just as the error was a way of living, so
is its opposite. We call this way of living the joy cycle. The
next chapter will discuss the results that seem to follow
when the joy cycle replaces the compulsive cycle as the
central coordinating process of an individual's life.

8

THE JOY CYCLE

The central message of this book is that compulsive behavior can be overcome. And yet, we agree with the idea first taught by alcoholic recovery programs that behavioral addicts can never say they are cured. "Once an alcoholic, always an alcoholic" is an accurate phrase in the sense that if you are vulnerable to an addiction in the first place, you are likely to remain vulnerable, even if you never again indulge in the activity. But aren't these two claims—that one can both overcome an addiction and remain vulnerable to it—contradictory?

They might be, but only if you define breaking a compulsive pattern as *leaving* the cycle of addiction. We have come to think that this destructive cycle is simply the counterfeit of an opposite cycle that operates in the life of virtually every happy person. It is one small part of the many patterns and influences by which our behavior is oriented. In the case of compulsive actions, the cycle becomes central to the individual's attention for the same reason that fresh air becomes central to our attention when we are smothering in smoke. A healthy, natural, and normal aspect of life has been replaced by a substitute that is unhealthy, unnatural, and abnormal. The counterfeit, in all its many forms, is what we have been referring to as the compulsive cycle. The "real thing" we call the joy cycle.

In the four chapters that described our concept of compulsive behavior, we went through the compulsive cycle once. The image evoked by our account and the diagram in Chapter 1 suggest a two-dimensional circle, like a wheel spinning around and around in the same location. But that is not an accurate portrayal of an addictive pattern. To complete the picture we need a third dimension: to north, south, east, and west, we must add up and down. The shape that describes the cycle best is a coil, like a spiral staircase. Imagine such a staircase spiraling eternally up, into light and happiness, and eternally down, into darkness and misery. Now imagine that the staircase is within you, is in fact part of you, and your soul moves on it as time passes. There is no apparent way off the staircase, and no way to move far in any direction without going either up or down—but it is up to you to determine which of these directions you will go. The spiral staircase is both the compulsive cycle and the joy cycle. It is a powerful thing, and like all powerful things it can move human beings to either great good or great evil, depending on how we decide to use it.

To the people we spoke with who were in the midst of a compulsive cycle, this spiral staircase was a shortcut to pain, fear, and sadness. The more times they went around the cycle, the deeper they sank. When they felt they must soon hit bottom, they found that the staircase went on down, down beyond depths they had never dreamed could exist, and then down further, and on down again. The deeper they descended, the faster they went and the harder it seemed to be to move back upward, even for a short while. Whatever lies at the bottom of this twisting staircase, it must be impressively large, for it seems to exert a profound gravitational force. But we believe the bottom is not reachable in this life. As long as a mortal being is able to make choices, the staircase within that person goes on and on. And no matter how long the journey or how far down the steps, as long as mortality continues there is always the opportunity to turn around.

Almost every compulsive-cycle addict we watched over a five-year period turned around at some point, usually at many. There were moments, or days, or weeks in all of their lives when some act of service or duty replaced an addictive action and when the person felt a rise in self-esteem because of it. There were times when a whole or partial disclosure of self chipped away at feelings of isolation. Most of these changes of direction, which came by substituting proper actions and feelings for destructive substitutes, addressed only some of the steps of the joy cycle. Before a whole turn upward was completed, the victim had become discouraged or tempted or simply tired of fighting gravity, and the descent down the staircase was resumed with more hopelessness than ever.

But some individuals attacked the compulsive cycle at every step, and continued to do so. It was always a struggle at first, and there were usually occasions when these people slid backwards, sometimes for quite a while. But as soon as they firmly understood the ways in which they could use their patterns of feelings and actions to ascend, rather than descend, they were no longer hopeless. In fact, for these people the staircase became a blessing rather than a curse, as much a shortcut to happiness as it had been to sorrow. In these cases, as time passed and the person climbed higher and higher, there seemed to be a point at which each of them began to realize that heaven, as well as hell, has its gravitational force. Climbing out of the densest darkness, they struggled along by sheer strength, which failed frequently. As the blackness gave way to grayness, the force pulling them down began to weaken, and they climbed a little faster, turned back a bit less often. Terrible compulsions became irritating, leftover habits. As the recovering addicts ascended into brightness, they felt the gravity downward being balanced and overcome by an even more powerful force from above. The intermittent descents all but stopped, and the addiction was officially broken — as long as there was no turning back. At this point most recovering behavioral addicts told us they were content: they could handle their addictions, and they wanted nothing more out of life. But, as they continued to move up the spiral staircase simply to keep from falling down it, they discovered that the cycle, which they knew could take them down beyond their worst imaginings, could also take them up beyond their wildest hopes. After a while, even though the possibility of backsliding was still there as long as there was a chance to turn back, the upward pull of the joy they experienced made these individuals' terrible temptations seem puny and ridiculous. The higher these individuals went, the stronger they got.

A disproportionate amount of space has been allotted to the counterfeit of the joy cycle, as opposed to the joy cycle itself, for the same reason that a disproportionate amount of literature has been devoted to describing conflict as opposed to concord. Because happiness is our natural state, happiness speaks for itself. We understand it. Unhappiness, being foreign to our natures, takes some explanation — and we all feel the need to puzzle it out, because it hurts and worries at all of us every day of our lives. Certainly the victims of compulsive cycles ponder and dissect and dwell on their discontent, whether they think of their addiction as poison or ambrosia. The amazing thing about the several dozen active behavioral addicts we spoke with was the similarity we noticed between their personalities, despite the apparent diversity of their lifestyles. After some of these people had been climbing the joy cycle for some time, the comparison was reversed: their life-styles became quite similar, and their personalities became marvelously divergent and unique. But they no longer felt any need to explain or justify either their behavior or their experiences. They were too busy enjoying themselves. A miserable life is more interesting to analyze, but a happy life is more interesting to live. For that reason,

261

we will spend only a chapter describing the joy cycle and the events we saw in the lives of individuals who learned to live the joy cycle. We will discuss the steps of the joy cycle one by one, compare them with the corresponding steps on the compulsive cycle, and attempt to show how each step leads into the next.

FEELINGS OF BELONGING

One of the most deadly things about the feelings of isolation that seem to lie at the root of compulsive cycles is that they are rarely recognized for what they are. The core of isolation within an addict is usually hidden under layers upon layers of other stresses as discontents. In their hearts, although not intellectually, victims of compulsive cycles seem to believe that they are essentially unlovable or perhaps that there is no such thing as love. Their lack of trust in their ability to find a sense of complete belonging often makes the acknowledgment that love is what they want and need too painful to face. Feelings of isolation go right to the core of the individual. They are felt not as a conscious awareness of the desire to be loved but as an indescribable void within the addict's soul. Actions of self-indulgence and other distractions serve to block the void temporarily, but it always returns when the distraction is removed.

This void is not simply emptiness. It is emptiness that yearns to be filled. It is characterized by longing, wistfulness, half-formed hopes, and bittersweet echoes of something the individual typically cannot identify. It craves some kind of satiation, but being wordless, it does not name the thing it craves. The void of isolation will not allow addicts to rest. It goads them to constant action the way hunger drives an animal to forage. It lies at the heart of a relentless search for satisfaction. Such satisfaction is never realized, however, by any of the frantic measures an addict uses to feed the internal void. Repeated attempts to block the void by worldly means leave him "even as when an hungry man dreameth, and, behold, he eateth; but he awaketh, and his soul is empty." (Isaiah 29:8.)

When victims of compulsive cycles (or anyone else, for that matter) are finally willing to acknowledge and reveal their dependency, their vulnerability, and their need for others—in other words, their essential loneliness—they have taken the first step toward replacing feelings of isolation with feelings of belonging. If such individuals present themselves without reservation before both God and their loved ones on earth, revealing their imperfections, sorrows, and weaknesses as well as their strengths and successes, they become both more lovable and more able to feel loved. This love grows as it is expressed in word and deed to fellow human beings and to the Lord. As addicts allow themselves to reach out fully to others, rather than locking parts of their experience within themselves, the aching void paradoxically becomes an overflowing abundance of joy.

"Blessed are they which do hunger and thirst after righteousness: for they shall be filled," said Jesus in His Sermon on the Mount. (Matthew 5:6.) A corollary we add from our research is that they who hunger and thirst after anything but righteousness, which is a closeness and similarity to God, never achieve a satiety of the soul nor any lasting fulness at all. In the scriptures, the word *joy* very often appears in the same sentence with the words *full, filled,* or *fulness.* In many of these instances, the "fulness of joy" is mentioned after an individual has experienced terrible isolation and then put forth a tremendous effort to reach out to God and to the people around him. Alma the Younger and the sons of Mosiah, after experiencing "the darkest abyss," decided that they "could not bear that any human soul should perish" in a similar condition. (Mosiah 27:29; 28:3.) They therefore embarked on a very difficult mission to the Lamanites. When the five met again, after "suffering all manner of afflictions," Ammon, one of Mosiah's sons, discussed his feelings in connection with his experiences: "Behold, my joy is full, yea, my heart is brim with joy, and I will rejoice in my God. . . . Yea, I say unto you, there never were men that had so great a reason to rejoice as we, since the world began." (Alma 26:11, 35.) The joy felt by Ammon and his friends sent them back into the mission field, where they performed some of the most impressive works and preached some of the greatest sermons ever recorded. They had reached out of the isolation of sin to serve others, and they seemed to gain more capacity to be filled with joy as they poured themselves out to God and his children in a seemingly endless flood of love.

One reason Alma and the sons of Mosiah were so able to experience great joy was precisely that they had "suffered much anguish of soul because of their iniquities, suffering much and fearing that they should be cast off forever."(Mosiah 28:4.) The fact that "there is an opposition in all things" (2 Nephi 2:11) creates a special form of justice in that it ensures that those who have felt deep anguish also possess the capacity to feel great rejoicing. The horror of the abyss carves out more space for joy, as long as the response to the yearning is not to pull things into one's self but to give things of the self away to others. No one ever encountered more isolation and darkness than Christ did at His atonement, and His response to that moment of the greatest possible need was to give the greatest possible gift. Like Ammon, who met again with his friend and brothers after a painful and difficult attempt to save souls, Christ spent the period immediately after His mortal mission meeting and talking with people who loved Him. The account of Christ's visit to the righteous part of the Nephites after the great destruction that accompanied His crucifixion hints that Jesus was affected by His experiences much as Alma and the sons of Mosiah were affected by theirs. After Christ told the Nephites about Himself and His doctrine, "it came to pass that Jesus spake unto them, and bade them arise.

"And they arose from the earth, and he said unto them: Blessed are ye because of your faith. And now behold, my joy is full.

"And when he had said these words, he wept, and the multitude bare record of it, and he took their little children, one by one, and blessed them, and prayed unto the Father for them.

"And when he had done this he wept again." (3 Nephi 17:19–22.)

The joy that emanated through and from the Lord, almost immediately after His having been so utterly forsaken during the time He had borne our sins, was "full" to the point that it overflowed in prayer, in expressions of tenderness and service to His people, and in tears. What a marvelously human reaction! The magnitude of this experience may be beyond our understanding, but the pattern is something familiar to everyone we interviewed who had finally felt belonging after being lost in isolation.

Feelings of belonging, like feelings of isolation, are not an end in themselves. Where isolation is a vacuum that must be filled, creating a constant hungering restlessness in those who experience it, the sensation of knowing one is loved and lovable is a spring of living water that seems to overflow in a spontaneous desire to do good. It creates an impulse, but the impulse is to give rather than to take, to supply rather than to consume. People who feel deeply alone know that they must somehow search out and obtain something—anything—to ease a limitless emptiness. People who feel deeply loved know that they must somehow—anyhow—find ways to share a limitless abundance. Thus both feelings of belonging and their opposite, feelings of isolation, are irresistible motivations to action. To someone who is locked in a compulsive cycle, the response will be an action of self-indulgence. But the only productive way to respond to either of these feelings is by performing some action of progression. That is how both Ammon and Jesus reacted to the isolation inherent in being mortal and individual, and that is how they came to feel the belonging inherent in godhood and at-one-ment. That joy is indescribable. "Behold," exulted Ammon, "I cannot say the smallest part which I feel." (Alma 26:16.) The people we interviewed who had replaced compulsive cycles with the joy cycle expressed the same inability to describe the joy that came from feelings of belonging. Instead of trying to talk about them, they allowed these feelings to be expressed in actions of progression.

ACTIONS OF PROGRESSION

In general we may say that actions of progression are any actions that increase both our capacity to love and our capacity to understand. You can imagine as many of them as you like, for the possibilities are as infinite as eternity and will continue to multiply throughout it. Unlike actions of self-indulgence, which are limited to a few predictable behaviors, actions of progression are as plentiful, beautiful, varied, and fresh as snowflakes in winter. In some cases they involve activities that can become mere empty pleasures when undertaken with the wrong motivation or in the wrong circumstances—sexual behavior is a good example. But actions of progression have some sure characteristics by which they can always be distinguished from actions of self-indulgence.

One of these characteristics is that someone engaged in mere actions of self-indulgence may be excited for a time but eventually becomes jaded and bored with the activity. The addict needs more and more of an addictive behavior to feel the same amount of interest, excitement, or pleasure, and the rest of life also becomes steadily less interesting as the person goes through the compulsive cycle again and again. Actions of progression, by contrast, enrich the remainder of life rather than dull it — and they are never boring. They may be difficult, tiring, even daunting, but they are *never* boring. Such actions are expressions of love and understanding, and through them love and understanding become concrete. That is not a boring process. It is gloriously interesting and exciting. To use the technical term, it is *fun.*

To some, *fun* is a word that has been corrupted to indicate mere pleasure. To others the concept is denigrated as childish — a sophisticated ennui is much more acceptable in worldly circles than a constant ebullition of fun. It is easy for Satan to convince vulnerable people that actions of progression are childish, because they are in fact thoroughly childlike. Children and young animals spend hours and hours in activities we call play, which we generally distinguish from serious, adult activities. Psychologists have long understood that this kind of play is not merely idle time-killing. It is an absolutely essential experience by which children learn how to interpret and manage information about themselves, each other, and the physical world. Through it, they gain in capacity to both love and understand. Play is the essence of an action of progression.

This capacity does not disappear with maturity. We all know people whose actions seem to spring spontaneously from within, instead of being imposed from without. These are the people who love their jobs, who are still curious about the world around them, who are delighted by both new and familiar experiences and people. We remember being called outside, as children, by parents who were entranced by a sunset and wanted us to see it. We remember being instructed by fathers and mothers in skills our parents seemed to love for their own sakes — skills that often touched on the work each of our fathers did to support our families. Both of us remember listening in on discussions during which our parents brought up and de-

267

bated new concepts about a wide variety of people, things, and events. Since both of us were later children in large families, our parents were not particularly young at the time. Apparently, however, they were not mature enough to have learned that grown-ups should not have fun.

Although actions of progression are fun, they are not silly or giddy. Watch a two-year-old playing contentedly, and you will see an expression on his face of great intensity, of complete absorption, not of glee. Watch an artist who is painting from the heart, or a parent playing with a new baby, or a mathematician working on a really intriguing theory, or two friends deeply engrossed in conversation, and you will see this same expression. The person involved in a true action of progression will continue for hours in complete absorption and identification with the process. Time seems to disappear, as does any conscious awareness that the actor is separate from the action. The dancer, to paraphrase Shelley, becomes the dance. Compared to the engrossing experience of love and understanding that accompanies actions of progression, the forced oblivion to one's own needs that arises from an action of self-indulgence is positively repugnant. The difference between these two types of action becomes even more glaring when we move to the next step on the joy cycle, the feelings that arise as a consequence of actions of progression.

FEELINGS OF SELF-ESTEEM

The feelings of self-hatred that follow the commission of a compulsive behavior are based on two comparisons: the comparison between what behavioral addicts aspire to do and what they have actually done, and the comparison between what they think other people are like and what they think they themselves are like. Both these comparisons involve, on the one hand, an intensive evaluation of the self. They draw the compulsive-cycle victim inward, to personal behaviors and personal emotions. On the other hand, these feelings also involve the addict in a scrutiny of others that is both inaccurate and incomplete. At this step on the compulsive cycle, victims dwell both on their own shortcomings and on their own images of other people's superiority. They exaggerate both the hatred they feel for themselves and the reaction others would have to them if the truth about the addiction were made public. Both these behaviors are equally self-centered, because in one case compulsive-cycle victims dwell on themselves, and in the other case they dwell on what other people think of them. The last thing a behavioral addict suffering feelings of self-hatred thinks about is what other people are actually doing and feeling. Furthermore, the pain created by self-hatred forces more attention to be focused on the self, which is experiencing the suffering.

Actions of progression, because they teach us how to deal with situations and beings other than ourselves, and because they allow us to lose ourselves in what we are doing, lead to feelings that are the opposite of self-hatred. We have called these feelings "self-esteem" because there is no more convenient brief term. What we mean by this term, however, is not self-congratulation but complete forgetfulness of self, utter lack of self-consciousness. The greatest works of mankind are accomplished when human beings, feeling the love of their Father in Heaven, express the joy of that love through actions of progression. The quality of objects and relationships produced by that process approach divine creations as nearly as human creations can, because they are made by the same methods employed by our Heavenly Father and in partnership with Him. The creation of a child or a family are examples of such projects, as are the creation of beautiful or useful objects and ideas.

Once the work has been done, the worker is understandably filled with pride at the quality of the product. But self-esteem is not the pride in which we decide that we are superior beings for having created good works. It is joy at being part of the awesome power of creation, which runs from God through mortal beings to the world around us. When Alma and the sons of Mosiah discussed their feelings about their missions, Ammon's brother Aaron expressed some concern that Ammon was falling into the error of focusing pride on his own actions and virtues. "Ammon," he said, "I fear that thy joy doth carry thee away into boasting." To this Ammon replied with one of the best descriptions of true self-esteem in the scriptures. "I do not boast in my own strength," he said, "nor in my own wisdom. . . . Yea, I know that I am nothing; as to my strength I am weak; therefore I will not boast of myself, but I will boast of my God, for in his strength I can do all things." (Alma 26:11–12.)

The submission to God that allows His light to shine in and through us, the love of others that makes us care for them as for ourselves, and the actions that spill over from the joy of belonging constitute the foundation of great and impressive works. But that foundation is by its very nature opposed to self-consciousness. It is a complete relinquishment of self that constitutes true self-love.

Christ taught that "whosoever will save his life shall lose it: but whosoever will lose his life for my sake, the same shall save it." (Luke 9:24.) "Losing" one's life and "saving " one's life can of course mean accepting death or seeking the continuation of mortality, but that is not necessarily what Jesus meant. For most of us, it seems more probable that He was using the terms *losing* and *saving* as we usually use them about objects. When we save something, we concentrate on it. We make sure we know what it is and where it is at all times. When we lose something, on the other hand, we lose track of it—simply forget where it is or even that it exists. The feeling of losing one's self in this way follows a true action of progression just as naturally as self-hatred follows a compulsive action of self-indulgence. It is the feeling we get from watching a child discover the perfect gift for which we searched and spent but which the child believes is from Santa. It is something that has nothing to do with how impressive we are, how we compare to others, or what those others must think of us. In true self-esteem, the self is forgotten. We can acknowledge our accomplishments and our worth without arrogance, because our whole attention is on the change for good that our actions of progression have wrought on the world and the people around us. Jesus proclaimed Himself "the way, the truth, and the life" because this was a matter-of-fact description of His role in the plan of salvation, not because it emphasized His own importance. (John 14:6.) In terms of his essential worth, Christ not only compares Himself but identifies Himself with the lowliest human beings. "Verily, I say unto you, Inasmuch as ye have done it unto one of the least of these my brethren, ye have done it unto me." (Matthew 25:40.) The feelings that follow actions of progression, which spring from feelings of belonging, tend to bring us closer to this divine attitude toward ourselves.

One consequence of this loss of self-consciousness that we call self-esteem is that the person who experiences it becomes much less concerned with protecting the reputation of the self by hiding its nature. For those who have no reason to feel guilty, open, unguarded communication of personal doings and feelings is not a threatening prospect. For the compulsive-cycle victim who has learned to follow the joy cycle, it means that telling the truth about past experiences or present struggles is much less frightening. There is no need to dwell on one's sins, but if discussing them will help accomplish good for someone else — if such a discussion can be seen as an action of progression stemming from feelings of love — the former addict who has learned to follow the joy cycle will gladly volunteer information about past experiences and feelings. For everyone, self-esteem combined with the need to trust and communicate with others tends to lead directly to the fourth step on the joy cycle, actions of self-disclosure.

ACTIONS OF SELF-DISCLOSURE

The deceptions meant to hide a behavioral addict's compulsion tended to have two devastating side effects. One was the tendency for "little" lies to spread out like the proverbial tangled web, so that finally the addicts found themselves lying about virtually every aspect of both inner life and behavior. The other was the truly terrifying capacity for this web of deception to interfere with the addicts' ability to recognize the truth and to lead the individuals toward eventual rejection of the discerning power of the light of Christ, which distinguishes truth from falsehood. Whereas actions of self-indulgence put compulsive-cycle addicts within the reach of misery, lies were the chains that bound them to it.

The two effects we saw resulting from self-concealment are reversed by full and honest self-disclosure. Just as addicts grow less capable of telling the truth about themselves with every turn down the compulsive cycle, so they becomes less capable of hiding themselves with every trip around the joy cycle. The first confession is usually very difficult. The more socially proscribed the addiction, the more difficult the confession. The second confession is somewhat easier. A common experience we saw in the lives of every person we met who broke an addiction was a phase following the initial confession when the recovering addict "told all" to a variety of close friends, relatives, Church leaders, and professional counselors, and spent a good deal of time with them revealing secrets.

Several factors seemed to be working in this broad dissemination of information. First of all, anyone who has been through a very traumatic experience is likely to discuss it and recount it a great deal during the initial aftermath. This process of communication allows the person to share the burden of grief and shock and to "touch base" with others as a person who has been changed by suffering. The experience of addiction, and the terrible effects compulsive behavior may have on the inner and outer life of the sufferer, constitute this kind of severe trauma. Second, recovering behavioral addicts we spoke with were astonished and thrilled by the discovery that others could accept them as they really were, and they wanted to make sure that they had this full acceptance from many of the people they cared about. Third, the recovering addicts knew that they simply could not overcome their compulsive behavior alone, and they wanted to enlist the largest support group possible to assist them. Finally, the act of telling the truth, which to habitually honest people seems as natural as blinking, was a source of great spiritual and emotional refreshment to the people we knew who had just broken compulsive cycles.

All of these factors working together had the interesting effect of making it eventually quite difficult for the former addict to lie well, if at all. One woman, a former bulimic, told us how for a year after her marriage she had lived in a typical network of deceptions, so that not even her husband knew how she spent her time. Finally, she broke away from her addictive bingeing by confessing her problems to her husband and enlisting his help in understanding herself and controlling her activity. After three years of climbing up the joy cycle, she told us, she was unable to lie convincingly to him even when she wanted to. "Now he always knows what I'm getting him for Christmas," she told us ruefully.

As the habit of lying is replaced by the habit of honesty, the addict's ability to trust others and interact with them freely increases. This, of course, accentuates feelings of belonging and love and sends the individual up another turn of the joy cycle, motivating more useful actions, which

273

further reduce self-consciousness and lead to even greater self-disclosure. Lying, which is a step down the compulsive cycle, begins to interfere with the feelings of belonging that bring so much joy. Eventually, the recovering addict learns to avoid any deceptive action whatsoever — perhaps more carefully than people who have not experienced the agony of living a lie.

When honest behavior returns to a recovering behavioral addict's life, so does the spirit of discernment. To tell the truth, one must know the truth, so in an effort to be as truthful as possible, the people who are climbing the joy cycle begin to think very carefully about what they inwardly know to be true. What exactly were the actions they performed? What actually were their motivations? The search for truth, for truth is recognized by the light of Christ, leads former addicts down paths of self-understanding they may never have known. "What did I actually do last night?" a recovering addict asks, quietly, without railing or rationalizing. The answer will be simple, factual, not decorated with exaggerations or excuses. "I got drunk," the answer might be, or "I committed a moral transgression." "Why did I do it?" is the next question the addict may ask, especially if others who know the truth are asking this question, too. "What were the feelings that led me to commit this error?" "Where did those feelings come from?" "What were the experiences that shaped my response to the feelings?" The answers may not be obvious. It may take a great deal of thought to come up with the truth, but when the truth is reached, the seeker recognizes it immediately. The whole process of psychotherapy is nothing more than a search for the truth about the links between our motivations and the events that create and arise from them. We met people who had changed their lives both with and without the help of people trained to ferret out these truths. But we never met anyone who overcame a compulsive cycle without complete honesty.

Even if a person is thoroughly honest about experiences and misconceptions that might have led to undesirable behaviors, however, it is impossible to draw correct motivations and behaviors simply from an accurate account of error. Once victims of compulsive cycles begin to understand the reasons that they have linked a search for joy with self-defeating actions, there is still a need for the great truths of the gospel. These provide us with a real understanding of our natures, our destination, our purpose, and the meaning of our lives. For instance, understanding that one or both of your parents set a bad example for you can help you stop from following in their footsteps, but it is not nearly so powerful as having a good example to emulate. Knowing that the steering wheel turns your car is essential to reaching your destination, but a map or a guide is also necessary to determining your direction if you have never been taught the way to reach your goal. Likewise, realizing the truth about the workings and reasons for your own behavior is an important step in gaining control over your actions, but the truth to be found in the scriptures is a map, and people who live the gospel are guides who can accompany you and show you the way to happiness.

That good people make good guides is especially true of people who have had experiences similar to our own. In the case of the behavioral addict, that truth is particularly relevant. A person who has never been involved in such habitual sins might tell the addict who is asking for directions, "Mister, you can't get there from where you are." That is certainly one message our interview subjects got from many people around them. But if there is someone who has traveled the road from the addict's situation to a condition of happiness, that person is able to point the way, describe the hazards, and encourage the traveler with real hope. Besides the common emphasis on submission to God that we found in organizations such as Alcoholics Anonymous, we were also impressed by the use of "buddy" systems, wherein a person just trying to break out of an addiction is paired with a person who has been climbing the joy cycle for some time. Often, as the members of these groups became stronger and stronger in their resistance to temptation, their role in the organization was more as a counselor than as a patient. The way they counseled was simply a constant self-disclosure of truths about their experiences (including mistakes), their feelings, and the things they had learned about themselves, other people, and their Father in Heaven (whatever name they used for Him).

Ironically, then, the behavioral addicts who had once lived in constant dread of being found out, now took every suitable opportunity to tell the truth about their addictions. Protecting themselves from social censure by actions of self-concealment had meant that these people were constantly on guard, that they rarely revealed their true feelings, and that they were pushed deeper into isolation. Self-disclosure, on the other hand, also created a form of protection—it is impossible to blackmail someone with information that is already public. At the same time, this sharing of personal thoughts and feelings, especially when done as a service to others, extended the former compulsive-cycle victims out beyond the abyss of loneliness and shame they had lived in while they kept themselves secret from others. Actions of self-disclosure create the opportunity for a free exchange of love and support from the addict to others and vice versa. The feelings that result from this interchange are the feelings of belonging, which continue the joy cycle. Every time a former addict honestly confides in others, whether in a full-blown confession or in simple sharing of thoughts and feelings unrelated to the addictive behavior, the force that would drag the person down the compulsive cycle grows weaker, the climb up the joy cycle becomes easier, and the light of happiness and understanding shines brighter.

The people we interviewed who had learned to live

the joy cycle testified that just as deception had wrapped them in chains, so they had also come to understand the meaning of the Lord's words, "and ye shall know the truth, and the truth shall make you free." (John 8:32.) As part of their newly adopted pattern of substituting honesty and altruism for deception and selfishness, they allowed us to probe into their experiences and feelings, both past and present, in the belief that someone who might be suffering as they had suffered could find helpful insight in their experiences. While we must repeat the caution that a victim of the compulsive cycle will always face opportunities to choose which way to move—up or down the cycle, and hence is never irrevocably cured—a brief look at how Ellen, Bill, and Warren deal with these choices daily shows that they now have a clearer understanding of the dynamics at work in their behavior, and therefore are far more likely to make good choices than bad ones. All of these people now agree that if they had been able to see themselves as they are today at a time when they despaired of ever obtaining happiness, the image would have given them hope. Now, their greatest hope is that their stories may give hope to others.

It is six o'clock on Saturday morning. Ellen forces her eyes open, then closes them again in an attempt to recapture a dream she can't remember but which feels unfinished. Her husband's side of the bed is empty. Ellen rolls over onto his pillow and feels the warmth still lingering where his head rested. The pillowcase smells faintly of aftershave and shampoo and the bakery where Matt is working nights to put himself through school. Ellen smiles and pulls the blankets up around her chin.

Matt's voice comes faintly through the wall from the other room of their tiny apartment. "Honey, where are the baby wipes?" Ellen sighs. So much for sleeping in. She yawns, climbs out of bed, and wraps herself in Matt's bathrobe. "I think they're on the changing table," she calls back.

"But I *looked* there, and they're *not!*"

Ellen opens the door of the bedroom and laughs. Sally, all eight pounds, three ounces of her, appears to have cornered her father somewhere near her bassinet. Matt stands helplessly holding Sally's tiny pink body above the grim contents of a very dirty diaper, looking for some way to clean up the mess without putting his daughter down. Sally wiggles her infinitesimal fingers, struggles to free her legs from hands that seem as big as she is, and lets out a frustrated wail. Matt looks up at Ellen, eyes wide with desperation.

"Help!" he croaks. "What do I do now?"

"An interesting question," says Ellen, leaning against the doorway. "Let's look at it strategically. How could foresight, planning, and decision making have prevented this problem? Now that the worst has happened, what measures might you take to solve the problem? Let's consider—"

"*Ellen!*" Matt explodes. "Come *on!*"

She laughs again, locates the baby wipes under the bassinet, spreads out a fresh diaper, and takes Sally from her distraught husband.

"And where were you when I had the same problem last Thursday?" she queries as she rediapers the baby. "I ended up putting her down on a towel. Had to do an extra load of laundry right then, just because I changed a diaper." She snaps up Sally's pink sleepsuit. Sally fusses, making noises like an asthmatic puppy. Ellen brushes the baby's cheek with her finger, and Sally opens her tiny mouth and turns her head toward her mother's hand.

"I thought women had some kind of diapering instinct," says Matt, going to the kitchen and opening the refrigerator. "I'm hungry," he adds thoughtfully, deliberating between English muffins and whole wheat toast.

"So's she," Ellen comments. She settles into their second-hand easy chair, and Sally nestles up to her, eager to be fed. A wave of absolute contentment sweeps through Ellen, tired though she is, as she watches Sally's wrinkled red face and feels the incredible, almost fuzzy softness of the baby's skin.

"I'm afraid none of it's instinctive," she says to Matt. "None of it. I mean, how would you feel if your body suddenly grew a new person and popped it out into the air? That's exactly how I feel. I mean, I know it happens to other people, but it seems totally bizarre that it should have happened to me." Sally's little body begins to relax in her arms. "But I'm glad it did," she adds.

Matt comes back from the kitchen with a glass of orange juice for Ellen. He stops in front of the easy chair and looks down at his wife and daughter. A smile spreads slowly across his face and stays there. Ellen looks up at him.

"What?" she queries. "What are you grinning at?"

"Oh, just you," he says.

"What about me?"

"You're beautiful."

Ellen blushes. "Are you kidding?" she says. "I haven't slept for two weeks, I have postpartum acne, my hair is falling out, and I've still got fifteen pounds to lose. I look like a walrus with beach rot."

Matt keeps smiling. "You're beautiful," he repeats.

"I'm not just going to snap back to normal, if that's what you're thinking," Ellen warns him. "I don't know what the old bod's going to do now, but I don't diet anymore, and I've already ruined my arches from too much jogging. So you'd better get used to me as is." She glances up at Matt to see how he will respond to this challenge. He puts the orange juice down next to the easy chair and sits down on the couch.

"Have some juice," he says. A copy of yesterday's paper sits folded up on the armrest, waiting for one or the other of them to find time to read it. More and more news-papers have gone unread since Sally was born. Matt un-folds the paper and glances at the headlines. The back page faces Ellen with a montage of slender models parad-ing their pencil-thin legs and torsos through a forest of fur coats. Ellen transfers Sally's sleepy little form to her other arm and sighs.

"Wouldn't you rather have a wife who looked like that?" she asks Matt, wistfully.

"What? Who?" says Matt, poking his head out from behind the paper.

"Like those women on the back," she says.

He looks at the ads. "Hmm," he says. "They look wimpy."

"If you really believe that," says Ellen, "You're a very rare man. Most guys would drop someone like me in a flash for someone like that."

Matt stares at her. "I do believe you're really worried about this," he says.

"Well, I am," Ellen replies. "I spent a long time think-ing thin was the answer to everything, and fat was the way to get dumped in the nearest home for the terminally unacceptable. I know we've talked about this stuff a million times, but it's different now. It's not easy for me to get used to the way my body's changed, so why should I expect you to get used to it?"

Matt puts down the paper and stares thoughtfully at the ceiling. "How shall I put this?" he ponders. "Let's see . . . if you ever weigh a great deal more than I do, one of us will definitely need to do something about it." He smiles brightly at Ellen. "How's that?" he asks cheerfully, and then, rather crestfallen, "Not good enough?"

Ellen shakes her head. "It could happen," she says grimly.

Matt laughs. "I don't think so," he says. "I really don't."

"Okay," says Ellen, "But suppose it did? I know it's dumb, but I still worry sometimes."

Matt stands up and walks over to the easy chair. He crouches down next to it, his elbows resting on his thighs so that his head comes just level with Ellen's. "Now, look," he says softly. Sally has fallen soundly asleep. Her small fists have drooped slowly open against the folds of her mother's robe, and the fine, fair curls of her eyelashes flutter occasionally, moved by some unfathomable newborn dream.

"Look," says Matt again. "Look what you made."

"We did," Ellen corrects him.

"All right, we. But at this point, you've got to admit you've done most of the work. My body didn't give her a place to grow. I didn't go through all those changes. You know how I felt when she was born?"

"Glad it wasn't you lying there squealing like a stuck pig?" Ellen guesses.

Matt shakes his head. "Just the opposite. I was so jealous. I was more jealous than I've ever been in my life."

"You're crazy," says Ellen.

"Am I?" he asks, looking at her.

Slowly, Ellen shakes her head. "No."

"Now, do you think I would walk away from the part I have in this thing just because you don't have hip bones that show, like those women in their wonderful fur coats?"

"No," she says again, and smiles.

Matt breathes a sigh of relief and stands up. "Well, then it's settled—again," he says. "How long is it going to take me to convince you once and for all?"

"Well, let's see," says Ellen. "At a rate of one conversation a week, maybe three years? Four? Of course, if you're willing to go to two a week, we could arrange the express treatment plan. You'd have Christmases off."

"The heck I would," says Matt cheerfully. He picks up

281

the paper and pores over the headlines, running a hand across the stubble on his chin.

Ellen puts Sally up against her shoulder in case the baby needs to burp. The aura of warmth around Sally's diminutive body and the feeling of her downy hair against Ellen's cheek seem to breathe sleep into the atmosphere like the poppies in *The Wizard of Oz*. Ellen closes her eyes and wonders if, when she falls asleep again, she will finish last night's interrupted dream.

It seems mildly insane to Bill that he and his companion should be visiting a lower-income housing development at seven o'clock on a Saturday morning. Not a soul seems to be awake yet, not even the bums sprawled out next to heat gratings under scraps of cloth and newspaper. Elder Thorsen told Bill that he scheduled their meeting with Mrs. Ramirez early on Saturday because she said that was the only time she was sure her husband would be home, but Bill is more impressed by the thought that his companion has arranged their visit to this area for a time when two squeaky-clean young Idahoans are least likely to get heckled, robbed, or pounded to a pulp. He envies the English-speaking elders in his mission, who not only escape having to struggle with Spanish but also get to avoid the scarier parts of town.

At least Elder Thorsen seems to know his way around. He picks his way through the garbage that festoons the inner courtyard between two tall apartment buildings and enters one of the buildings through a cracked glass door. He presses the call button by the Ramirezes' name. The answer comes back immediately, and Bill understands, "Who is it?"

Elder Thorsen replies, and Bill's attention drifts away from the incomprehensible conversation that follows. Looking back through the door, he can see three small children in bare feet chasing a flock of pudgy and reluctant pigeons away from their morning snack of breadcrumbs. The children's faces are like sunlight glancing off dark water. There is a loud buzz, and Elder Thorsen pulls open the inner entry door.

The Ramirez family live on the third floor. In the elevator, Elder Thorsen explains what is going on. "She didn't want to let us in," he says. "She was nice, but she said she'd changed her mind about meeting with us. I asked her if we couldn't just come in for a minute, and she said okay, but I want you to know we shouldn't push it, all right?"

"All right," says Bill. As if he can "push" anything! He was one of the worst Spanish students in the whole MTC, and they hadn't even told him that the Spanish they spoke in there had nothing to do with the Spanish people speak out here. If I get the urge to "push" the Ramirezes, Bill thinks to himself, I'm going to have to do it with my hands.

Mrs. Ramirez is a short woman with dusty-looking black hair that is greying at the roots and eyes the color of chestnuts. As she opens the door to her apartment, Bill and his companion smell beans and tortillas cooking inside. She invites them in with a weariness Bill understands much more clearly than her words. Elder Thorsen says something polite, and the missionaries sit down on the family's shabby sofa. Bill can feel the sharp point of a loose spring against the back of his thigh, and he shifts uncomfortably in his seat. Mrs. Ramirez excuses herself and goes into the tiny kitchen. Bill looks around the apartment. It is tidy but very poor, much of the furniture patched together from old pieces collected, Bill suspects, from trash dumps or alleys. A gaudy picture of Christ wearing his crown of thorns decorates one wall, and a crucifix hangs on another.

A small boy bursts around the corner by Bill's elbow and dashes across the room. He stops, turns around, and aims an imaginary gun at the missionaries. Bill throws his hands into the air in mock terror, and the boy advances menacingly. Bill tries to remember the word for *Help!* but all he can conjure up is the word for *mercy* from the discussions, and he's not sure that is a word Spanish-speaking children use in play. He settles for an exaggerated show of fear, which elicits a hearty laugh from the boy. Bill smiles back.

Mrs. Ramirez emerges from the kitchen and apologizes for keeping them waiting. She goes on: Bill gathers that she is very busy and that things are not going well for her family. Mr. Ramirez is nowhere to be seen. Elder Thorsen responds with a question. What is wrong? Is there anything the missionaries can do to help? Mrs. Ramirez seems flustered by the inquiry. No, it is nothing, it is nothing, she says, only . . . and here Bill loses the thread again. It is frustrating, because there is obviously something very wrong. Mrs. Ramirez's voice is breaking, and tears are appearing at the corners of her tired eyes. Elder Thorsen is nodding sympathetically and responding with a few simple questions, which Bill can understand.

"How old is Romulo?" Elder Thorsen asks.

"Fifteen," says Mrs. Ramirez. "He is a good boy." And then she begins to cry in earnest. She puts her head down and hurries back to the kitchen, mumbling an apology under her breath. The little boy crouches under a ramshackle table, quiet and very small.

"What is going *on* here?" Bill whispers to his companion. "Did somebody die or something?"

"No," Elder Thorsen whispers back. "Their son Romulo got arrested. Her husband is downtown right now trying to bail him out. I guess he's into drugs, and he's been stealing to get them. His parents just found out. I was going to try to set up an appointment, but I think we should probably come back some other time, huh?"

Bill's answer is cut short by Mrs. Ramirez's return from the kitchen. Her eyes are bloodshot but determinedly dry. Elder Thorsen begins a polite departure, apologizing for the interruption and hinting about coming back when it is more convenient. Bill has heard this all before, so he understands it fairly well, but he has no time to think about it. His brain is searching furiously for the words he needs to say, and his heart races with adrenaline as he prepares to say it.

"Mrs. Ramirez!" he blurts out suddenly. Elder Thorsen stops in midsentence and turns toward him, a shocked expression on his face. The woman and the little boy stare at Bill, as if they had been convinced up to now that he was deaf and dumb. Bill feels his face go cold and then flaming hot.

"Mrs. Ramirez," he says again, his voice softer this time but still a bit too loud. "I know the message we bring can save your son." Bill blushes even more violently at the overdramatic effect of the word *save*, but he can't for the life of him remember how to say *help* in Spanish. All he can do is repeat himself: "I know that the message we bring can save your son. I know this. I know this." A peculiar sensation begins to spread from the center of Bill's chest out to his arms and legs and then to the very tips of his fingers and toes. He feels as though every hair on his head is charged with some kind of strange electricity that burns but does not hurt.

Mrs. Ramirez looks at him for a long moment, her sad chestnut eyes gazing into his young blue ones. Elder Thorsen glances from her face to Bill's and back again in complete bewilderment. Bill gazes back, remembering every easy excuse for a fix he ever made, every evasion of his morals to get some drug or other, every terrible moment when he finally refused to give in to temptation, and every surge of his strength when he began to overcome the temptation, one day at a time. He tries to tell her all of it, every bit, with the simple, inarticulate openness of his eyes.

"I believe you," she says quietly.

The little boy under the table smiles. Elder Thorsen

breaks in with fluent, excited Spanish, setting up an appointment for next week, when Mr. Ramirez might be home, and even possibly Romulo himself. Mrs. Ramirez is no longer crying. There is a trace of hope in her expression that was not there when she had opened the door — only a slight trace, but definite. Bill looks around the room again, at the broken furnishings and dilapidated decor, and wonders what this peculiar electricity is and why it does not go away. The room, for all its shabbiness, suddenly seems as clear and valuable as daylight. He is somehow aware of the carefulness of the work that went into the patched lamps and chairs, and the picture of Christ in its cheap, gaudy frame seems to symbolize every noble spirit trapped in impoverished surroundings. Bill realizes with a jolt that this feeling is exactly the sensation which he almost, but never quite, achieved with drugs. The clarity, the vividness, the ideas that go beyond what he would have thought on his own, are all the elusive experiences drugs had let him think he glimpsed but which they had never truly shown him.

Bill looks at the little boy, who peeks back at him from under the table and smiles shyly. The guilelessness of that smile brings an unexpected catch to Bill's throat, and he looks away quickly, embarrassed. He feels as though he will burst with the strange, thrilling feeling that vibrates more and more powerfully through his body. He wonders if Elder Thorsen would be willing to spend more time in this area, with these people who need so much. One thing Bill knows for sure: however he does it, he will come back.

The door buzzer sounds at exactly seven-thirty. Warren hops over to it, pulling on one running shoe with his left hand and trying not to spill the glass of orange juice he holds in his right. The buzzer goes off again as he finally gets the shoe in place and presses the intercom control.

"Yo!" he says into the microphone. "That you, Brian?"

"What's keeping you?" Brian's voice crackles through the intercom.

"I'm coming, I'm coming," Warren drains his orange juice in one long gulp, grimaces at his unshaved reflection in the mirror by the door, makes sure he has his keys before he leaves the apartment. He runs down the stairs, four at a time, knowing that Brian will already be warmed up and ready for a good fast pace.

Brian is waiting in the lobby, jogging in place to keep from cooling off. "My, don't we look chipper this morning," he says with a grin as Warren bursts through the stairwell door.

"I've decided to give up showering and shaving for Lent," says Warren.

"And combing your hair, and tying your shoes?" Brian inquires.

"All right, so I slept in. I was working late at the crisis center last night. A twelve-year-old runaway called looking for help. I was there until three." The two of them trot out of Warren's apartment building into the glow of the California morning. The dew on the grass sparkles like liquid crystal, and the air is soft with humidity.

"Nice day," says Brian as they fall into a steady, even pace.

"Yeah," Warren agrees. "Let's go around the park."

Brian nods. "So," he says, "How are things going?"

"Great," Warren answers, "How about you?"

"Pretty good. Better since Karen isn't so sick anymore."

"Oh, yeah?" Warren responds. "How's she doing?"

"Well, she seems fine. A little emotional, maybe. Sleeps a lot, accuses me of being a worm because it's my baby too but I don't have to deal with it, that sort of stuff. But at least she's not nauseated. Seems like all I've done for the last three months is bring her Popsicles and help her stop crying after she's seen sentimental telephone commercials on TV. Her obstetrician told her she gets sicker

287

than most women. But the first three months are supposed to be the worst."

Warren shakes his head incredulously. "The whole thing is so wild. Karen's usually such a mellow person. I just can't imagine what it would be like to have all those things going on in your body."

"Yeah," Brian agrees. "Sometimes it's frustrating, you know. I try to understand, but I just have no real idea what she's going through."

"As Dr. Freud said," Warren switches to German, "Women—what do they *want?*"

"You figure that one out, and I'll pay for your lecture tour myself," says Brian.

They run on, easing into a comfortable rhythm, their feet making soft thuds in unison on the moist earth.

"Speaking of women," says Brian, "how are things going with Kim?"

Warren wipes the sweat off his forehead. "Okay, I guess," he responds.

"Just okay? Things cooling off a bit between you two?"

Warren shakes his head. "Oh, no, nothing like that. She still really wants to get married."

"So, what's the trouble? Don't you want to marry her?"

Warren laughs ruefully. "Are you kidding? You'd better believe I want to marry her. Do you know what I would give to be where you are? Do you know what I would give to go home and see her every night, and have to bring her Popsicles because she's having our baby? Seriously, Brian, you don't know how lucky you are."

"Oh, I do too. I just complain because that's what my dad always did—it's a family tradition," Brian answers. "But I still don't understand. If Kim wants to marry you and you want to marry her, what's the problem?" He glances sharply at Warren. "Is it the same old stuff?" he asks. "Are you having problems again?"

Warren shakes his head. He looks at Brian and smiles,

288

his uncombed hair bouncing into his eyes with each step. "You know," he says, "I'm doing better with that stuff than I ever thought I would. It's amazing. It's like I just don't have time for it anymore. I spend all my time at work or at the crisis center or trying to talk things out with Kim. No, I really haven't had a problem since that time I talked to you about it a year ago. It's been getting easier all the time."

"That's terrific!" said Brian. "So that's not the problem with Kim, then?"

"Well," Warren's voice is uneasy. "I guess it is, sort of. Yes, it definitely is."

"So, what do you mean? Is Kim worried about it?" Brian asks.

"Well, I guess so. I mean, yes, of course she worries about it. But mostly it's me that gets worried. I mean, I'm doing all right at the moment, but what if something happens in the future? What if I can't trust myself? I can't let Kim take a risk like that."

"It's her risk, Warren," says Brian softly.

"Maybe. I guess so," says Warren. "But it's my responsibility. How can I do something like that to her, anyway, saddling her with a husband who has problems like mine?"

"What does she think about it?" Brian asks.

"She says we'll just keep working on it. Right when we first started getting serious, she said she wouldn't marry me if I was the only one who told her I could get over it, but she would marry me if the Lord told her I could."

"And did He?" says Brian casually.

"She says so," answers Warren. "I don't know. We're going to fast and pray about it over the weekend and go to the temple, and then we're going to ask President Stott what he thinks."

"So, as I understand this thing," says Brian, plucking

a leaf from a shrub as they pass by and snapping it in two with his fingers, "Kim loves you, you love her, you haven't been having problems being a good boy, and she feels good about marrying you, but you don't trust yourself. Are those the facts?"

Warren sighs. "Yeah, I guess so." He shakes his head. "You know, Bri, women really are unbelievable. They never do what you expect. Half the time Kim acts like you could knock her over with a feather. You know, she absolutely dissolves watching *Bambi* or something."

"Yeah, I know," says Brian with a smile.

"And yet, you get to an issue that you think would just about crumble anybody, and she's so strong and so brave. She knows about me, Brian. I mean, I've told her *everything*. And she cries, and gets hurt, and I feel like I've lost her, and then she says, 'Let's get married. We can work on this together.' I keep reading her stories about women who married gay men and then the guy runs off with some man and leaves the woman with twenty-seven children. It scares *me* to death, I'll tell you. But she just looks at me and says that if Heavenly Father wants us married, He'll help us make it work. I don't know, Brian. I think she's crazy."

Brian knits his brows thoughtfully and grabs another leaf from a eucalyptus tree, bringing a shower of dew down on Warren's head.

They move up behind an elderly couple in matching sky-blue sweatsuits, who move politely out of the jogging path to let the young men go by.

"So you don't think you're a good risk?" Brian asks when they are out of the couple's earshot.

Warren glares at him. "No," he says succinctly. "Do you?"

"Well, Warren, I don't know," Brian muses. "In a lot of ways I wouldn't have thought so. Anyway, Heavenly Father apparently does."

290

"Does what?" says Warren.

"Thinks you're a good risk."

"What's that supposed to mean?" Warren scowls at the toes of his shoes, which thud on the ground beneath him in steady alternation.

"Elder White, I feel impressed to call you as the second counselor in the bishopric of our ward," says Brian. He runs on, several strides, before he notices that Warren is no longer running with him. He stops and looks behind him. Warren is standing in the grass of the park as though he has been planted there. His mouth is open, and his expression is perfectly blank.

"Come off it, Brian," he says as his friend turns around and walks back to where he is standing.

"It's 'Bishop' to you," answers Brian, wiping the sweat from his forehead.

"Come off it, Bishop," says Warren. "Quit rubbing it in. You know God doesn't want someone like me in that kind of position. What if I ever, you know, did something? What if someone found out?"

"Do you intend to, you know, do something?" asks Brian, looking into Warren's eyes.

"No," Warren answers. "I don't. But how can I be sure? You know what I am."

"No," says Brian, "I know what you've done. I don't know what you are. Your problem is, you won't let what you really are get away from what you've done."

"What do you think I really am?" asks Warren. He is still standing in the same spot, arms at his sides.

Brian looks over at a group of teenage boys shooting baskets in the court at the center of the park. "I think you're a great player who got drafted by the wrong team for a while," he says. "But you're back on the Lord's side now, and I think he wants you off the bench."

Warren doesn't answer for a while. The morning sun shines through the new green of the eucalyptus leaves,

291

and the dew settles through the mesh of his running shoes. He studies the shoes with his eyes. Finally he murmurs, almost to himself, "I just don't see how, I just don't see how . . . after everything I've done. . . . "

"Warren, look at me," says Brian. Warren looks, reluctantly, eyes up but head still bent.

"What makes you think you're so special, Warren?" says Brian. "What makes you think that your sin is so all-fired special that you can never get away from it? What about me? You think I don't have sins? You think I don't struggle? You think I didn't cry myself to sleep every night for a week after they called me to be bishop? It's a tough life, Warren, but it's tough for all of us. Of course you're not going to be perfect all your life. Of course it's not absolutely safe. That's what it's all about, buddy, that's what we're here for. You mess up, you repent. I mess up, I repent. And you better believe we're both going to keep messing up. I, for one, intend to keep repenting, too. Now, what about you?"

Warren's eyes are fixed on his friend's face. "I intend to keep repenting, too," he whispers.

"Then, Warren, don't you understand? Once you've repented of something, it's *gone*. Kaput. Zilch. A big goose egg. God doesn't even remember it anymore, so what gives you the right to?"

Warren swallows. He looks intently at Brian from behind the thick black hair that has fallen over his eyes. "Do you really think so?" he asks. "Even for me?"

Brian folds his arms across his chest and looks up at the open sky. "Warren," he says. "I would never have thought of you to fill this calling. I had the same problem you do—I thought you were somehow different or incapable of it or something. I didn't even realize I felt that way, but I did. I admit it. But when I was praying about who I should call to replace Brother Harker, I knew you were the one. I never really understood you until then, Warren.

I didn't understand that really, when it all comes down to it, you're just like me. Better, in some ways."

Warren gives a snort of disbelief.

"No, Warren," says Brian earnestly. "I mean it. What I felt when that impression came about you was that I don't have the faintest idea what it's like to repent like you've repented. I mean I sort of go along in life, trying to be a good guy and hoping I'm doing all right, but you've gone right down into your guts and hauled them all up and given them away. You may make mistakes again, buddy, but right now you're as clean as a newborn baby."

Warren says nothing. His head drops and he looks at his shoes, digging one foot into the damp clay of the park lawn.

"Okay?" Brian queries.

He stoops a little to look at Warren's face under the shock of hair. "Okay?" He sounds concerned. Warren's face under the stubble of his beard is very pale, and a bright red spot burns in the center of each cheek.

Warren nods, begins to lift his head, then turns downward abruptly and wipes a hand across his face. Brian coughs and looks away.

"Well, listen, Warren," he says, "I'm going to let you have some time alone to think about this calling, okay? I'm going to go on ahead—I'll get back to you tomorrow. I know it's a lot of responsibility, but I think you'll find it's the right thing. All right?"

Warren nods wordlessly, head down. Brian looks at him for a moment, then says, "Okay. I'll see you." He gives Warren a pat on the shoulder and jogs away.

Warren tries to call to Brian, to raise a hand and beckon him back, but he seems unable to lift either his voice or his arm. He wants to tell Brian that he knows it's the right thing, that he will accept the calling. He wants to tell him that he knows now it could all happen, all the things he had long ago given up wanting, all the things his patriarch had promised him before his hope had died. He wants to tell Brian about the wife and family in that blessing, the ones he'd decided belonged to someone else. He wants to tell him about the place in the celestial kingdom. But he can't. He stands in the park, not moving, his eyes leaking foolishly, as helpless as a chick with its feathers still wet from the egg.

The old couple in their matching jogging clothes shuffle past, looking curiously at Warren out of the corners of their eyes, but he is too limp to move. All strength and solidity seem to have utterly left him: he feels as though he might be blown away by the breeze in the wake of their sky-blue sweatsuits. But although all his own strength seems to have disappeared, Warren is aware of nothing but strength. Up and down, around and through, over and under him, he feels the swelling of a strength so powerful he knows that it could flick him across the park and into the street. It could scatter him into shreds without a ripple of effort; it could crush him like a blade of grass. The strength seeps into every fiber of Warren's body, every muscle, every molecule, leaving him as weak as a soggy paper doll and as strong as sunlight. He wonders why he is not afraid, but at the moment he cannot even remember what fear is like. The strength that runs through him seems to remove all fear, all sadness, all recrimination, loneliness, and pain from his existence. It bathes him in gentleness. Warren feels himself relaxing, feels the sweat and tears mingling on his cheeks and running down his neck. He lifts his head and looks at the sky, and the morning beams down on him as brightly as though there had never been a night.

Tomorrow, Ellen Schor Marshall, Bill Stewart, and Warren White will each put on Sunday clothes and go to a sacrament meeting in a Latter-day Saint meetinghouse. One of them may be in your chapel, sitting next to you, sharing your hymnbook and passing you the sacrament tray. They will not look different from thousands of other Church members all over the world, and in many ways they will not be different. Like Ellen, Bill, and Warren, every one of us, no matter how well meaning, well brought up, or well disciplined, is born into this difficult mortal estate with the objectives of gaining a body and being tested. Every one of us started life as confused by our new identities as if we had been shoved into a moving vehicle with no idea how the thing should be driven. Each of us has made mistakes in learning to control the natural man and bring this nature into harmony with spiritual development. During the trial-and-error process of learning to match our human natures to our divine potential, each of us has repented and been forgiven, by God, ourselves, and others, of countless blunders large and small. All of us must continue to learn and repent, virtually without ceasing, if we are to achieve lasting happiness. In these respects, any one of us might be Ellen Schor Marshall, Bill Stewart, or Warren White.

In some ways, however, those who have been the victims of compulsive cycles are different from those who have not. Perhaps the distinction lies in their having been born or raised in such a way that they are susceptible to behavioral addictions, or perhaps it is simply that they, more than many others, realize the universal vulnerability of the human condition. Certainly, the Ellens, Bills, and Warrens we see around us differ from many others in having been the battlefields upon which all-out, unseen wars have been fought between good and evil, between heaven and hell, between the divine and demonic aspects of their own personalities. Because of this, there may be some other differences between these recovering addicts and the other Latter-day Saints who sit around them tomorrow in church. Ellen, Bill, or Warren may be more quick than the rest of the congregation to see the profundity in simple words or the shallowness of glib ones. They may be more alert to the struggles behind their neighbors' smiles or the questions behind their confidence. They may be less likely than some to pass over the sacrament as a habitual ritual while they wait for an interesting speaker. To them, the words, "that they do always remember him," "that they may always have his spirit to be with them," will never be matter-of-fact or casual, for they remember, more clearly than most of their fellow Latter-day Saints, a time when they had all but forgotten Him and assumed that His spirit could never be with them again. They have a little more than the usual understanding of the pain He suffered for them at His atonement. As we interviewed such people, we heard echoes of that pain in their voices and saw it in their eyes. There are no words to describe it. But language is even more inadequate to convey the fulness of joy that followed when a victim of compulsive behavior turned back and learned to live according to a process of happiness. To all those who still struggle with addictive behaviors, who live through a continual descent with nothing but a hopeless hope that their longings will ever be known or satisfied, we join the recovering addicts we interviewed in pointing out the invitation of Jesus Christ:

"Come unto me, all ye that labour and are heavy laden, and I will give you rest.

"Take my yoke upon you, and learn of me; for I am meek and lowly in heart: and ye shall find rest unto your souls.

"For my yoke is easy, and my burden is light." (Matthew 11:28–30.)

We fervently believe that the atonement of the Redeemer is the way, the *only* way, by which the vicious cycle of compulsive behavior can be broken. Through Christ, the lives of behavioral addicts can be salvaged and made better than they were before. We know that this is true: we have seen it happen. During the research and writing of this book, we have seen many hearts broken and many spirits bruised by addiction. The ravages of the compulsive cycle reach into the lives not only of its victims but of all those who care for them. But there is no reason to abandon hope. In providing those affected by addictions with broken hearts and contrite spirits, Satan has put his own plan at great risk, for these things are all our Heavenly Father asks of us in exchange for eternal life. If we offer our hearts, souls, and lives to Him in complete humility, the Lord will help us turn back from the forces which pull us downward. He will forgive us, help us, and teach us to climb upward with our own strength until we are able to return and live with Him in the place we came from, the place we yearn for, the place where finally, after all our wanderings, we can know that we are home.

INDEX

Abstinence, simple, is not enough, 19

Actions: of self-indulgence, 17, 66, 70; of self-concealment, 18; abstaining from, is not enough, 19; of progression, 20, 266–68; of self-disclosure, 20–21; influence of, on spirit, 66–67; work in concert with spiritual commitments, 68–69; all, have consequences, 69–70; pleasurable, 71–72; restricting, will not break compulsive cycle, 184–88; are less important than motivations, 186; loved ones' tendency to focus on, 193–94; changing, addicts should concentrate on, 199–200; impelled by feelings of belonging, 265–66

Addictions. *See* Behavioral addictions

Adultery: woman taken in, 104; rationalization about, 135

Alcoholics Anonymous, 211, 275

Alcoholism: genetic factors in, 39; bishop counsels man involved in, 105–7; changing public awareness of, 213

Alma, 33–34, 36, 39, 263

Ammon, 264, 270

Anger, effective expression of, 224–25

Appearances, deceptively calm, 11

Atonement: recovery depends on gift of, 23–24; reconciled mercy and justice, 36–37

Ballet teacher, 145–48

Behavioral addictions: common patterns in, 11, 17, 40, 61–62, 72–73, 92–94; Latter-day Saints involved in, 12–14; understanding, assists in controlling, 14–15, 38–39; common types of, 17, 72; life-style of deception accompanying, 18, 132; spiritual component in, 22–23; roots of, 33; genetic predisposition toward, 39–40; feelings leading toward, 43; transmitting, to others, 75–76; exclusionary nature of, 76; planning a routine around, 76–78; willingness to talk about, 79–80; "anesthetizing" effects of,

95–96; devastating effects of labeling in, 101–3; concealing, 128–30; likened to foggy cliff, 172–78; misunderstanding, as "simple" sins, 192; connecting, to need for joy, 197–98; changing public awareness of, 213–14; vulnerability to, 258

Belonging, feelings of, 21, 262–66

Bingeing, 83–84, 108

Bodies, physical: importance of, in plan of salvation, 27–28, 29, 66–67; religious view of, as inherently sinful, 28; perfect, stereotyped conceptions of, 28–29; rationalist view of, as all-important, 29–30; and spirits are not mutually exclusive, 31; "natural" inclinations of, 33–34; capacity of, to feel physical pleasure, 71–72

Bridle, imagery of, 39

Candy, stealing, illustration of, 189–92

Carnal mind, inclinations of, 33–34

Change: power for, rests in individual, 218–19

Childbirth, woman gains new insights through, 222

Church disciplinary councils: purpose of, 207–8; actions taken by, may vary, 213

Church leaders, confessing to, 21, 213; difficulty of, 206–8

Coaddiction, 137, 223

College: as typical breeding ground of compulsive cycle, 13

Communication: as equals, 232–34

Compulsive cycles: common patterns in, 11, 40, 61, 72–73, 92–94; susceptibility to, in young adulthood, 13, 40, 128; broken versus unbroken, 13–14, 170; four steps of, 15–19; diagram of, 16; physical nature of, 26; roots of, 33; genetic predisposition toward, 39–40; type of, based on early experiences, 46; likened to leprosy, 95, 100; division of, along two axes, 15–16, 193; "unlearning" erroneous ideas about, 195; downward spiral of, 259. See also Compulsive cycle, breaking

Compulsive cycle, breaking: involves substituting constructive steps, 15, 19–22, 197, 201–2; requires participation of others, 19–21, 198, 234; requires power of God, 23, 211; possibility of, 170–71, 196; is process, not single event, 181–84, 217, 260; abandoning hope of, 182–83; cannot be done by force, 184–88, 218–19; hampered by misdirected focus, 192–94; first step in, is understanding cycle, 196–97; requires simultaneous attack on all four steps, 197, 260; is process of substitution, not of abstinence, 201–2; importance of confession in, 205–8, 212; summary of procedures in, 209–10, 234; seeking help in, 210–13; potential for growth in, 217–

18; draws people together, 234–35; requires complete honesty, 273–74; "buddy system" in, 275–76; great happiness resulting from, 296–97

Conditioning, 33

Confession, 20–21; importance of, in overcoming addiction, 205–8, 212; risk involved in, 212; effective manner of, 214–15; possible reactions to, 215–16; treating, with empathy, 227–28; in rehabilitation program, 242–43; becomes easier with practice, 272

Consequences: all actions have, 69–70; failure to recognize, 85; difficulties in facing up to, 180

Control: loss of, 78–79, 84–85, 92, 96–97; through force, 186–87; surrendering, to God, 188, 211–12

Counterfeits for joy, 65–66, 70, 92–93, 178, 258

Creation, joy of, 269–70

Cynicism, 144

Debating, 133

Deception: life-style of, accompanying addiction, 18, 131–32; and coaddiction, 223; spreading web of, 272. *See also* Lying

Despair. *See* Self–hatred, feelings of

Dieting, obsession with, 81–82

Discernment: losing power of, 143–45; regaining abilities of, 274

Dorm mates, confusion of,

over addict's behavior, 150–53

Double identity of behavioral addicts, 18, 110–12

Down's syndrome child, 25–26

Drug addict: case study of, 4–7, 50–53, 85–88, 113–18, 153–59, 240–48, 282–86; family plans special vacation for, 138–39

Drugs: "enhancing" life through, 74–75; regulating life with, 86–87

Eating disorder, case study of, 1–4, 47–50, 80–85, 108–13, 145–53, 235–40, 277–82

Employer, confusion of, over addict's behavior, 153–55

Family members, confusion of, over addicts' behavior, 148–50, 157–59, 161–65. *See also* Loved ones

Feelings: of isolation, 15, 17, 18–19, 43–46; of self-hatred, 17–18; of belonging, 21, 262–66; of self-esteem, 21, 268–72; leading toward behavioral addiction, 43; addicts' tendency to focus on, 193; cannot be changed without changing actions, 199; loved ones should focus on, 227, 230–31; being honest but nonaccusatory about, 232–34

Focus: misdirected, in reacting to addictive behavior, 192–94; switching, to help break compulsive cycle, 194–95

Fog, analogy of rescue from, 172–78

Force, ineffectiveness of, in

breaking compulsive cycle, 184–88, 218–19
Free agency, 218
Friends: confusion of, over addicts' behavior, 155–57, 159–61, 165–69; new, can help in overcoming addiction, 245–46. *See also* Loved ones
Fulness of joy, 263–65
Fun, 267–68

God: unconditional love of, 45; drawing closer to, through physical actions, 67; two types of activities of, 204; seeking help of, to break cycle, 210–12
Grandmother, confusion of, over addict's behavior, 148–50
Guilt: healthy versus unhealthy, 17–18, 98–99, 104–7; and self-esteem, 100–101; proper, labeling is not part of, 103

Hawaii vacation, family plans, for teenage son, 138–39
Holy Ghost, denial of, 37–38
Homosexuality: case study of, 7–10, 53–61, 88–92, 118–25, 159–69, 248–56, 286–94; devastating effect of labeling in, 102–3; can be overcome, 103
Honesty: courageous, of recovering addicts, 41; about feelings, 232–34; developing habit of, 273; complete, required to break cycle, 273–74
Humiliation as wounded pride, 207–9

Humility: as weapon against humiliation, 207–8; exhibited by Christ, 208–9; seeking Lord's help in, 297

Inadequacy, feelings of, 45
Innocence, loss of, 117–18
Intelligence: sin presupposes, 34–35; utter denial of, constitutes unforgivable sin, 38
Isolation, feelings of, 15, 17, 43–46; temporarily blocked by actions of self-indulgence, 17, 62, 70, 96; intensified by compulsive cycle, 18–19; universality of, in mortality, 43–44, 71; case histories describing, 47–61; repressing, 62; are not inherently destructive, 62; cannot be resolved by actions of self-indulgence, 63; as opposite of joy, 70–71; potential usefulness of, 95; increased by self-concealment, 169; overcoming, importance of confession in, 205–8; are increased by judgmental attitudes, 222; focusing on eliminating, 228; dispelled by nonjudgmental listening, 231–32; subconscious nature of, 262

Jesus Christ: atonement of, recovery depends on, 23–24; needed to obtain body, 27; assumed consequences of our sins, 36; loneliness felt by, 43; gospel of, is one of integration, 71; asks for repentance, not self-hatred,

104; understands suffering of sinners, 126–27; perfect understanding of, 180; humility exhibited by, 208–9; emulating, in helping addict, 219–21; did not compromise with sin, 223–24, 225; fulness of joy experienced by, 264–65; invites all to come to Him, 296

Joy: as purpose of life, 64–65, 240; Satan's counterfeits for, 65–66, 70, 92–93, 178, 258; need for, connecting addictive behavior to, 197–98; and sorrow are not mutually exclusive, 226; intense, offered by Spirit, 226–27; fulness of, 263–65; increased capacity for, 264

Joy cycle: substituting, for compulsive cycle, 15, 19–22, 216–17, 257; diagram of, 16; as great source of happiness, 22, 261, 296–97; as upward spiral, 259, 261; illustrated in case studies, 277–94

Judgment: harsh, of behavioral addicts, 18, 104–5; belongs to Lord, 104, 220; resisting tendencies toward, 220; requires perfect understanding, 221; we set our own standards of, 221–22; increases feelings of isolation, 222

Justice and mercy, 36

Labeling, 101–3, 109

Latter-day Saints: involved in behavioral addictions, 12–14;

difficulties of, in confessing to Church authorities, 206–8

Leprosy, 95, 100

Life, purpose of, 64–65

Listening, 228–32

Loneliness, 44–45; willingness to acknowledge, 263. See also Isolation, feelings of

Love: search for, 44; unconditional, of God, 45; contrasted with sexual encounters, 91; increasing capacity for, 204; regardless of sin, 220; showing increase of, after reproving, 224

Loved ones: participation of, is mandatory in overcoming compulsive cycle, 19–21, 198; exclusion of, by addicts, 93–94; desire of, to believe addicts' rationalizations, 136–37; confusion of, over addicts' lies, 139–40; relationships with, destroyed by lying, 140–42, 169, 216; confusion of, illustrated in case studies, 145–69; dilemmas faced by, in trying to help addicts, 179; confessing to, 212–16; responsibility of, for own attitudes, 219; coaddiction of, 223; growth of, regardless of addicts' actions, 226, 227; should focus on addict's feelings, 228

Lying: unlimited ways of, 131; to conceal behavioral addictions, 132; confusion engendered by, 132, 138; omission and commission in, 138; relationships destroyed by, 140–42, 169,

216; convincing manner of, 142; destroys power of discernment, 143–45; and coaddiction, 223; keeps addict bound in cycle, 272

Mercy and justice, 36
Misinterpreting cues, 62
Mission: recovering addict decides to go on, 246–48; of sons of Mosiah, 263–64; of recovering drug addict, 282–86
Moses, law of, 67
Mosiah, sons of, 263–64
Moslems, 67–68
Motivations: are more important than actions, 186; varying types of, behind sin, 188–92; must be understood before judging, 221; learning to recognize, 274

Needs, recognizing, 197–98

Ordinances, proxy, 68–69

Parents, difficulties of, in helping addicted children, 179–80
Passions, bridling, 39, 224
Patterns, similar, in behavioral addictions, 11
Perdition, sons of, 37–38
Physical nature: role of, in compulsive cycles, 26, 32; incorrect ideas concerning, 26–32; resolving apparent conflicts regarding, 32; understanding, helps us control, 37–39; and pleasure, 71–72. See also Bodies, physical

Prayer: power of, in breaking compulsive cycle, 211; open invitation to, 229
Pride: repentance blocked by, 188; humiliation is grounded in, 207–9
Progression, actions of: replacing addictive behavior with, 20, 201–5; definition of, 20, 202; are essence of salvation, 202; choosing, from childhood favorites, 202–3; exercising talents as, 203–4; recognizing, through their fruits, 204–5; spring naturally from feelings of belonging, 266; fun involved in, 266–68

Rationalism, focus of, on physical, 29–30
Rationalization: as initial self-deception, 132; definition of, 133; any position is subject to, 133–34; popular forms of, 134–35; constant, of behavioral addicts, 136; loved ones' desire to believe, 136–37
Rehabilitation program, addict checks into, 242–43
Rejection: fear of, 212; deception causes, more than confession does, 216
Repentance: persistent attempts at, 22; possibility of, provided by Christ, 37; sorrowing unto, 98–99, 104–7; is continuing process, not single event, 181–84; involves confessing and forsaking sin, 200
Restitution, attempting to make, 243–44

Revenge, avoiding tendencies toward, 220

Righteousness: flows without compulsory means, 187; personal, determine's individual's happiness, 227; hunger and thirsting after, 263

"Rooms," life separated into good and bad, 88–89

Routine established around actions of self-indulgence, 77–78, 93, 96–97; entire, must be eliminated, 200–201

Satan: incorrect ideas propounded by, 31, 35; chose damnation, 38; offers counterfeits for joy, 65–66; mortal world is province of, 71; message of, is constantly changing, 131; is father of lies, 145

Scriptures, substituting own name in, 122–23

Sealing power, 44

Schor, Ellen, 1–4, 47–50, 80–85, 108–13, 145–53, 235–40, 277–82

Self-concealment, actions of: as reaction to shame, 18; effectiveness of, in maintaining exterior, 128–30; motivations for, 130–31; confusion involved in, 131; two categories of, 131–32; increase feelings of isolation, 169–70; replacing, with self-disclosure, 205–8

Self-disclosure, actions of: replacing deception with, 20–21, 205–8; humility involved in, 208–9; to oneself, 210; to Heavenly Father, 210–11; to loved ones, 212–16; developing habit of, 273; helping others through, 276

Self-esteem, feelings of: replacing self-hatred with, 21–22; effect of, on guilt, 100–101; self-forgetfulness implied in, 269–71

Self-hatred, feelings of: following actions of self-indulgence, 17–18, 97; differentiated from sorrowing unto repentance, 98–99, 104–7; increase in, over time, 99–100; enhanced by labeling, 101–3; viewed as "payment" for sins, 104–5; demonstrated by alcoholic, 105–7; involve comparisons, 268–69

Self-image, low, of behavioral addicts, 100–101

Self-indulgence, actions of: feelings of isolation blocked by, 17, 70, 96; feelings of self-hatred following, 17, 97; as counterfeits for joy, 66, 70, 92–93, 178; any action can become, 72; fascination with, prior to committing, 73, 93; initial exposure to, 73–74; placing, at center of life, 74–75; stretching, through planning routines around, 76–78, 93; addict's reactions to, 99–100; pleasure of, eventually disappears, 100; extreme difficulty of giving up, 178–79; forsaking, involves eliminating entire routine, 200–201; substituting actions of progression for, 201–5

Service, forgetting self in, 237
Sexual behavior: double
   standard of, 101–2; labeling
   in, 102; rationalizing, 135;
   lying about, relationship
   destroyed by, 140–42; as
   addiction, difficulty in
   classifying, 214. *See also*
   Homosexuality
Shoplifting, 77–78; illustration
   of, 189–92
Silence, productive, 229–30
Sin: different views of, based
   on motivations behind, 188–
   92; no one is without, 220;
   understanding, does not
   imply compromising with,
   223–24, 25
Sinners: suffering of, Christ
   understands, 126–27;
   condemning, is grave error,
   220–22
Smith, Joseph, 65, 187, 240
Spirit: denial of, by Western
   rationalism, 29–30; and body
   are not mutually exclusive,
   31
Spirit of the Lord: loss of,
   through deception, 144–45;
   fruits of, 204–5; remaining
   sensitive to, in dealing with
   addicts, 225–26; intense joy
   offered by, 226–27
Stewart, Bill, 4–7, 50–53, 85–88,
   113–18, 153–59, 240–48, 282–
   86
Structural barriers,
   ineffectiveness of, in
   breaking compulsive cycle,
   184–88

Suffering of sinners: society's
   view of, 125–26; Lord's
   understanding of, 126–27
Suicidal tendencies, 111, 125
Sunday School class, 11–12
Support group, addict gets
   help from, 236–37

Talents, exercising, 203–4
Temple work, 68–69
Temptation: existence of,
   despite repentance, 183–84;
   varying levels of complexity
   in, 188–92
Trust, lack of, resulting from
   deception, 143–44
Truth: learning to discern, 31;
   is unchangeable, 131; losing
   power to discern, 143–45;
   need for, 275; makes us free,
   277

Understanding: perfect, of
   Christ, 126–27, 180; is first
   step to conquering
   addiction, 196–97; growth
   in, through helping addicted
   loved one, 217–18; tempers
   judgmental attitudes, 222;
   increasing, through
   listening, 229; increased, of
   recovering addicts, 295–96
Unpardonable sin, 37–38

White, Warren, 7–10, 53–61,
   88–92, 118–25, 159–69, 248–
   56, 286–94
Willpower, insufficiency of, in
   overcoming addiction, 187–
   88
Word of Wisdom, 67, 92